The politics of global atmospheric change

Issues in Environmental Politics

series editors Tim O'Riordan, Arild Underdal *and* Albert Weale

The politics of global atmospheric change

Ian H. Rowlands

Manchester University Press
Manchester and New York
Distributed exclusively in the USA and Canada by St. Martin's Press

Copyright © Ian H. Rowlands 1995

Published by Manchester University Press
Oxford Road, Manchester M13 9NR, UK
and Room 400, 175 Fifth Avenue, New York, NY 10010, USA

Distributed exclusively in the USA and Canada
by St. Martin's Press, Inc., 175 Fifth Avenue, New York,
NY 10010, USA

British Library Cataloguing-in-Publication Data
A catalogue record for this book is available from the British Library

Library of Congress Cataloging-in-Publication Data
Rowlands, Ian H.
     The politics of global atmospheric change / Ian H. Rowlands.
          p.   cm. — (Issues in environmental politics)
          ISBN 0–7190–4094–9. — ISBN 0–7190–4095–7 (pbk.)
          1. Ozone layer depletion—International cooperation.   2. Climatic
     changes—International cooperation.   3. Man—Influence on nature–
     –International cooperation.   I. Title.   II. Series.
     QC879.7.R684   1995
     363.73'87—dc20   94-31959

ISBN   0 7190 4094 9 *hardback*
        0 7190 4095 7 *paperback*

Photoset in Linotron Sabon
by Northern Phototypesetting Co. Ltd, Bolton

Printed in Great Britain by
Bell and Bain Ltd, Glasgow

Contents

Contents

Figures

To my mother and father

Acknowledgements

This book could not have been completed without the support and assistance of numerous individuals and organisations. It is my pleasure to be able to acknowledge them here.

This book grew out of a doctoral dissertation that was completed under the supervision of Michael Banks of the Department of International Relations at the London School of Economics and Political Science. Michael initially sparked my interest in the study of international relations, and he has remained a source of great inspiration and encouragement ever since. Others associated with the Department have also provided me with a large measure of intellectual stimulation and personal support, both during and after my studies – in particular, Malory Greene, Mark Hoffman and Kathleen Newland. Further assistance and backing have also been gratefully received from a number of others at the LSE – in particular, John Harriss, Peter Odell and Meghnad Desai.

I would also like to express my appreciation to the numerous people in international organisations, government, industry, nongovernmental organisations and elsewhere who took time off from their busy schedules to agree to be interviewed by me.

I thank those organisations that provided financial assistance during the course of the research for this book: the Commonwealth Scholarship Commission in the United Kingdom, the Canadian Institute for International Peace and Security, the Committee of Vice-Chancellors and Principals of the Universities of the United Kingdom, the Edward Boyle Memorial Trust, the London School of Economics, the Centre for the Study of Global Governance and the Centre for Social and Economic Research on the Global

Environment.

Michael Nicholson and Oran Young each read a earlier version of the manuscript, and I am especially grateful to them for their comments. Richard Jerram, Jeremy Larkins, Annie Taylor and Tim Woolf each read and commented upon parts of the work. Their time and insights are also appreciated.

Richard Purslow at Manchester University Press was always supportive, while the series editors – in particular, Tim O'Riordan and Arild Underdal – provided both encouragement and critiques.

The constant support that I have received from my family is especially appreciated. I would also like to express, in particular, my appreciation to Barbara, for helping me to complete this project. Finally, I would like to thank my parents for a range of things much too long to enumerate. As a small token of this gratitude, I dedicate this book to them.

A chronology of the politics of ozone layer depletion

1840   – Ozone is first discovered.

1879–81   – Ozone is first detected in the earth's stratosphere.

1930   – British chemist Sydney Chapman puts forth the first theory of ozone generation and destruction.

1957–58   – The first significant amounts of data on stratospheric ozone are collected during the International Geophysical Year.

1966   – John Hampson is the first to argue that hydrogen compounds may be able to alter the ozone balance.

1970   – The first suggestions that nitrogen compounds may be able to destroy stratospheric ozone are proposed by Paul Crutzen and Harold Johnston.

1971   – The United States Congress orders a report on the potential damage to the ozone layer by supersonic transports (SSTs).

1973   – Delegates at a conference in Kyoto, Japan discuss the suggestions that free chlorine in the atmosphere may be able to affect ozone levels in the stratosphere (September).

1974   – The US Department of Transport's Climate Impact Assessment Program publishes its report, arguing that a large fleet of SSTs would have posed significant danger to the ozone layer.

          – A paper putting forth the theory that CFCs may destroy significant amounts of stratospheric ozone is published in *Nature* (June).

1975   – The report of the US Task Force on Inadvertent

Modification of the Atmosphere finds that the CFC theory is a 'legitimate cause for concern' (June).

1976   – At the fourth session of the United Nations Environment Programme (UNEP) Governing Council, initial steps are taken to convene an international meeting to consider the CFC–ozone link (March–April).

– The United States National Academy of Sciences (NAS) releases its first report on the ozone layer, predicting most likely depletion to be between 6 and 7.5 per cent (September).

1977   – The United States hosts the first intergovernmental meeting in Washington, DC to discuss international regulation of CFCs (April).

– The first meeting of the UNEP-sponsored Co-ordinating Committee on the Ozone Layer is held in Geneva (November).

1978   – CFCs are banned as propellants in non-essential aerosols in the United States (October).

1979   – A second NAS report is released in the United States. It estimates eventual ozone layer depletion to be 16.5 per cent (November).

1980   – The European Communities, having reduced aerosol use by 30 per cent, enact a cap on capacity.

– The UNEP Governing Council calls for reductions in the production of CFC-11 and CFC-12 (April).

1981   – The UNEP Governing Council releases a statement that argues for 'the desirability of initiating work aimed at the elaboration of a global framework convention [for the protection of the ozone layer]' (May).

– US EPA Administrator nominee Anne Gorsuch testifies at her confirmation hearings that she considers the CFC–ozone theory to be highly controversial (May).

– NASA scientist Donald Heath announces that satellite records show that there has been a loss of some ozone in the stratosphere (August).

1982   – UNEP convenes the first meeting of the *Ad Hoc* Working Group of Legal and Technical Experts for the Preparation of a Global Framework Convention for the Protection of the Ozone Layer in Stockholm (January).

– A third NAS report, which predicts eventual ozone

layer depletion to be between 5 and 9 per cent, is released in the United States (March).

1983 — Officials from Norway, Sweden and Finland propose both a worldwide ban on CFCs in aerosols and limitations on all uses of CFCs (April).

1984 — A fourth NAS report is released in the United States. It predicts an eventual level of ozone depletion to be between 2 and 4 per cent (February).

1985 — The Vienna Convention for the Protection of the Ozone Layer is opened for signature (March).

— In a paper published in *Nature*, members of the British Antarctic Survey present evidence of significant destruction of the ozone layer over Antarctica (May).

1986 — A NASA–UNEP report finds evidence of reduced levels of stratospheric ozone (January).

— The First Part of the Workshop on the Control of CFCs – part of a series of informal workshops designed to advance the drafting of a Protocol – is held in Rome (May).

— CFC manufacturers suggest that safe substitutes for the chemicals might be possible, if the price were high enough (June).

— Thirteen US scientists depart for Antarctica on the National Ozone Expedition. Although they discover significant destruction of stratospheric ozone, their findings do not resolve the debate about causation (August).

— The Second Part of the Workshop on the Control of CFCs is held in Leesburg, VA (September).

— The Alliance (an industry group) announces that it will support limits on CFC production (September).

— The first session of the *Ad Hoc* Working Group of Legal and Technical Experts for the Elaboration of a Protocol on the Control of CFCs to the Vienna Convention for the Protection of the Ozone Layer is convened in Geneva (December).

1987 — A UNEP meeting of scientists – convened to discuss models of ozone depletion – takes place in Wurzburg, West Germany (April).

— Informal Consultations toward the Elaboration of a

Protocol on the Control of CFCs to the Vienna Convention for the Protection of the Ozone Layer are held in Brussels (June).
– After much discussion and debate, the Montreal Protocol on Substances that Deplete the Ozone Layer is opened for signature (September).
– Members of the Airborne Antarctic Ozone Experiment conclude that chlorine chemicals are the primary cause of ozone depletion in Antarctica (October).

1988   – Members of the Ozone Trends Panel not only formalise the results of their Antarctic trip, but also announce that they have discovered ozone losses over the northern hemisphere (March).
– Du Pont announces that it will cease manufacture of CFCs as substitutes become available (March).
– The Vienna Convention enters into force (September).
– The Ozone Depletion Conference is held in London (November).

1989   – The Montreal Protocol enters into force (January).
– European countries and the United States agree to faster CFC reductions, but developing countries oppose the new timetable, citing the prohibitive costs of substitutes. They call for a fairer arrangement (March).
– The Saving the Ozone Layer Conference is held in London (March).
– The First Meeting of Parties to the Montreal Protocol takes place in Helsinki (May).
– Working groups are formed to consider revisions to the Montreal Protocol (August). They continue to meet through the second half of 1989 and the first half of 1990.
– UNEP publishes a *Synthesis Report*, incorporating results of scientific, environmental, economic and technical assessments (November).

1990   – The Second Meeting of the Parties to the Montreal Protocol is held in London, at which substantial amendments to the original terms of the Protocol are agreed (June).
– The Interim Multilateral Ozone Fund is established. With its secretariat located in Montreal, its primary purpose is to provide assistance to countries of the

developing world so that they can reduce their use of ozone-depleting chemicals (September).

1991   – The Third Meeting of the Parties to the Montreal Protocol is held in Nairobi (June).

– The World Meteorological Organisation (WMO) and UNEP release a report that suggests that destruction of the ozone layer has advanced far more rapidly than predicted (October).

1992   – The London Amendments to the Montreal Protocol enter into force (August).

– The Fourth Meeting of the Parties to the Montreal Protocol is held in Copenhagen, at which substantial amendments to the original terms of the Protocol are agreed (November).

– The Multilateral Fund is established.

1993   – The Fifth Meeting of the Parties to the Montreal Protocol is held in Bangkok (November).

1994   – The Copenhagen Amendments to the Montreal Protocol enter into force (June).

A chronology of the politics of climate change

1273   – The first air pollution law to deal with the deleterious effects of fossil fuel combustion is passed in London.

1661   – John Evelyn writes about the harmful effects caused by coal burning.

1827   – Baron Jean-Baptiste-Joseph Fourier sets out the analogy between the behaviour of heat in the atmosphere and its behaviour in a greenhouse.

1865   – John Tyndall builds upon the theories originally put forward by Fourier.

1896   – Svante Arrhenius puts forth the theory that rising concentrations of atmospheric carbon dioxide would lead to global warming.

1938   – G.D. Callendar, a British meteorologist, tries to persuade an audience at the Royal Society in London that the global warming that had occurred since the 1880s was the result of increasing carbon dioxide levels in the atmosphere. His ideas attract little support.

1957   – An atmospheric carbon dioxide measuring station is established at Mauna Loa observatory in Hawaii as part of the International Geophysical Year.

        – A paper suggesting that the oceans had not absorbed as much carbon dioxide as previously assumed is published in *Tellus*.

1965   – The US White House initiates a study into the burning of fossil fuels and its relations to the steadily rising atmospheric concentrations of carbon dioxide.

1970   – 'The study of critical environmental problems', a symposium to investigate such issues, is held at MIT in Cambridge, USA (July).

1971   – The first international meeting of scientists to discuss long-term climate change is held in Wijk, Sweden (August).

1972   – The United Nations Conference on the Human Environment is held in Stockholm, Sweden (June).

1975   – A WMO-sponsored International Symposium on Long-Term Climate Fluctuations takes place in Norwich, England (August).

   – One of the first major governmental studies to investigate the causes and consequences of climate change is published by the NAS in the United States. It highlights the need to improve the science on the climate change issue.

1977   – Another report is prepared by the US NAS, and, like its predecessor, it calls for further investigations. Nevertheless, it also warns that the implications of projected climate change 'warrant prompt action' (July).

1979   – The First World Climate Conference is convened in Geneva by the WMO (February).

   – At its Eighth World Meteorological Congress, the World Climate Programme (WCP) is created by the WMO.

1980   – As part of the WCP, an international conference to address climate change is held in Villach, Austria (November).

1982   – An NAS report in the US reinforces the emerging consensus that a doubling of carbon dioxide concentrations in the atmosphere would cause a global warming of between 1.5°C and 4.5°C.

1983   – Reports in the United States by the NAS and the EPA draw different conclusions from seemingly similar findings.

1985   – Participants in the International Conference on the Assessment of the Role of Carbon Dioxide and Other Greenhouse Gases in Climate Variations and Associated Impacts (held in Villach, Austria) agree that global warming could occur (October).

1987   – WMO and UNEP agree to establish an intergovernmental mechanism to assess the scientific data and to formulate response strategies for climate change (June).

– A workshop to investigate further the question of global warming is held in Villach, Austria (September–October).

– The previous month's Villach meeting is followed-up by another gathering in Bellagio, Italy. Together, the findings from these two conferences not only highlight the problem, but also put forward proposals for policies (November).

– The World Commission on Environment Report publishes its report, entitled *Our Common Future* (commonly referred to as the 'Brundtland Report').

1988   – In testimony to the US Senate Energy Committee, NASA's James Hansen asserts that he is 99 per cent certain that the warming of the 1980s is not a chance event, but is, instead, causally linked to global warming (June).

– A conference on The Changing Atmosphere: Implications for Global Security is held in Toronto (June). Its delegates conclude that humanity is 'conducting an unintended, uncontrolled, globally pervasive experiment whose ultimate consequences could be second only to a global nuclear war' (June).

– The first meeting of the Intergovernmental Panel on Climate Change (IPCC) is held in Geneva (November).

– A United Nations General Assembly resolution charges the WMO and the UNEP to initiate a comprehensive review and to make recommendations on possible responses to mitigate the impact of adverse climate change, as well as on elements for inclusion in a possible future international convention on climate (December).

1989   – Protection of the Atmosphere: International Meeting of Legal and Policy Experts is held in Ottawa, Canada (February).

– Summit Meeting on the Protection of the Atmosphere takes place in The Hague. Delegates call for the formation of new global institutions to meet the challenges of global atmospheric change (March).

– The UNEP Governing Council requests that the heads of UNEP and WMO 'begin preparation for negotiations on a framework convention on climate' (May).

– A Ministerial Conference on Atmospheric Pollution and Climatic Change takes place in Noordwijk, the Netherlands (November).

– The Dutch government, by introducing plans to stabilise carbon dioxide emissions at the 1989/90 level by the year 2000, becomes the first to set a target on the global warming issue.

1990 – The White House Conference on Science and Economics Research Related to Global Change is held in Washington (April).

– The first reports of the IPCC's three working groups are released (May).

– A meeting of the United Nations Economic Commission on Europe, called as a follow-up to the report of the World Commission on Environment and Development, is held in Bergen, Norway (May).

– The IPCC reports are finalised in Sundsvall, Sweden (August).

– The Second World Climate Conference is held in Geneva (November).

– With its resolution on the 'protection of global climate for present and future generations of mankind', the United Nations General Assembly takes primary responsibility for the climate change issue (December).

1991 – The first meeting of the Intergovernmental Negotiating Committee for a Framework Convention on Climate Change (INC) is held in Washington, DC (February).

– Meetings of the INC continue in Geneva (June), Nairobi (September) and Geneva once again (December).

– Leaders of over forty developing countries issue the 'Beijing Declaration', in which they reinforce their demands for resource transfers on the global warming issue (June).

1992 – The IPCC publishes its updated report.

– In New York, at the fifth INC, negotiators agree the Framework Convention on Climate Change (May).

– The United Nations Conference on Environment and Development (UNCED, or the 'Earth Summit') is held in Rio de Janeiro, Brazil (June).

– At the Earth Summit, the Framework Convention on Climate Change is opened for signature (June).

– A meeting of the INC is held in Geneva (December).

1993   – Meetings of the INC are held in New York (March) and Geneva (August).

– The fiftieth ratification of the Framework Convention on Climate Change is received (December).

1994   – The ninth session of the INC is held in Geneva (February).

– At a meeting in Geneva, agreement is reached on a restructured GEF (March).

– The Framework Convention on Climate Change enters into force (March).

Abbreviations

AAOE	Airborne Antarctic Ozone Experiment
AOSIS	Alliance of Small Island States
BCSD	Business Council for Sustainable Development
BTU	British thermal unit
CBA	cost–benefit analysis
CCOL	Co-ordinating Committee on the Ozone Layer
CEC	Commission of the European Communities
CFC	chlorofluorocarbon
CH_4	methane
CIAP	Climate Impact Assessment Program
CIS	Commonwealth of Independent States
CO_2	carbon dioxide
CSD	Commission on Sustainable Development
DDT	dichloro-diphenyl-trichloroethane
EC	European Communities
EEC	European Economic Community
EPA	Environmental Protection Agency
EU	European Union
GATT	General Agreement on Tariffs and Trade
GDP	Gross Domestic Product
GEF	Global Environment Facility
GNP	Gross National Product
G7	Group of Seven
HCFC	Hydrochlorofluorocarbon
HFC	Hydrofluorocarbon
HMSO	Her Majesty's Stationery Office
HST	Hegemonic Stability Theory
ICC	International Chamber of Commerce

ICI	Imperial Chemical Industries
ICSU	International Council of Scientific Unions
IEA	International Energy Agency
IFI	international financial institution
IMO	International Meteorological Organisation
IMOF	Interim Multilateral (Ozone) Fund
INC	Intergovernmental Negotiating Committee for a Framework Convention on Climate Change
IPCC	Intergovernmental Panel on Climate Change
IUCN	World Conservation Union
MIT	Massachusetts Institute of Technology
NO_x	nitrous oxides
NAS	National Academy of Sciences
NASA	National Aeronautics and Space Administration
NGO	non-governmental organisation
NIEO	New International Economic Order
ODA	Official Development Assistance
OECD	Organisation for Economic Co-operation and Development
OPEC	Organisation of Petroleum Exporting Countries
SST	supersonic transport
TCE	tonnes coal equivalent
TNC	transnational corporation
UK	United Kingdom
UN	United Nations
UNCED	United Nations Conference on Environment and Development
UNCTAD	United Nations Conference on Trade and Development
UNDP	United Nations Development Programme
UNEP	United Nations Environment Programme
UNGA	United Nations General Assembly
US	United States
USSR	Union of Soviet Socialist Republics
VA	Virginia
WCP	World Climate Programme
WCED	World Commission on Environment and Development
WMO	World Meteorological Organisation
WTO	World Trade Organisation

Introduction

Human activity is causing considerable damage to the global environment. Evidence to support this statement has been accumulating steadily during the past four decades. The 1962 publication of Rachel Carson's *Silent Spring* was one of the first events to draw significant attention to ways in which human actions were interfering with the planet's environment.[1] Other studies published since that time have also highlighted the problem – for example, the Club of Rome's 1972 report on the *Limits to Growth*, the 1980 *Global 2000 Report to the President of the U.S.* and the Brundtland Commission's 1987 report on *Our Common Future*.[2] Accidents have further focused attention – the 1967 crash of the supertanker, the Torrey Canyon, the 1979 nuclear reactor explosion at Three Mile Island and the 1986 spill of toxic chemicals into the Rhine river are but three cases. As recognition of environmental damage has become more widespread, environmental issues have ascended political agendas around the world. Support for this assertion can be found at both the state level – for example, the creation of governmental agencies with environmental management responsibilities in over one hundred countries during the 1970s and 1980s – and the inter-state level – for example, the convening of the 1972 United Nations Conference on the Human Environment in Stockholm and the 1992 United Nations Conference on Environment and Development in Rio de Janeiro.

Simple recognition of any problem in itself, however, does little to improve the quality of the environment. No matter how many reports are written and no matter how many conferences are convened, only substantive action will slow the degradation and repair the damage already done. For some environmental problems the necessary action can be executed by a person working on her or his own – for example, replacement of harmful asbestos insulation in a home. Other environmental problems are bigger than the individual and require all members of a community, be it a city, a province or even a country, to commit themselves to action – for example, cleaning a neighbourhood playground, a cottagers' lake or a national park. Still other environmental problems are too large to be handled within a single state, and they require individuals from each of a number of different countries to take action.

This book is concerned with this last kind of environmental problem – namely, those that are international. Even restricted in this manner, however, international environmental problems still constitute a relatively large set of issues. Acid precipitation, pollution of multinational waterways, depletion of biological diversity and desertification are just four examples of issues that have international dimensions. Rather than consider the whole range, this book explores two in particular – namely, the global atmospheric problems of ozone layer depletion and climate change. This focus is warranted for two reasons. The first is normative: a better understanding of the political dynamics associated with global atmospheric change will facilitate our efforts to achieve global sustainable development. The second is analytical: an examination of these two issues in parallel will enhance our understanding of international co-operation.

Global atmospheric problems are relatively recent concerns for the world's inhabitants. Traditionally, the atmosphere had been thought to be a bottomless receptacle, into which any amount of waste could be cast. It was, in the language of the economist, a 'free good'. Certainly, there was some price to be paid – primarily deterioration in local air quality – but it was generally assumed that, with sufficient commitment and resources, any damage could be repaired without undue delay. In this way, it was thought that atmospheric problems could be contained over both space and time.

This presumption is now known to be false. Two findings in particular have revealed that the global atmosphere is not a limitless sink. The first came in 1988, when scientific investigations after the discovery of an ozone 'crater' above Antarctica revealed that chlorofluorocarbons and other widely used chemicals were destroying the earth's protective ozone layer.[3] The second came in 1990, when an international group of scientific experts declared that 'emissions resulting from human activities are substantially increasing the atmospheric concentrations of the greenhouse gases. ... These increases will enhance the greenhouse effect, resulting on average in an additional warming of the Earth's surface'.[4] It was thus evident that the release of trace particles was disturbing the long-term equilibria of the global atmosphere. In other words, people's everyday activities were generating environmental problems that could not be contained over either space or time.[5]

Changes in the composition of the global atmosphere would have significant consequences. As the ozone layer thinned, the incidence of skin cancers, cataracts and infectious diseases among humans would increase, agricultural yields of certain crops would decrease, many manufacturing materials would weaken prematurely and ecosystems would be destabilised. An increase in average global temperatures, meanwhile, would raise sea levels, shift climatic zones and also destabilise ecosystems. Therefore, if people continued to treat the global atmosphere as a limitless sink, then there would not only be significant changes in the chemical composition of the atmosphere, but also enormous repercussions for life on earth.[6] A departure from the world's business-as-usual path would thus seem desirable.

Changes in behaviour among all of the world's inhabitants, however, are much easier to seek than to achieve. Niccolò Machiavelli recognised this four hundred years ago, and his comments are just as relevant today:

> It must be considered that there is nothing more difficult to carry out, nor more doubtful of success, nor more dangerous to handle, than to initiate a new order of things. For the reformer has enemies in all those who profit by the old order, and only lukewarm defenders in all those who would profit by the new order, this lukewarmness arising partly from fear of their adversaries, who have the laws in their favour; and partly from the incredulity of mankind, who do not truly believe in anything new until they have had actual experience of it.[7]

Social change does not come easy. Moreover, the particular characteristics of global atmospheric issues make it that much more difficult.

Imagine an individual who decided that he or she wanted to avoid the outcomes that would result from a thinner ozone layer or a warmer climate. He or she might then endeavour to cease any activities that contributed to global atmospheric change. That individual's unilateral actions, however, would not necessarily bring about the desired result. Because access to the global atmosphere is free and unrestricted – in other words, the atmosphere is a 'global commons' – all of the world's inhabitants would have to be committed to its stabilisation. If only one person were to change her or his usual practices, while others maintained theirs, then the composition of the atmosphere would still be altered. Consequently, our individual (and, indeed, everyone else as well) would still be affected by global atmospheric change. Not wanting to be duped, he or she might well decide to forget about changing behaviour after all.

This kind of dilemma is not unique to issues of global atmospheric change. Individuals may find themselves in other situations that are no one's ideal – that is, there is an alternative arrangement that all would prefer. Still, in the absence of any enforcement mechanisms, everyone is loath to change his or her behaviour, lest others maintain theirs, which could lead them to be even worse off than they were in the first place. In this way, it is in everyone's rational interest to maintain the status quo, and the result is that outcomes are suboptimal for all.

The general dilemma has been formalised in the literature this century as the 'problem of collective action'.[8] The difficulty itself, however, has been recognised for much longer. Aristotle, for one, alluded to it over three thousand years ago, and his comments still carry significant relevance today:

> What is common to the greatest number gets the least amount of care. Men pay most attention to what is their own: they care less for what is common. . . . When everyone has his own sphere of interest . . . the amount of interest will increase, because each man will feel that he is applying himself to what is his own.[9]

Taken together, these observations from the social sciences suggest that international co-operation may be difficult to achieve. History, indeed, provides support for this assertion.

Studies of war and peace – the traditional mainstays of international relations – have contributed a wealth of examples. Arms races have frequently left all participants worse off. Some – for example, the one between Britain and Germany at the beginning of this century – have led to war between the antagonists, while others –

for example, the one between the United States and the Soviet Union during the Second Cold War – have not. Regardless, both parties in both instances could envisage a better outcome than the one that transpired.

More recently, enquiries in international political economy have produced additional illustrations. Protectionist tendencies have often reduced the welfare of all adversaries. After a number of countries adopted mercantilist-inspired policies during the 1930s, for example, not only did economic welfare collapse but also eventually so too did the borders of many of those same countries.

Still more recently, scholars have noted that the competitive use of natural resources often leads to a tragedy of the commons, a situation in which everyone loses as a result of the degradation, or even destruction, of the particular resource.[10] The depletion of certain fish stocks in the world's oceans is but one of many international cases. Together, these examples suggest that international co-operation can often be elusive, with the result being that every actor is worse off.

Other stories, however, have had different endings. At times, the members of international society have been able to overcome the obstacles to change and co-operation in order to escape sub-optimal outcomes. There are illustrations from questions of war and peace – for example, the reduction in strategic arms during the late 1980s. Additionally, there are illustrations from international political economy – the progress made in the successive GATT rounds is but one instance. Finally, environmental issues also provide a number of cases – the agreements to clean up regional seas is perhaps one of the clearest. Thus, arrangements to resolve collective action problems have sometimes been created internationally.

Returning to our two issues under investigation in this book, a closer inspection of the ozone layer depletion and climate change challenges reveals that this contrast between relative success and relative failure is also apparent here.

In the face of ozone layer depletion, a substantial degree of international co-operation has been realised, as evidenced by the respect given to the terms of the 1985 Vienna Convention for the Protection of the Ozone Layer, the 1987 Montreal Protocol on Substances that Deplete the Ozone Layer, and the 1990 London and 1992 Copenhagen Adjustments and Amendments to the Protocol.[11] Although the problem is by no means totally solved, significant progress has been made. Consequently, the ozone layer arrangement is often cited as a paradigm for the resolution of international environmental problems.

This is in sharp contrast, however, with the climate change challenge. Although some degree of international co-operation is evident – in particular, the Framework Convention on Climate Change, which was opened for signature at the 1992 Earth Summit[12] – the consequent changes in actors' behaviour will not solve the problem. Why, then, has there been relative success on one, but not on the other?

Combine this with the numerous other examples that have been cited above, and I can pose this question more generally: Why are some international collective-action problems successfully resolved, while others remain intractable? This question has engaged scholars of international relations for many years. In response, a number of different explanations have been offered, the vast majority of which direct attention to one of three factors. Let me briefly review each of these in turn.

First, some argue that the key determining variable is the distribution of power. International co-operation is only possible when one actor has a preponderance of power. Even then, however, international co-operation is by no means guaranteed. Only if the dominant actor chooses to exercise its power will international co-operation be realised. *Power-based* is the term often used to refer to this sort of explanation.

Second, others maintain that the interests of the key actors determine the presence or absence of international co-operation. The world can be thought of as a collection of self-interested utility maximisers. These actors, who continuously assess the relative costs and benefits of the policy-alternatives that they face, will always choose the option that will maximise their own welfare. International co-operation will be realised when all of the key actors conclude that co-ordinated action is their preferred option. *Interest-based* is the label often applied to this sort of explanation.

Finally, still others contend that international co-operation and discord can be best explained with reference to the ways in which actors receive, process, interpret and adapt to new information. The existence of a consensus regarding the problem's causal relations, and its subsequent acceptance by key actors, will generate international co-operation. Alternatively, any disagreements will ensure international discord. *Knowledge-based* is what this sort of explanation has often been called.

Who is right? Which group of scholars can best explain absences and instances of international co-operation? Because persuasive case-studies are offered to support each of the three different sorts of explanations, a single answer is difficult to deduce. Consequently, a general explanation remains elusive.

This, however, does not preclude the utility of any or all of these scholars' contributions. Indeed, in spite of the fact that these three alternatives offer different, even contradictory, explanations for the presence and absence of international co-operation, one does not need to 'triumph' in order for any of them to be useful. Instead, each explanation can help to shed light on some parts of the dynamics associated with international co-operation.

Consequently, I begin this study of the politics of global atmospheric change by reviewing and analysing each of the three sorts of explanations. Their insights, supplemented by a number of independent observations, generate four hypotheses for international co-operation. These four hypotheses are:

1) A consensus regarding the problem's causal relations is necessary for international co-operation.
2) A situation in which all key actors, operating as self-interested utility maximisers, calculate the benefits of co-ordinating their policies to be greater than the costs, is necessary for international co-operation.
3) Adequate resolution of North–South issues – that is, developing countries' concerns about 'equity' – is necessary for international co-operation.
4) The prospects for international co-operation will increase when any of four catalysts – namely, political entrepreneurs, non-governmental organisations, issue tangibility and a conducive international environment – are present.

The four hypotheses are derived, defended and elaborated in Part I.

In Parts II, III, IV and V, the hypotheses are tested. Within each Part, one of the different hypotheses is investigated, with the study proceeding in three chapters. The first two consider the ozone layer depletion and climate change issues separately. The third presents a number of findings and conclusions relevant to the particular hypothesis under examination, along with a range of observations about global environmental politics more generally. In the Conclusions, I identify a number of findings, arising out the analysis, that have implications for the study and practice of international relations more broadly.

Thus, in this book, I document the ways in which humanity has responded to the changes they have imposed upon the earth's atmosphere. I also offer explanations as to why the politics of the two issues of global atmospheric change have unfolded as they have. Although the investigation has a relatively narrow objective – that is, attempting to explain why the ozone layer problem has been largely resolved, while the climate change problem has remained largely intractable – I am also concerned with more general enquiries – namely, attempts to explain why some international collective action problems are resolved, while others remain intransigent. Consequently, the book aims to contribute to both specific discussions about the issues of global atmospheric change, and the more general debate about international co-operation.

Global atmospheric change would cause broader transformations in the earth's environment. These would have the potential to create significant turmoil among the world's inhabitants. If this is to be avoided, then some level of international co-operation will have to be achieved. Overcoming the obstacles to co-operation on international collective action problems, however, is a daunting task. Thus, the effectiveness of international agreements designed both to halt and to reverse ozone layer depletion is noteworthy. The barriers to international co-operation to deal with the climate change issue, however, have yet to be surmounted. By focusing upon the theoretical dilemmas and the historical evidence, this book seeks to contribute to the general discussion as the members of international society attempt to build co-operative structures to address not only the challenges of climate change but also global environmental issues more generally.

Notes

1   Rachel Carson, *Silent Spring* (New York, Fawcett Crest, 1962).
2   Donella H. Meadows, Dennis L. Meadows, Jorgen Randers and William W. Behrens III, *The Limits to Growth* (New York, Universe Books, 1972); Gerald O. Barney, *The Global 2000 Report to the President of the U.S.* (Oxford, Pergamon, 1980); and World Commission on Environment

and Development, *Our Common Future* (Oxford, Oxford University Press, 1987).

3   Robert T. Watson, F. Sherwood Rowland and John Gille, *Ozone Trends Panel: Executive Summary* (Washington, DC, NASA, 1988).

4   *The Policymakers' Summary of the Report of Working Group I to the Intergovernmental Panel on Climate Change* (Geneva, WMO and UNEP, 1990), p. 2.

5   For scientific assessments of these two issues, see Daniel Albritton and Robert T. Watson (eds), *Scientific Assessment of Ozone Depletion: 1991* (Geneva, WMO, Global Ozone Research and Monitoring Project – Report No. 25, 1991); and J.T. Houghton, B.A. Callander and S.K. Varney (eds), *Climate Change 1992: The Supplementary Report to the IPCC Scientific Assessment* (Cambridge, Cambridge University Press, 1992).

6   For descriptions of the potential impacts of these two issues, see J.C. van der Leun and M. Tevini (eds), *Environmental Effects of Ozone Depletion: 1991 Update* (Nairobi, UNEP, 1991); and W.J.McG. Tegart, G.W. Sheldon and J.H. Hellyer (eds), *Climate Change 1992: the Supplementary Report to the IPCC Impacts Assessment* (Canberra, Australian Government Publishing Service, 1993).

7   Niccolò Machiavelli, *The Prince* (1513), translated by Luigi Ricci, revised by E.R.P. Vincent, in *The Prince and The Discourses* (New York, The Modern Library, 1950), p. 21.

8   See, for example, Russell Hardin, *Collective Action* (Baltimore, Johns Hopkins University Press, 1982); and Mancur Olson, *The Logic of Collective Action: Public Goods and the Theory of Groups* (Cambridge, Harvard University Press, 1965).

9   Aristotle, *Politics*, Book II, Chapters 3 and 4, quoted in: 'Preface: the evolution of cultural norms', in Garrett Hardin and John Baden (eds), *Managing the Commons* (San Francisco, W.H. Freeman, 1977), p. xi.

10   Garrett Hardin, 'The tragedy of the commons', *Science*, 162 (13 December 1968), pp. 1243–8.

11   The Vienna Convention, the Montreal Protocol, the London Adjustments and Amendments, and the Copenhagen Adjustments and Amendments are reprinted in *International Legal Materials*. Respectively, each appears in: 26 (1987), pp. 1516–40; 26 (1987), pp. 1541–61; 30 (1991), pp. 537–54; and 32 (1993), pp. 874–87.

12   The Climate Change Convention is reprinted in *International Legal Materials*, 31 (1992), pp. 849–73.

I
Theory

1

Explaining international co-operation

Co-operation occurs when 'actors adjust their behavior to the actual or anticipated preferences of others, through a process of policy coordination'.[1] Robert Keohane presented this definition in 1984, and since then it has gained considerable acceptance in international relations. In addition to presenting what co-operation is, Keohane also outlined what co-operation is not: it is not only distinct from 'discord' (the most obvious antithesis of co-operation) but also from 'harmony'. Discord is present when each actor's behaviour is detrimental to the goals of other actors. Before there can be co-operation, there must necessarily be discord. Harmony, alternatively, is present when each actor's behaviour is naturally conducive to the goals of other actors. The presence of harmony precludes the need for co-operation.

Given the nature of collective action problems, however, a condition of harmony will tend to be the rare exception rather than the rule. Much more common will be the transition from discord to co-operation. When will each actor adjust his or her behaviour so that it corresponds to the preferences of all other actors? Although there is substantial consensus surrounding the definition of what constitutes co-operation, there is much less agreement about the conditions under which it is likely to emerge. Within the literature, scholars have offered a number of explanations for the absence and presence of international co-operation.[2] The vast majority of these focus upon one of three key factors: power, interests or knowledge. I begin this chapter by reviewing each of these three sorts of explanations for international co-operation.

Power-based explanations

One sort of explanation is distinguished by the emphasis its proponents place upon the concept of power. Although writers from a number of diverse perspectives are grouped together here, all nevertheless share the belief that the distribution of power (however defined) within the international system (constituting whatever units) is the key factor determining the prospects for international co-operation. The two most significant approaches within this set of explanations, which is often called 'power-based', are, first, associated with traditional realist ideas and, second, inspired by Marxist scholarship.

So-called realists in the international relations literature argue that states are 'preoccupied with their security and power; by consequence, states are predisposed toward conflict and competition, and they often fail to cooperate even when they have common interests'.[3] Many of these scholars maintain that international co-operation is only possible if a single actor has a preponderance of power. This actor is identified as a 'hegemon', and the theory has become known as 'Hegemonic Stability Theory' (HST). In Keohane's words, HST 'predicts that the more one such power dominates the world political economy, the more cooperative will interstate relations be'.[4] Although the theory first attracted significant attention in the study of international political economy,[5] it has also been applied to other kinds of issues.

Duncan Snidal makes a useful distinction between two sorts of HST. On the one hand, he identifies a 'benign version', as developed by Charles Kindleberger and, in his earlier writings, Keohane.[6] The benign hegemon induces a change in the behaviour of others by agreeing to bear the full costs of international co-operation. It accepts this burden because it anticipates that it will accrue even larger benefits. These may either be tangible (for example, peace, security or economic prosperity) or intangible (for example, prestige, glory or immortality[7]). The benign hegemon, therefore, uses its power to make all members of international society better off.

Snidal suggests, on the other hand, that a hegemon can be motivated by different incentives. Labelled the 'malevolent version', he identifies Robert Gilpin and Stephen Krasner as two of its best-known proponents.[8] Once again, international co-operation can occur as a result of the actions of the hegemon. But this time, instead of shifting to a policy that will be in the longer-term interests of all members of international society, the malevolent hegemon considers only its own short-term interests when making policy. Thus, these theorists agree with their 'benevolent-view' colleagues that co-operation may occur when a single actor has power resources sufficient enough to transform the arrangements within international society. They disagree, however, in their view that not all members of international society will be better off as a consequence. Instead, the new arrangements will yield the highest net benefits for the hegemon, most probably at the expense of others. Still, all HST theorists contend that in order to explain the absence or presence of international co-operation, the manner in which the hegemon has transformed international structures must be investigated.

The 1973 publication of Kindleberger's *The World in Depression*[9] is often cited as the first major study giving prominence to HST. Nevertheless, ideas about the role of 'great powers' have deep roots in both the study and the practice of international relations.[10] Moreover, a course of policy that could well have been prescribed by HST proved to be irresistible to United States policy-makers after the Second World War. More specifically, some suggested that strong 'policing' interventions by the US in world affairs would be necessary if any sort of co-operation and order were to be achieved.[11]

Since the publication of Kindleberger's work, scholars have continued to develop ideas about the influence that powerful actors can have in the quest for co-operation. This has been undertaken not only within the HST discourse but also outside of it. Oran Young's work on 'imposed regimes', for example, has obvious parallels. He argues that such regimes are 'established deliberately by dominant actors who succeed in getting others to conform to the requirements of these arrangements through some combination of coercion, cooperation, and the manipulation of incentives'.[12]

The number of authors cited in reference to HST thus far should make it clear that the theory has attracted a number of adherents within international relations scholarship.[13] Even Keohane, who himself has undergone an intellectual transformation on this issue, recognises that the 'dominance of a single great power may contribute to order in world politics, in particular circumstances . . .'.[14] Donald Puchala and Raymond Hopkins, furthermore, identify 'revolutionary change' as one of two sources of regime change.[15] In this instance, they argue that the dominant power(s) imposes a new order that has to be accepted by others. Moreover, shifts in power capabilities usher in corresponding shifts in co-operative arrangements: '. . . previously disadvantaged but newly powerful participants ascend to dominance and impose new norms favouring their own interests'.[16] This, they claim, is the 'most frequent pattern of regime change'.[17] Arthur Stein also identifies the domination of the weak by the strong as a key determinant of co-operation.[18] Meanwhile, even Young, who is certainly no friend of the approach, notes that any criticisms laid upon HST do not 'exhaust the potential linkages between power and regime formation; it is not difficult to see opportunities to formulate a number of other propositions relating structural power or the distribution of such power to regime formation and to apply them to the realm of environmental concerns'.[19] Notwithstanding this use and support, a number of problems with HST have also been identified.

Keohane is one who subjects the explanation to fairly rigorous testing to illuminate its empirical weaknesses.[20] HST, he argues, cannot explain 'lags between changes in power structures and changes in international regimes'.[21] Moreover, why does there appear to be much more extensive co-operation now in world politics than during earlier periods (such as the late nineteenth century) of supposed hegemonic leadership?[22] Given such inconsistencies, Keohane concludes that the 'empirical evidence for the general validity of hegemonic stability theory is weak'.[23] Magnifying this sentiment Peter Mayer and colleagues, after reviewing two major research efforts, report that the 'power-based hypotheses, in particular the theory of hegemonic stability, did rather badly'.[24]

Aside from its failures in the face of application, the theory is also challenged on conceptual grounds. In an oft-cited article, Snidal lays out one of the most comprehensive theoretical attacks upon HST. Using formal models, he comes to a conclusion that contradicts HST – namely, that international co-operative arrangements can not only persist in the face of declining hegemony, but that they can even be strengthened. This, he argues, shows that hegemonic stability is only a special case of international co-operation.[25]

In addition, Stein challenges the HST theorists' assertion that changes in the distribution of power will lead to changes in co-operative arrangements. He argues, instead, that more subtle factors are at work within world politics:

If interests intervene between structure and regimes, then only those structural changes that affect patterns of interest will affect regimes. Further, since other factors also affect interests, it may be that the impact of changing power distributions on actor preferences can be negated by other structural changes, such as those in technology.[26]

And although Keohane does not complement his rigorous empirical testing with an equally comprehensive conceptual analysis, he nevertheless maintains that the 'argument that hegemony is necessary for cooperation is both theoretically and empirically weak'.[27] The conclusion in light of such observations is, Young contends, that 'the hegemonic-stability hypothesis is dead'.[28] Although this declaration might be premature, it is clear that HST's utility has been effectively challenged.

Among those who look at the distribution of power internationally in order to explain the presence or absence of co-operation, there is a second predominant strand of thought. Inspired by Marxist scholarship, it has often been labelled 'dependency theory'.[29] Effectively summarising its basic tenets, Samir Amin, Giovanni Arrighi, Andre Gunder Frank and Immanuel Wallerstein − four of the most famous scholars working within this tradition − write that:

> [There] is a social whole that may be called a capitalist world-economy . . . this capitalist world-economy came into existence a long time ago, probably in the sixteenth century, and that it had expanded historically from its European origins to cover the globe by the late nineteenth century . . . it can be described as capitalist in that endless accumulation is its motor force. . . . the appropriation by the world bourgeoisie of the surplus value created by the world's direct producers has involved not merely direct appropriation at the market place, but also unequal exchange, transferring surplus from peripheral to core zones.[30]

In contrast to the HST theorists, who study the distribution of military power among states, these scholars argue that the distribution of economic power among classes should be the primary focus of any analysis. International co-operation, they maintain, can be explained by looking at the way in which the most powerful actors structure the capitalist world-economy so that their economic interests are advanced at the expense of the weak. Though divisions between economic classes do not always follow international borders, the vast differences in wealth between countries of the

North and countries of the South nevertheless mean that when international co-operation does occur, it is always in the interests of the Northern capitalist nation-states.

In spite of the attention accorded the ideas of these scholars by other academic disciplines, their theories do not receive as much attention as HST in the literature on international co-operation. Many, in fact, overlook their ideas altogether.[31] Others, nevertheless, do take note. Peter Haas, for one, identifies this group of scholars as being members of the 'historical materialist' school.

Dependency theory grew out of the conviction that the dominant post-Second World War prescription for Third World development was inadequate. That prescription, perhaps best exemplified by the 'stages of growth' model,[32] was that sound domestic economic management, coupled with infusions of foreign aid, would permit poor countries to 'take off'. Challenging this view most ardently were a number of Latin American scholars during the 1950s and 1960s. They argued that, even though the colonial period was formally over, the North's domination and exploitation of the South continued. The control, however, now took economic, rather than political, forms.

A full exploration of the critiques levelled, and the alternatives proposed, by such theorists is well beyond the scope of this study. Nevertheless, having laid out its basic contribution to the study of international co-operation, let me briefly specify a few of its identified strengths and weaknesses.

The dependency story seemed to fit well with much of what was happening in the world: it accurately described the low level of development of many of the world's inhabitants. In this way, it presented a penetrating critique of naive developmentalism. These theorists' ideas, moreover, provided support for new and different understandings of world politics. By helping to supplement the dominant state-centric analysis, dependency theory focused attention upon, in particular, the globalisation of the world economy.

Although the theories offered some valid descriptions, they could not, however, account for some apparent anomalies in the world. Why, for example, has the development experience of Australia and Argentina (two countries which were, at one time, similar in many respects) been so different during the past one hundred and fifty years? More recently, why has the pattern of development been so uneven within the Third World? Additionally, although the notion that the North had consciously 'underdeveloped' the South is attractive,[33] such a proposition seems to credit the North with much more co-ordination, control and rationality than could have conceivably been possible. Is it simply not an excuse for directing attention away from the problems of domestic management? Indeed, dependency, apart from import substitution, offers few policy prescriptions short of revolution. Finally, with the collapse of communism in Eastern Europe, some considered the approach to have been sent into total disarray. Consequently, by the beginning of the 1990s, the intellectual credibility of both strands of power-based explanations – that is, hegemonic stability theory and dependency theory – had been severely challenged.

Interest-based explanations

A second sort of explanation begins with the assumption that the world can be envisaged as a collection of self-interested utility maximisers. Choosing continually among available policy alternatives in such a way as to maximise his or her own welfare (irrespective of the impact of such policies upon others), international co-operation will only be realised when each of these actors finds it in their own particular self-interest to co-ordinate their policies with the rest. As Joshua Goldstein and John Freeman note, '[a]ccepting most realist assumptions, this school attempts to show that it is possible to achieve cooperation even under conditions of anarchy. This school synthesises two traditions in international relations theory, bringing together "neorealism" and studies of "international interdependence." '[34] 'Interest-based' is the term often used to describe this sort of explanation.

The analysis borrows many concepts from microeconomics and suggests that actors may engage in international co-operation in order to 'overcome the barriers to more efficient coordination identified by theories of market failure'.[35] Indeed, Robert Keohane, who along with Robert Axelrod and Kenneth Oye, is one of its leading proponents, maintains that this kind of approach 'can be used to explore the conditions under which cooperation takes place, and it seeks to explain why international institutions are constructed by states'.[36] It is, according to Oran Young, easy enough to see why actors may be able to solve a collective action problem and realise international co-operation:

To the extent that they find themselves involved in interdependent decision making (a pervasive condition in the realm of international relations), such actors are bound to discover that individually rational behavior regularly produces suboptimal (sometimes even disastrous) outcomes and that they (as well as other members of the group) can benefit from accepting the constraints of institutional arrangements.[37]

Given the extent to which this tool of analysis is used within international relations scholarship, it is not surprising to find a variety of different labels for it – these include 'neoliberal institutionalism',[38] 'situational models',[39] 'structural analysis'[40] and 'co-operation under anarchy'.[41] What is more surprising, however, is that some have failed to recognise its close links with game theory. Many theorists who use this approach have used 'games', such as the Prisoner's Dilemma, in order to model collective action problems that face the members (most commonly, states) of international society.[42] Although games should be considered alongside interest-based explanations, some scholars separate the two concepts explicitly. (Haggard and Simmons, for example, have distinguished between the 'game theoretic' and the 'functional' approaches.[43]) This separation may be incorrectly predicated upon a perceived distinction between theory and method. Just as it was eventually recognised that behavioural studies did not, in themselves, constitute a new theory in the field of international relations, but simply did present a new method for realism,[44] game theory is merely a formalisation of the interest-based scholars' theme. Consequently, interest-based explanations and games are considered together here.

Even though both games and interest-based approaches have been evident in international relations scholarship for a number of years,[45] they did not gain considerable attention until the early 1980s. In light of the perceived decline of American hegemony during the 1970s and 1980s, such explanations were thought to be more appropriate for an increasingly multipolar world. Goldstein and Freeman, however, identify an even more pressing impetus:

> The anarchic nature of international relations is very troubling to these theorists because the prospect of a continuing free for all in the nuclear age is so undesirable. Thus these international relations theorists are quite interested in formal models that propose possible resolutions of such a dilemma.[46]

Regardless of the inspiration, their visibility has meant that interest-based explanations have come under much scrutiny. Let us consider some of the identified strengths and weaknesses.

Focusing specifically upon game theory, Robert Jervis identifies a number of its advantages:

> [I]t builds upon central characteristics of international politics –
> anarchy, the security dilemma, and the combination of common and
> conflicting interests. . . . the approach is parsimonious and lends itself
> to deductive theorizing . . . it seeks to bring together the study of
> conflict and the study of cooperation, and tries to explain a wide range
> of phenomena encompassing both security and political economy.[47]

Furthermore, Keohane maintains that these 'models, especially Prisoner's Dilemma, draw our attention to ways in which barriers to information and communication in world politics can impede cooperation and create discord even when common interests exist'.[48] By illuminating counter-intuitive findings, game theory may be able to provide a framework for both discussion and analysis of various international collective action problems. The main insight developed by such approaches is that equilibrium outcomes in non-cooperative games may be sub-optimal; or, in less technical language, rational actions may not necessarily produce the most favourable outcome for society as a whole. In this way, interest-based theorists in general, and game theorists in particular, attempt to formalise the traditional collective action problem.

Despite their concentration upon collective action problems, these theorists, as mentioned above, do not claim that the world is condemned to sub-optimal outcomes. Indeed, another perceived strength of the approach is that the models can identify conditions that encourage co-operation.[49] First, the 'mutuality of interests' can be a key determinant.[50] States will engage in co-operative actions if it is in their rational self-interest to do so. By examining how the payoff matrices are calculated, analysts and policy-makers may be able to discern how these values might be changed, so that co-operation can be fostered.[51]

Second, the 'shadow of the future' is an important determinant of co-operation. As Young notes: 'Parties expecting to engage in a long-running relationship are apt to find that the shadow of the future exerts considerable pressure on them to behave co-operatively at the outset.'[52] Axelrod, in his book *The Evolution of Cooperation*, makes this point, while supporting his argument with both empirical case-studies and an analysis of an innovative computer tournament.[53] Again, quoting Young:

> [Axelrod's work] demonstrates that purely self-interested actors may develop effective rules or social conventions through an interactive learning process involving trial and error coupled with a kind of behavioral natural selection, so long as they expect to interact with each other repeatedly and employ relatively low discount rates in computing the present value of future benefits.[54]

Axelrod and Keohane, furthermore, emphasise the importance of anticipated future interactions. They argue that a norm of reciprocity, which can help promote international co-operation, is more likely to develop if three conditions are satisfied: '(1) players can identify defectors; (2) they are able to focus retaliation on defectors; and (3) they have sufficient long-run incentives to punish defectors'.[55]

Third, interest-based analyses highlight the significance of the number of players involved in the particular issue. Building upon findings made famous by Mancur Olson,[56] many have argued that a greater number of actors increases a whole range of transaction costs[57] (for example, surveillance).[58] Consequently, fewer players will increase the prospects of international co-operation.[59]

However, in addition to the insights that this set of theories can provide in the study of international co-operation, there are also a number of problems with both game theory in particular and the entire approach more generally. The first difficulty is encountered when one attempts to determine the objects of the analysis – that is, for which actors should the costs and benefits of policy alternatives be calculated? Some choose the nation-state. In a world where some transnational corporations are more influential than many nation-states, however, can this choice be adequately defended? Moreover, how can influence be measured? Should it be in the coin of guns or butter, or perhaps something else? Perhaps influence is only specific to particular relationships, and, accordingly, cannot be assessed in a general case. Proponents of power-based explanations, moreover, maintain that interest-based theorists 'assume too easily that actors' decisions are in some meaningful sense voluntary, thus running the risk of ignoring inequalities of power among actors'.[60] In short, this kind of approach may not be appropriate in some international predicaments.[61]

Once the 'most significant' actors have been selected for the analysis, further difficulties will be encountered when attempts are made to operationalise the explanation by constructing the model. How can a single interest be determined for each of the actors? As scholars working on 'bureaucratic politics' effectively demonstrate, different elements within 'an actor' may value the same policy differently.[62] It is, therefore, wrong to assume that the actor's 'interest' is somehow 'given'. It may be equally wrong to attempt to add together these individual competing interests in order to discover an 'aggregate interest' for the actor. Instead, different factions may exercise different degrees of influence at different times. At a minimum, one should acknowledge that some explanation of group politics is necessary.[63]

Determining the preferences of even an individual, however, will also be problematic. One must wonder whether anyone, in a real-world situation, is ever faced with a well-defined pair of alternatives ('co-operate' or 'defect', in the usual language of game theory) or even some sort of continuum of choices. Thus, identifying the dominant policy options may be a demanding task. Additionally, given the difficulty of assigning ordinal numbers to the boxes (that is, ranking preferences), it is that much more difficult if one has to establish cardinal values (that is, ranking preferences and intensities) for the outcomes. Can all of the contributing factors to policy preferences really be measured? Keohane, for one, accepts this criticism by recognising that the conclusions of such analyses depend upon the model chosen. He also admits that the choice of model necessarily depends upon contextual factors – such as history – which do not enter the interest-based theorists' considerations.[64]

Further, this type of approach tends to be static, while, in reality, the world is quite dynamic. Not only will preferences change as consensual knowledge grows and as actors learn but also the individuals who occupy the important decision-making positions may be replaced over time and these transformations may affect the actor's priorities. Peter Haas notes that because 'many neorealist authors use game-theoretic techniques in their analysis, they are unlikely to consider the possibility of learning that recognises and transcends the limitations of the game being played'.[65] Indeed, the payoffs may shift to such an extent that the very nature of the policy dilemma fundamentally changes.

Another problem with the interest-based approach is that it assumes that states choose independently, ignorant of the choices of others. This can be questioned, because technological improvements in remote sensing and the greater importance attached to verification mean that actors now have a greater understanding of the actions of others.

Finally, each game must be placed within the context of a larger game – namely, all international activities. Many issues are linked to others, and therefore cannot be examined in complete isolation. In this way, a variety of games – that may be compatible or incompatible – must be considered. The fact that many game theorists fail to do so substantially weakens their analysis.

Moving from the theoretical to the empirical, a number of authors question the explanatory value of interest-based approaches. More specifically, and more importantly for the purposes of this book, scholars note that these analytical tools may have more to say about the maintenance of co-operative arrangements than about their formation. Even Keohane, who is one of the approach's major articulators and proponents, recognises that the theory has not been used much to explain the creation of institutions.[66] Young reiterates this observation by noting that: 'While the logic behind each of these propositions is straightforward, an initial assessment of the evidence regarding the formation of environmental regimes raises significant questions about their explanatory power.'[67] The approach is thus not only questioned on theoretical grounds, but it also encounters problems in the face of empirical testing.

Knowledge-based explanations

A third sort of explanation directs attention to the ways in which actors receive, process, interpret and adapt to new information. Such a focus, proponents argue, helps to explain the absence and presence of international co-operation. International co-operation will only be possible after a convergence of key players' understandings of the problems at hand. This set of explanations has often been labelled 'knowledge-based'.

Peter Haas, one of the foremost such theorists, argues that:

> Writers from this tradition look at policymaking in terms of such nonsystemic variables and actors as ideas, knowledge, beliefs, experts, and scientists. Arguing that structural analysis alone overpredicts

interstate conflict and underpredicts cooperation, such writers rely on insights from organization theory, policy sciences, social psychology, the philosophy and history of science, the sociology of knowledge, and international relations to explain the choice of state ends to which resources will be deployed and the preconditions for and forms of international cooperation.[68]

Knowledge is the key to understanding the decision-making process. Those who are perceived to have a monopoly on knowledge, or at least privileged access to it, are highly valued in times of policy uncertainty. As a consequence, they may be given greater access to decision-makers. Therefore, to explain instances of international co-operation, one should look to those who control knowledge (be they individuals or groups) and the ways in which they interact with those in decision-making circles.

This type of approach is not unrelated to dependency theory, which is considered above with different power-based explanations. The difference, however, is that here I am focusing explicitly and primarily upon the dominance of ideas. Dependency theorists are obviously interested in the dominance of ideas, but focus primarily upon one major idea – namely, capitalism. This then allows them to focus upon the forces that advance the interests of the capitalist class. I adopt a similar tack here, but open it up so that many different ideas are considered. Propositions like 'the language of consensus is a language of common interest expressed in universalist terms, though the structure of power underlying it is skewed in favor of dominant groups'[69] capture some of the flavour of the sort of explanations under examination in this section. Young effectively distinguishes between the two by noting that knowledge-based explanations (versus power-based explanations) stress 'the importance of hegemony in the Gramscian, in contrast to the material, sense in accounting for successes and failures in efforts to form international regimes'.[70] Scholars exploring the value of such sorts of explanations include Emanuel Adler, Hayward Alker, Richard Ashley, Peter Haas, Friedrich Kratochwil and John Ruggie.

Many scholars, while constructing their respective typologies of the literature on international co-operation, identify this as a unique grouping. There is little agreement, however, upon the appropriate label to apply. Haggard and Simmons, for example, identify 'cognitive approaches' as one of four branches in the literature. They argue that by focusing on 'the intersubjective meaning structures that bind actors together, [cognitivist theorists] necessarily see a looser fit between structural constraints, interests, and choices'.[71] Goldstein and Freeman offer 'psychological models' as one of their three general classifications. They note that some scholars attempt to fill in the game-theorists' black-box by looking at the motivations, cognitive abilities and perceptions of the players in the game.[72] Additionally, while identifying two types of regime change, Puchala and Hopkins note that there may be an evolutionary change – that is, institutional arrangements:

> may change qualitatively because those who participate in them change their minds about interests and aims, usually because of changes in information available to elites or new knowledge otherwise attained. . . . Such change, undisturbing to the power structure and within the regime's 'rules of the game,' is rather exceptional and characteristic mainly of functionally specific regimes.[73]

Young, furthermore, identifies a group of scholars who harbour the view that co-operation can 'only come into existence in the presence of widely shared visions of the problems at stake and the appropriate solutions'.[74] Additionally, in a bipartite division of the study of international institutions, one of Keohane's categories can be considered to be a grouping of such theories. Referring to it as a sociological approach and formally labelling the adherents as 'reflective writers', he notes that this type of analysis 'stresses the role of impersonal social forces as well as the impact of cultural practices, norms, and values that are not derived from calculations of interests'.[75]

Although knowledge-based theories have gained significant prominence only relatively recently, ideas which are true to their basic tenets can be traced back much earlier in the international relations literature. Concepts like security communities,[76] functionalism and neo-functionalism,[77] integration theories,[78] transnationalism[79] and cybernetic theories[80] – all of which were developed during the 1960s or early 1970s – direct scholars' studies (admittedly to varying degrees) to the importance of cognitive factors in international co-operation.

Commentators have identified three particular strengths of the knowledge-based explanations. First, by maintaining that the analysis of international co-operation should not be wholly consumed with the state (either on its own [as in some interest-based explanations] or in combination, thereby defining structure [power-based/HST explanations]), these scholars have highlighted the importance of non-state actors that are made up of individuals acting across national boundaries – for example, epistemic communities, political elites and pressure groups. With greater global inter-dependence, a broadening of the analysis to include such players is surely welcome.

Knowledge-based explanations also encourage the analyst to consider domestic politics as one of the determinants of international politics. Citing this as one of the most important reasons for their explicit endorsement of cognitive approaches, Haggard and Simmons maintain that it is vital to direct attention to domestic political processes, which, they argue, have been ignored in the past.[81] Although the knowledge-based explanations cannot claim to have determined how domestic processes should be analysed, they nevertheless have done more to permeate the realists' billiard-ball – the dominant image in the international relations literature for much of the post-Second World War period – than many others.

A third strength of this approach is that its explanation is dynamic. Recognising one of the weaknesses of his own preferred methodology, Keohane notes how these writers have properly included an endogenous dynamic, which Alker calls 'historicity' and E. Haas calls 'learning'.[82] This addresses one of the major problems with many traditional approaches – namely, that preferences (be they of the power-based hegemon or the interest-based 'major actors') are assumed to be fixed. With the accelerating rates of change in our world today, an approach that is better able to handle evolution in social institutions would seem to have greater promise.

The potential contribution of knowledge-based explanations is recognised by scholars who are not necessarily identified with this particular strand of thought. Arthur Stein, for example, notes that changes 'in the nature of human understanding about how the world works, knowledge, can also transform state interests and therefore the prospects for international cooperation and regime formation'.[83] Even Stephen Krasner (although still defending the validity of his preferred power-based theories) accepts that the knowledge-based theorists may have a contribution to make: 'Knowledge alone is never enough to explain either the creation or the functioning of a regime. Interests and power cannot be banished. But knowledge and understanding can affect regimes. If regimes matter, then cognitive understanding can matter as well.'[84] In general, it seems that this is, at present, the most 'fashionable' of the three approaches identified in this chapter.

This popularity has, inevitably, led these scholars' ideas to be placed under greater scrutiny. Such an examination prompts Keohane to suggest that the approach has, at this stage, more to say about the weaknesses of other methods than the strengths of its own particular ideas:

> Reflective approaches are less well specified as theories: their advocates have been more adept at pointing out what is omitted in rationalistic theory than in developing theories of their own with a prior content. Supporters of this research program need to develop testable theories, and to be explicit about their scope.[85]

More recently, Young suggests that the argument about epistemic communities 'requires further elaboration and may not stand up in its strongest form . . .'.[86] Greater critical analysis will presumably take place as the concepts of this group's adherents are further developed and elaborated.

The framework for analysis

Most scholars striving to explain the presence or absence of international co-operation argue that attention should be focused upon either power, interests or knowledge. Thus far in this chapter, I have examined each of these different sorts of explanations. From this review, it appears that no single one is able to produce all of the answers. Although each captures at least one important aspect of the process of international co-operation, each nevertheless has little to say about other vital elements. As a result, an unwavering commitment to any one could cause important elements to be neglected, and therefore leave the analysis wanting. To avoid this predicament, some synthesis of the three seems desirable. By presenting a framework for analysis in this section that is informed by all three sorts of explanations, I attempt to give substance to this ambition. This framework is subsequently used in the following chapters to investigate the politics of global atmospheric change.

Although most scholars in international relations have concentrated upon one of the three, a minority have attempted to make use of more than one explanation for international co-operation.

Christer Jonsson, for one, explicitly uses a number of established theoretical ideas in his study of the creation, change and maintenance of the international aviation regime. 'Rather than relying on any one model, [Jonsson probes] the ability of several models to account for the observed regime dynamics.'[87] Although his different models have varying degrees of explanatory power, each contributes to a better understanding of at least part of the story. As Jonsson admits, the inspiration for this approach includes the comments of Robert Keohane and Joseph Nye, who, ten years earlier, suggested that: 'It would not be wise to develop a single amalgamated model; but under different conditions, different combinations of the models will provide the best explanations of international regime change and political outcomes.'[88] Oran Young advances similar ideas. When discussing various models of regimes, he argues that each 'captures some important features of reality but none offers a satisfactory account of the full range of observable phenomena'.[89] Indeed, in a study of international regime formation in the Arctic (with Gail Osherenko), he explicitly employs a multi-faceted approach, suggesting that a number of key components and linkages must be considered in order to understand more fully instances of international co-operation.[90] Furthermore, Vinod Aggarwal assembles different ideas to inform his analysis of the international politics of textiles. He uses 'the expectations generated from the theoretical ideas ... to investigate regime transformation. This method provides [him with] the first step in utilizing cases systematically'.[91] Thus, the precedence of using more than one approach is well established.

There exist sound arguments, therefore, for proceeding with a multidimensional approach to study the politics of global atmospheric change. The question that remains, however, is: what elements should be included? More specifically, what hypotheses for international co-operation should guide this study of ozone layer depletion and climate change?

To arrive at an answer, I take direction from two quarters. First, insight is distilled from the existing literature on international co-operation – that is, each of the three identified sorts of explanations provides considerable guidance. After review, it appears that each has retained sufficient plausibility to deserve inclusion, in some shape or form, in the derived set of hypotheses. Consequently, recognition of the potential influence of power, interests and knowledge is retained. Second, a number of independent observations, with particular relevance to the issues of global atmospheric change, are also made. They are revealed below, in the elaboration of each element of the framework. Together, then, a literature assessment and a number of independent observations help to generate the testable hypotheses. Having thus spelt out the inspiration for the set of hypotheses, I now present the theoretical framework that is used in this book to study the politics of global atmospheric change.

The first hypothesis is that *a consensus regarding the problem's causal relations is necessary for international co-operation*. This hypothesis relates directly to the work of scholars advancing knowledge-based explanations. Given the uncertainty regarding the value of this sort of explanation (as outlined above),[92] any opportunity for additional testing should be taken. Moreover, global atmospheric issues appear to be particularly well-suited case-studies. Like other environmental issues, they involve a good deal of 'natural' and 'applied' science. Such was the major inspiration for the inclusion of this first hypothesis.

In Part II, this hypothesis is explored. The investigation examines the ways in which knowledge of atmospheric dynamics was attained, legitimated and transmitted. Additionally, it studies the ways in which this knowledge entered into, and existed within, political processes. Like most other hypotheses for international co-operation, therefore, this one directs our attention to policy-making. Unlike others, however, it also focuses explicitly upon scientific knowledge, and how it affected the quest for international co-operation.

The second hypothesis is that *a situation in which all key actors, operating as self-interested utility maximisers, calculate the benefits of co-ordinating their policies to be greater than the costs, is necessary for international co-operation*. This hypothesis relates closely to the work of scholars advancing interest-based explanations. Utilisation of their work is justified not only by the widespread use of such ideas,[93] but also by the more recent results of two major research efforts. The hypothesis, however, also relates to one strand of power-based explanations. Despite the apparent difficulties encountered by the hegemonic stability theory (HST),[94] some consideration of the ways in which powerful states affect the interests of others was thought necessary. Consequently, inspired by HST, this hypothesis also directs attention to the exercise of so-called structural power, and the ways in which it can affect the interests of both 'source' and 'target' actors.[95] These ideas motivated the inclusion of this second hypothesis.

In Part III, this hypothesis is explored. It directs our attention to the ways in which the values of different policy alternatives – in particular, 'do nothing' or 'take action' – were evaluated. In the face of global atmospheric change, the costs and benefits of a 'do nothing' policy alternative stemmed from the shifts caused by the global atmospheric change. Alternatively, a 'take action' policy resulted in costs and benefits that had two primary elements: associated not only with the shifts in those activities that were causing the atmosphere to change, but also with the avoidance of global atmospheric change itself. I explore the ways in which the different calculations affected efforts to realise international co-operation.

The third hypothesis is that *adequate resolution of North–South issues – that is, developing countries' concerns about 'equity' – is necessary for international co-operation.* This hypothesis relates to one strand of the power-based explanations – namely, that body of work which has been identified as dependency theory. I have selected this because North–South issues have received relatively little attention in studies of international co-operation. This may be explained by the fact that the dominant issues within the post-Second World War study of international relations have been either strategic (primarily analysed along the US–USSR axis) or economic (primarily analysed among countries of the triad). However, the global reach of the atmosphere, coupled with recent political developments (particularly the 1992 Earth Summit and its follow-up), encouraged inclusion of this third hypothesis.[96]

In Part IV, this hypothesis is explored. Attention is directed to the major actors in both the North and the South, in order to discover how they defined and attempted to achieve 'equity'. The ways in which the international negotiations were subsequently affected by these understandings are also examined.

The fourth hypothesis is that *the prospects for international co-operation will increase when any of four catalysts – namely, political entrepreneurs, non-governmental organisations, issue tangibility and a conducive international environment – are present.* Many of these factors have not been considered systematically in much of the literature on international co-operation. Consequently, they are not directly related to any one of the three identified sorts of explanations. Nevertheless, recent propositions about the importance of leadership[97] and contextual factors[98] encouraged the identification of political entrepreneurs[99] and a conducive international environment, respectively.[100] While more general expositions about the role of social movements[101] motivated inclusion of the other two factors.[102] By identifying these elements as 'catalysts', I am proposing that they have a secondary impact – though not 'necessary', their presence would nevertheless accelerate the processes associated with international co-operation. In Part V, the influence of these four catalysts is explored.

The following chapters cover wide expanses in both space and time. On their own, each of eight of them (that is, Chapters 2, 3, 5, 6, 8, 9, 11 and 12) tell a story about the relationship between a key factor and an issue of global atmospheric change. Whereas each of the other four (that is, Chapters 4, 7, 10 and 13) develops a number of ideas about the role of science, interests, equity or catalysts in global environmental politics more generally. Each individual chapter, however, is also part of a larger story. The twelve chapters, together, strive to explain the factors that affect international co-operation, not only on the two issues of global atmospheric change but also on international collective action problems more generally.

Notes

1   Robert O. Keohane, *After Hegemony: Cooperation and Discord in the World Political Economy* (Princeton, Princeton University Press, 1984), p. 51.

2   Keohane goes on to define 'intergovernmental co-operation' as taking place *'when the policies actually followed by one government are regarded by its partners as facilitating realization of their own objectives, as the result of a process of policy coordination'* (Keohane, *After Hegemony*, pp. 51–2. Emphasis in original). Alternatively, I will preserve the term 'international co-operation', looking not just at governments, but at all sorts of actors working across international borders.

3   Joseph M. Grieco, *Cooperation Among Nations: Europe, American, and Non-tariff Barriers to Trade* (London, Cornell University Press, 1990), p. 4.

4   Keohane, *After Hegemony*, p. 34. Snidal credits Keohane with coining the term (Duncan Snidal, 'The limits of hegemonic stability theory', *International Organization*, 39:4 (Autumn 1985), p. 581, n. 4).

5   See, for example, Charles Kindleberger, *The World in Depression*,

1929–1939 (Los Angeles, University of California Press, 1973).

6 Snidal, 'The limits of hegemonic stability theory', pp. 580–1. Kindleberger's first writings on the subject include: *The World in Depression*; and 'Systems of international economic order', in David Calleo (ed.), *Money and the Coming World Order* (New York, New York University Press, 1976). Keohane's earlier works include: 'The theory of hegemonic stability and changes in international economic regimes, 1967–1977', in Ole R. Holsti, Randolph M. Siverson and Alexander L. George (eds), *Change in the International System* (Boulder, Westview Press, 1980), pp. 131–62.

7 Charles P. Kindleberger, 'International public goods without international government', *The American Economic Review*, 76:1 (March 1986), p. 8.

8 Gilpin's works include: *U.S. Power and the Multinational Corporation: the Political Economy of Foreign Direct Investment* (New York, Basic Books, 1975); and *War and Change in World Politics* (Cambridge, Cambridge University Press, 1981). Krasner's writings include: 'State power and the structure of international trade', *World Politics*, 28:3 (April 1976), pp. 317–47.

9 Kindleberger, *The World in Depression*.

10 See, for example, Hedley Bull, *The Anarchical Society: a Study of Order in World Politics* (Basingstoke, Macmillan, 1977), Chapter 9.

11 Isabelle Grunberg exposes the ethnocentric appeal of the theory, showing how some scholars (particularly Kindleberger) have stressed the moralistic mission of the hegemon both to engage in self-sacrifice and to work for the benefit of the entire international community (Isabelle Grunberg, 'Exploring the "myth" of hegemonic stability', *International Organization*, 44:4 (Autumn 1990), pp. 431–77).

12 Oran R. Young, *International Cooperation: Building Regimes for Natural Resources and the Environment* (London, Cornell University Press, 1989), p. 88.

13 No doubt that, as a tool of analysis, one of the attractions of HST is its parsimony. It invites the scholar to study the relative power capability of the dominant state in world politics and to speculate upon the prospects for international co-operation from there.

14 Keohane, *After Hegemony*, p. 46.

15 The other that they identify is 'evolutionary change', which I consider below (Donald J. Puchala and Raymond F. Hopkins, 'International regimes: lessons from inductive analysis', in Stephen D. Krasner (ed.), *International Regimes* (London, Cornell University Press, 1983), pp. 61–91).

16 Ibid., p. 66.

17 Ibid., p. 90.

18 Arthur A. Stein, 'Coordination and collaboration: regimes in an anarchic world', in Krasner, *International Regimes*, p. 136.

19 Oran R. Young, 'Global environmental change and international governance', in Ian H. Rowlands and Malory Greene (eds), *Global Environmental Change and International Relations* (Basingstoke, Macmillan, 1992), p. 11.

20 Keohane, *After Hegemony*, Chapters 8–10.

21 Robert O. Keohane, 'The demand for international regimes', in Krasner *International Regimes*, p. 142.

22 Ibid., p. 142.

23 Keohane, *After Hegemony*, p. 38.

24 Peter Mayer, Volker Rittberger and Michael Zurn, 'Regime theory: state of the art and perspectives', in Volker Rittberger (ed.), *Regime Theory and International Relations* (Oxford, Clarendon, 1993), p. 413.

25 Snidal, 'The limits of hegemonic stability theory', pp. 597–612.

26 Stein, 'Coordination and collaboration', p. 138. We should recognise, nevertheless, that Stein also acknowledges the importance of the distribution of power in the international system (ibid., p. 135).

27 Keohane, *After Hegemony*, p. 38.

28 Young, *International Cooperation*, p. 204.

29 Though united by some fundamental premises, a variety of different perspectives are still discernible within 'dependency theory'. For one survey, see Chris Brown, 'Development and dependency', in Margot Light and A.J.R. Groom (eds), *International Relations: a Handbook of Current Theory* (London, Frances Pinter, 1985), pp. 60–73.

30 Samir Amin, Giovanni Arrighi, Andre Gunder Frank and Immanuel Wallerstein, *Dynamics of Global Crisis* (Basingstoke, Macmillan, 1982), p. 9.

31 In one of the most-cited syntheses of the literature on international co-operation, this sort of analysis does not appear, explicitly, in the review of four types of scholarship (Stephan Haggard and Beth A. Simmons, 'Theories of international regimes', *International Organization*, 41:3 (Summer 1987), pp. 491–517).

32 W.W. Rostow, *The Stages of Economic Growth: a Non-Communist Manifesto* (Cambridge, Cambridge University Press, 1971).

33 See, for example, Andre Gunder Frank, *Capitalism and Underdevelopment in Latin America* (Harmondsworth, Penguin, 1971).

34 Joshua S. Goldstein and John R. Freeman, *Three-Way Street: Strategic Reciprocity in World Politics* (London, University of Chicago Press, 1990), p. 11.

35 Keohane, 'The demand for international regimes', p. 151.

36 Robert O. Keohane, 'International institutions: two approaches', *International Studies Quarterly*, 32:4 (December 1988), p. 381.

37 Young, *International Cooperation*, p. 211.

38 Grieco, *Cooperation Among Nations*. See, also, Robert O. Keohane, 'Neoliberal institutionalism: a perspective on world politics', in Robert O.

Keohane (ed.), *International Institutions and State Power: Essays in International Relations Theory* (London, Westview Press, 1989).

39   Christer Jonsson, *International Aviation and the Politics of Regime Change* (London, Frances Pinter, 1987), p. 158.

40   Young, 'Global environmental change', p. 10.

41   Kenneth A. Oye (ed.), *Cooperation Under Anarchy* (Princeton, Princeton University Press, 1986).

42   See, for example, Michael B. Nicholson, *Formal Theories in International Relations* (Cambridge, Cambridge University Press, 1989).

43   Haggard and Simmons, 'Theories of international regimes', pp. 504–9. Haggard and Simmons, nevertheless, do acknowledge the close links between the two.

44   See Michael Banks, 'The inter-paradigm debate', in Light and Grooms *International Relations*, p. 11; and John Vasquez, *The Power of Power Politics: a Critique* (London, Frances Pinter, 1983), especially Chapter 2.

45   Games were developed in the social science literature during the Second World War, and so-called 'adjustment theories' were in evidence from the 1970s. For the former, see John Von Neumann and Oskar Morgenstern, *The Theory of Games and Economic Behavior* (Princeton, Princeton University Press, 1944); while, for the latter, see Paul Taylor, 'A conceptual typology of international organisation', in Paul Taylor and A.J.R. Groom (eds), *International Organisation: a Conceptual Approach* (London, Frances Pinter, 1978), pp. 119–20.

46   Goldstein and Freeman, *Three-Way Street*, p. 11.

47   Robert Jervis, 'Realism, game theory, and cooperation', *World Politics*, 40:3 (April 1988), p. 319.

48   Keohane, *After Hegemony*, p. 69.

49   Kenneth A. Oye, 'Explaining cooperation under anarchy: hypotheses and strategies', in Oye, *Cooperation Under Anarchy*, pp. 1–24.

50   Robert Axelrod and Robert O. Keohane, 'Achieving cooperation under anarchy: strategies and institutions', in Oye *Cooperation Under Anarchy*, p. 227.

51   Robert Axelrod, for one, has attempted this. See his 'Conflict of interest: an axiomatic approach', *Journal of Conflict Resolution*, 11:1 (March 1967), pp. 87–99, where he explicitly examines the calculation of payoff matrices.

52   Young, 'Global environmental change', pp. 10–11.

53   Robert M. Axelrod, *The Evolution of Cooperation* (New York, Basic Books, 1984).

54   Young, *International Cooperation*, p. 202.

55   Axelrod and Keohane, 'Achieving cooperation', p. 235.

56   Mancur Olson, *The Logic of Collective Action: Public Goods and the Theory of Groups* (Cambridge, Harvard University Press, 1965).

57   Young, 'Global environmental change', p. 10.

58   Peter M. Haas, *Saving the Mediterranean: the Politics of International Environmental Cooperation* (New York, Columbia University Press, 1990), p. 45.

59   Young and Osherenko argue that these three conditions are 'inadequate to explain or predict the formation of international regimes'. Alternatively, in their discussion of 'interest-based hypotheses', they present ten different hypotheses 'pertaining to regime formation' (Gail Osherenko and Oran R. Young, 'The formation of international regimes: Hypotheses and cases', in Oran R. Young and Gail Osherenko (eds), *Polar Politics: Creating International Environmental Regimes* (London, Cornell University Press, 1993), pp. 11–19).

60   Keohane, *After Hegemony*, p. 70. Some interest-based theorists who can also be labelled 'modified structuralists' (this is Krasner's terminology (Stephen D. Krasner, 'Structural causes and regime consequences: regimes as intervening variables', in Krasner, *International Regimes*) do acknowledge this point, for they argue that 'regimes cannot be relevant for zero-sum situations in which states act to maximize the difference between their utilities and those of others' (ibid., p. 8).

61   Jervis makes a similar argument (Jervis, 'Realism, game theory', p. 334). Keohane also recognises that actors' choices 'will be constrained in such a way that the preferences of the most powerful actors will be accorded the greatest weight' (Keohane, *After Hegemony*, p. 71).

62   Graham T. Allison, *Essence of Decision: Explaining the Cuban Missile Crisis* (Boston, Little, Brown, & Company, 1971).

63   See, for example, James Rosenau, 'Before cooperation: hegemons, regimes, and habit-driven actors in world politics', *International Organization*, 40:4 (Autumn 1986), pp. 849–94; and Helen Milner, 'International theories of cooperation among nations: strengths and weaknesses', *World Politics*, 44:3 (April 1992), pp. 466–96.

64   Keohane, 'International institutions: two approaches', p. 388.

65   Haas, *Saving the Mediterranean*, p. 61.

66   Keohane, 'International institutions: two approaches', p. 387. Keohane's use of the term 'institution' is sufficiently similar to our term 'co-operation' so as to make the comparison valid.

67   Young, 'Global environmental change', p. 11.

68   Haas, *Saving the Mediterranean*, p. 52.

69   Robert W. Cox, 'Labor and hegemony', *International Organization*, 31:3 (Summer 1977), pp. 385–424. See, also, Robert W. Cox, 'Gramsci, hegemony and international relations: an essay in method', *Millennium: Journal of International Studies*, 12:2 (Summer 1983), pp. 162–75, in which he notes the importance of the ways in which international organisations universalise the norms supported by the leaders of the dominant state.

70   Young, 'Global environmental change', p. 341.

71   Haggard and Simmons, 'Theories of international regimes', p. 499.
72   Goldstein and Freeman, *Three-Way Street*, pp. 14–22.
73   Puchala and Hopkins, 'International regimes: lessons', pp. 65–6.
Their other type of regime change – revolutionary – is noted above.
74   Young, 'Global environmental change', p. 11.
75   Keohane, 'International institutions: two approaches', p. 381.
76   Karl W. Deutsch, *The Nerves of Government: Models of Political Communication and Control* (New York, The Free Press, 1966).
77   David Mitrany is considered to be the 'founder' of the functionalist school of thought, while Ernst Haas and Leon Lindberg elaborated the idea of 'neo-functionalism'. For a review of these ideas, along with further references, see Jeppe Tranholm-Mikkelsen, 'Neo-functionalism: obstinate or obsolete?: a reappraisal in the light of the new dynamism of the EC', *Millennium: Journal of International Studies*, 20:1 (Spring 1991), pp. 1–22.
78   Taylor, 'A conceptual typology', p. 126.
79   See, for example, Robert O. Keohane and Joseph S. Nye (eds), *Transnational Relations and World Politics* (Cambridge, Harvard University Press, 1972).
80   John D. Steinbruner, *The Cybernetic Theory of Decision* (Princeton, Princeton University Press, 1974).
81   Haggard and Simmons, 'Theories of international regimes', p. 517. See, also, Milner, 'International theories of cooperation'.
82   Keohane, 'International institutions: two approaches', p. 390.
83   Stein, 'Coordination and collaboration', p. 136.
84   Stephen D. Krasner, 'Regimes and the limits of realism: regimes as autonomous variables', in Krasner, *International Regimes*, p. 368.
85   Keohane, 'International institutions: two approaches', p. 393.
86   Young, 'Global environmental change', p. 11.
87   Jonsson, *International Aviation and the Politics of Regime Change*, p. 152.
88   Robert O. Keohane and Joseph S. Nye, *Power and Interdependence: World Politics in Transition* (Boston, Little, Brown & Company, 1977), p. 59.
89   Young, *International Cooperation*, p. 213.
90   Oran R. Young and Gail Osherenko, 'International Regime Formation: Findings, Research Priorities, and Applications', in Young and Osherenko, *Polar Politics*, pp. 246–51.
91   Vinod K. Aggarwal, *Liberal Protectionism: the International Politics of Organized Textile Trade* (London, University of California Press, 1985), p. 39.
92   See notes 85 and 86 and accompanying text.
93   One of the studies finds that interest-based behaviour was the factor most consistently emphasised by contributing case-studies (Young and Osherenko, 'International Regime Formation', p. 232), while the other

concludes that the interest-based hypothesis (that is, 'situation-structural hypothesis', in the study's terminology) holds the most promise (Peter Mayer, Volker Rittberger and Michael Zurn, 'Regime theory: State of the art and perspectives', in Rittberger, *Regime Theory and International Relations* (Oxford, Clarendon, 1993), p. 413).

94   See the discussion above, particularly note 24 and accompanying text.

95   See, for example, Susan Strange, *States and Markets: an Introduction to International Political Economy* (London, Pinter Publishers, 1988).

96   Recognise also that Oran Young maintains that the 'availability of arrangements that all participants can accept as equitable (rather than efficient) is necessary for institutional bargaining to succeed' (Oran R. Young, 'The politics of international regime formation: managing natural resources and the environment', *International Organization*, 43:3 (Summer 1989), p. 368).

97   See, for example, Oran R. Young, 'Political leadership and regime formation: on the development of institutions in international society', *International Organization*, 45:3 (Summer 1991), pp. 281–308.

98   See, for example, Young, 'Global environmental change', p. 12.

99   For the purposes of this book, a political entrepreneur is defined as a person who finds it in her/his private interest to use her/his distinctive personal qualities to facilitate efforts to realise international co-operation. (Compare with, for example, the definition proposed by Hardin: a person who for 'career reasons, find[s] it in [her/his] private interest to work to provide collective benefits to relevant groups' (Russell Hardin, *Collective Action* (Baltimore, Johns Hopkins University Press, 1982), p. 35.))

100   I use the term 'a conducive international environment' to capture the same ideas to which Osherenko and Young refer:

> The state of the broader political environment is a key determinant of the prospects for regime formation in specific issue areas. Sometimes the political environment is conducive to efforts at institution building; it may even provide a powerful impetus toward regime formation, regardless of the content or coherence of specific proposals. . . . By the same token, the broader political environment may impose severe constraints on regime building in specific issue areas.

(Gail Osherenko and Oran R. Young, *The Age of the Arctic: Hot Conflicts and Cold Realities* (Cambridge, Cambridge University Press, 1989), pp. 260–1.)

101   See, for example, Ronnie D. Lipschutz and Ken Conca (eds), *The State and Social Power in Global Environmental Politics* (New York, Columbia University Press, 1993).

102   Non-governmental organisations are those 'non-profit organisations, whose actions are substantially independent of governments or the

private for-profit sector – and whose activities are directed toward a clearly defined set of goals that they perceive to be in the interest of society as a whole' (Navroz K. Dubash and Michael Oppenheimer, 'Modifying the mandate of existing institutions: NGOs', in Irving M. Mintzer (ed.), *Confronting Climate Change: Risks, Implications and Responses* (Cambridge, Cambridge University Press), p. 266. Issue tangibility, meanwhile, relates to the extent to which the issue is 'perceptible by touch; definite, clearly intelligible, not elusive or visionary' (*The Concise Oxford Dictionary*).

II
Science

2
Science and ozone layer depletion

The word 'ozone' is derived from the Greek word *ozein*, which means 'to smell'. Scientists first used the term in the middle of the nineteenth century to describe a ground-level substance that was characterised by a pronounced, pungent smell. The suggestion that ozone might also be present in the stratosphere (that is, in what we now call 'the ozone layer') was not made until the latter part of the same century. Even after that point, however, relatively little scientific attention was paid to stratospheric ozone. That had to wait another fifty years. In 1930, Sydney Chapman proposed that the amount of ozone present in the stratosphere was dictated solely by the concentrations of atomic oxygen, molecular oxygen and ozone. His work became the accepted foundation of this branch of atmospheric chemistry for many years.[1]

Chapman's hypotheses, however, were eventually challenged. Following an investigation of new data collected after the International Geophysical Year (1957–58), scientists suggested that other atmospheric trace gases, particularly hydrogen and nitrogen compounds, also affected the density of the ozone layer. This discovery meant that a number of everyday human activities had the potential to affect the concentration of ozone in the stratosphere. Consequently, these suppositions launched the political debate about the ozone layer.

Supersonic transports in the ozone layer

With this knowledge, some looked upwards to determine if any of these suspect compounds were reaching the ozone layer. A possible culprit was soon identified. It was the supersonic transport (SST).

By the 1960s, plans for a high-capacity, long-distance passenger airplane had been drawn up and were being developed. The SST attracted the ire of some environmentalists and scientists because it would fly higher than other airplanes – in the stratosphere, in fact – and would therefore release hydrogen and nitrogen compounds directly into the ozone layer.[2] At this time, three programmes were underway. The one in the United States, led by the Boeing Corporation, was by far the most ambitious. The others were being undertaken by the Soviets (who were building a prototype, the Tupolev 144) and the French and the British (who were collaborating on the Concorde project). One estimate suggested that there could eventually be over a thousand SSTs flying around the world, leading many to argue that the damage to the ozone layer could be significant.

With concerns mounting, studies were launched in order to investigate the potential impact of SSTs upon the ozone layer. One of the most significant was initiated by the US Department of Commerce in September 1970. Soon after its establishment, it convened a workshop of experts in the field of stratospheric chemistry in Boulder, Colorado on 18 and 19 March 1971.

At this meeting, it was evident that there was substantial disagreement concerning the possible causes of ozone layer depletion. James McDonald, from the University of Arizona, was one of the most vocal supporters of the hypothesis that water vapour caused the destruction of stratospheric ozone. He warned of the potential increase in cancer rates among the human population should this destruction be allowed to occur. McDonald's views, however, did not go unchallenged. Arnold Goldburg, chief scientist of Boeing's SST Division, vigorously contested the theory's validity. Lydia Dotto and Harold Schiff report that:

> Goldburg became obsessed with recent measurements that indicated that ozone had been increasing in the atmosphere and that water-vapour levels had also been going up at the same time. This was not what the water-vapour theory predicted would happen, and Goldburg clearly believed these data to constitute a virtual death blow to McDonald's ozone-depletion calculations.[3]

Of course, anything that challenged the validity of the hypothesis would probably bring much pleasure to Boeing officials, so

Goldburg's zeal may not be so surprising. Nevertheless, he was a respected scientist, and his attacks upon McDonald's arguments were well-substantiated.

The theory that nitrogen compounds caused depletion of the ozone layer also came under scrutiny at the Boulder meeting. Harold Johnston, from the University of California at Berkeley, had been one of the first to put forward the proposition, and he unyieldingly pushed it at this time. Johnston believed that the scientific community was too concerned with the, as he saw it, relatively less important question about the influence of water vapour. The real threat, Johnston argued, was from nitrous oxides. In 1971, he had calculated that if SSTs were allowed to operate, then there would be 'average global [ozone] reductions ranging from 3 to 23 per cent, with 50 per cent local reductions near zones of high SST traffic'.[4] Johnston also used the highly emotive issue of increased cancer rates and other health ailments to help illuminate the consequences of a depleted ozone layer. Just as the water-vapour thesis had come under attack, however, some participants had substantial reservations about the nitrous oxide hypothesis. Consequently, no consensus about the possible causes of ozone layer depletion could be reached at this workshop.

Details of the meeting and its enduring scientific disagreements had a revealing impact upon the political process. Dotto and Schiff report that:

> news of the heated debate in Boulder had rapidly reached the ears of John Ehrlichman – then the top domestic adviser to [US President] Nixon – who was reported to have said that if these scientists couldn't agree with one another, the White House wouldn't pay any attention to any of them. This was later confirmed publicly by Hubert Heffner, former deputy director of the White House's Office of Science and Technology. In a speech, Heffner suggested that when scientists reach opposite conclusions based on the same evidence, the public and government officials tend to disregard their views on political issues. He is quoted as saying that such lack of public confidence enabled Ehrlichman to dismiss Johnston's calculations by saying, 'No one believes scientists anyway.'[5]

The message seemed to be clear: without some level of agreement among members of the scientific community, its influence upon the political process would be minimal.

Without a consensual scientific opinion, a range of projections, from 'nothing' to 'catastrophe', remained tenable. Therefore, the US Government decided to investigate further the possible dangers of SST flights, and Congress ordered a report in 1971.[6] This report, initiated by the US Department of Transport and undertaken by the Climate Impact Assessment Program (CIAP), involved 1,000 individuals from ten countries and cost US$40 million. The final report, which was the most thorough study of the SST–ozone layer relationship ever undertaken, was completed in 1974.[7]

In response to the concerns that had prompted the investigation in 1971, the final report concluded that a 500-plane fleet of Boeing SSTs would cause a 16 per cent depletion of stratospheric ozone in the northern hemisphere and an 8 per cent depletion in the southern hemisphere. It confirmed the hypothesis that Johnston had put forward about nitrous oxide, although predicting less depletion. However, since the commissioning of the report, the circumstances surrounding it had changed. Most importantly, the US Senate, in May 1971, had cancelled the SST programme. Not only was the environmental impact of its operation being questioned but the SST's economic non-viability also played a major role in the final decision. Therefore, in order to try to retain some relevancy for their investigations, the CIAP's members put forth their estimates for a smaller fleet of SSTs. The researchers concluded that 125 SSTs would have to be in operation before any ozone layer depletion would be detectable.

The use of two scenarios – large-fleets and small-fleets – generated some confusion. Because the report seemed to be noting that a small fleet was environmentally acceptable, while only a larger fleet would be damaging, it offered some support to a variety of political positions. To add to the confusion, the manner in which the CIAP report was packaged ensured that the ozone layer–environment nail was not driven deeply into the coffin of the SST project. More specifically, although the 7,200 pages of the report presented a comprehensive overview of the issue, the 27-page executive summary did not, many scientists believed, accurately represent the committee's findings, because it made only oblique references to the harmful consequences of projected ozone layer depletion. Some journalists, therefore, concluded that the SSTs had been found 'innocent' – the headline, for example, in the 22 January 1975 edition of the *Washington Post* was 'SST Is Cleared on Ozone'. Moreover, a writer in *Science* at this time argued that: 'The result has been, temporarily at least, to publicly discredit those scientists who initially raised a quite justified concern about SSTs and to raise a credibility gap in regard to the still more serious threat of ozone depletion by halocarbons and other chemicals.'[8] At the beginning of 1975, therefore, an assortment of scientific views about the causes and consequences of ozone layer depletion by SSTs was still credible among members of both the scientific and the political communities.

The fact that agreement could not be reached, however, was relatively inconsequential, because the threat – that is, the operation of SSTs – was quickly evaporating. With the cancellation of the American programme, along with the termination of the Soviet one, global SST activity was virtually limited to the Concorde project. This, meanwhile, had been significantly scaled back, primarily because of its commercial limitations. (There have never been more than fourteen Concordes in operation.) Thus, the scientific debate about SST-induced ozone layer depletion became largely theoretical and, as such, a matter primarily for scientists once again.

Other possible threats to the ozone layer

During the early 1970s, other potentially significant threats to the ozone layer were identified. One was the consequences of nuclear explosions. This issue would have received greater attention if international agreements to restrict above-ground nuclear tests had not been concluded during the 1960s. In 1974, it was found that the 'effects of nuclear bomb tests around 1960 on ozone are only marginally detectable'.[9] With Test-Ban treaties being respected by the United States and the Soviet Union, the threat to the ozone layer receded. As a consequence, there was less reason for the issue to develop politically.

At this time, fertilisers were also identified as a possible threat to stratospheric ozone. Because their use in agriculture causes nitrogen compounds to be released, some individuals were suggesting that they could be a potentially significant cause of ozone layer depletion. Their likely impact was still, however, a matter of much debate, and the fertiliser–ozone layer link did not substantially impact the political agenda.

The proposition that chlorine could be a cause of ozone layer depletion was also forwarded during the early 1970s. Once again, some looked skywards to determine if any chlorine compounds were reaching the ozone layer. And, once again, a possible culprit was soon identified. This time, it was the space shuttle.

During the early 1970s, the space shuttle was being developed by the National Aeronautics and Space Administration (NASA) in the United States. The first significant elaboration of the chlorine–ozone layer hypothesis was offered at a scientific gathering in Kyoto, Japan on 10, 11 and 12 September 1973, when Richard Stolarski and Ralph Cicerone, both from the University of Michigan, presented the findings from their research. Responding both to pressure from outside the academic community (in particular, NASA, who were understandably eager to avoid the same sort of politics that had helped to terminate the SST project) and to their own uncertainties (neither were 'true' atmospheric chemists – the former had trained in physics, the latter in electrical engineering), however, they did not mention the space shuttle, but instead framed their ideas within a broader discussion about the impact of volcanic eruptions (which are the largest natural sources of chlorine). Because no one was expecting a significant increase in the incidence of volcanic eruptions, many considered their suggestions to be curious, at best.

Although the hypothesis had potentially explosive political implications, NASA's adept ability in public relations, coupled with the fact that the shuttles were not expected to be used extensively (as had been initially envisioned for the SSTs), effectively kept the issue off the political agenda.[10] Thus, as Sharon Roan reports, the 'chlorine issue was dropped. Other than volcanic emissions and exhaust produced by the space shuttle, which wasn't even built then, there was no other known source of free chlorine in the stratosphere'.[11] Although it did not acquire significant political dimensions, the space shuttle issue is nevertheless noteworthy. By bringing the issue of chlorine into the ozone layer discussions for the first time, it helped to set the stage for the ensuing debate.

Spray cans and the ozone layer

The scientific debate about the ozone layer entered new territory after the 1974 publication of a paper in the scientific journal *Nature*.[12] In this paper, Mario Molina and Sherwood Rowland, both from the University of California at Irvine, argued that we should not only be looking skywards in order to discover possible ozone-depleting activities. Rather, they hypothesised that the chlorine found in chlorofluorocarbons (CFCs) – substances used in a variety of applications at ground-level – had the potential to rise through the troposphere and to destroy substantial amounts of stratospheric ozone. With this supposition, the international political debate about the ozone layer was also launched into a new dimension.

Molina and Rowland's paper advanced unexpected findings that had wide-ranging implications. Given this, it sent tremors through the scientific and political communities: Were they right? Definitive answers, however, could not be found. Despite the substantial research that had been undertaken on the SST issue, Dotto and Schiff report that the stratosphere was still 'dubbed the "ignorosphere" because aeronomers had paid so little attention to it in the past'.[13] With so little data available, the Molina/Rowland hypothesis could only be based upon theoretical assumptions and limited laboratory observations. Consequently, there were many differing opinions about the validity of the two chemists' work.

In response, the US Government elected to examine the hypothesis further. A major report was subsequently undertaken by the US National Academy of Sciences (NAS).[14] This study, convened under the Academy's 'Climatic Impact Committee' (later renamed the 'Committee on Impacts of Stratospheric Change') was initiated in April 1975 and was due to be completed in 1976. Anticipation of its publication was high, and Dotto and Schiff argue that the NAS essentially became the 'scientific Supreme Court' in the CFC case.[15]

The much-awaited NAS report was finally released in September 1976. Its conclusions, however, were somewhat unclear. On the one hand, it confirmed the hypothesis, for it predicted an eventual 2 to 20 per cent depletion of stratospheric ozone, with a most likely depletion level between 6 and 7.5 per cent. This suggested a degree of urgency. On the other hand, it did not recommend any immediate ban upon the use of CFCs, but instead asserted that some regulation was almost certain to be necessary at some time and to some degree of completeness.[16] This suggested a degree of indifference. Effectively reflecting this ambiguity, two major US newspapers reported the NAS's study differently. The headline in the *New York Times* on 14 September 1976 was 'Scientists Back New Aerosol Curbs to Protect Ozone in Atmosphere', while the *Washington Post*'s headline on the same day was 'Aerosol Ban Opposed by Science Unit'. The 'court' seemed to have returned a mixed verdict.

Nevertheless in 1977, lawmakers decided to take action. In May of that year, legislation was set in train in the United States which would enact a ban on CFCs in non-essential aerosols by the end of 1978. This was achieved, and subsequent scientific reports seemed to vindicate this decision. More specifically, in November 1979, a second report was published by the NAS in the United States. It highlighted the potential significance of the CFC–ozone link, estimating eventual ozone layer depletion at 16.5 per cent.[17] This report from the Academy further argued that a 'wait-and-see' approach was not advised, and it encouraged the United States both to foster and to lead international efforts to protect the ozone layer. In this way, its findings suggested that politicians should be addressing the issue with some degree of urgency.

Although the NAS reports were essentially endorsing the CFC theory and suggesting that ozone layer depletion should be considered seriously, there was still some disagreement evident. Scientists employed by the major CFC producers were the most vocal individuals who challenged the NAS position. Although their interest in challenging the Molina/Rowland hypothesis may appear self-evident, the strength of some of their assertions was not in doubt. For example, in 'a 1979 statement, Du Pont officials stated: "No ozone depletion has ever been detected despite the most sophisticated analysis. . . . All ozone-depletion figures to date are computer projects based on a series of uncertain assumptions." '[18] These weaknesses in the scientific case, which were highlighted by industry's representatives, were unassailable at this time.

Attention thus far has been focused solely upon the United States. The reasons for this are that most expertise in atmospheric chemistry – both institutionally and individually – was located in the US, and that most scientific investigations were being conducted in the US.[19] Nevertheless, some research was being carried out in other places.

Elsewhere, the most substantial investigations into the CFC–ozone layer hypothesis were being conducted in Europe, particularly the United Kingdom. Though reports emerging from across the Atlantic were reaching broadly similar conclusions, their tone was markedly different. A study released by the UK government in late April 1976, for example, foresaw a potential 8 per cent depletion of stratospheric ozone in 100 years; yet it did not view this potentiality as significant.[20] Similar sentiments were expressed in another British report the following year. The Environment Secretary's Clean Air Council found the evidence linking CFCs and ozone depletion to be

tenuous and inconclusive and therefore recommended the con-
tinuation of the British Government's 'wait and see' approach. In a
remark that is oft-cited, the UK Royal Commission on Environmental Pollution's Chairman, Professor Hans Kornberg, said that
although the CFC–ozone link:

> ... may give rise to concern, there is certainly no need for panic. ...
> We feel that, even if production were to continue at the present rate,
> the evidence suggests that, at worst, over the next ten years the
> decrease in the ozone layer would result in an increase in ultraviolet
> radiation of biologically harmful wavelengths *which would roughly
> correspond to moving from the North of Scotland to the South of
> England.*[21]

In 1979, additionally, the British government published a follow-up
report, which suggested that basic scientific understanding,
'although progressing rapidly, is still inadequate in many respects'.[22]
British studies during the 1970s were thus emphasising the need for
more research. Only after conclusions became more reliable, they
argued, might policy changes need to be considered.

During the late 1970s, the National Academy of Sciences in the
United States and the Department of the Environment in the United
Kingdom arrived at rather similar findings with respect to possible
ozone layer depletion. They differed, however, in their recommendations arising from these findings. The Americans brought in
new legislation, while the British preserved the status quo. In 1978,
James Lovelock, arguably Britain's foremost scientist in this field,
maintained that 'no one can be sure which if any of the reported
analyses of atmospheric concentrations in the published literature
are correct';[23] and in 1979, a writer from the British journal *New
Scientist* argued that: 'On balance, the evidence that is now available
suggests that nothing mankind is now doing will have a disastrous
effect on the ozone layer . . .'.[24]

These differences affected the international political negotiations.
In December 1978, for example, representatives from fourteen
countries met in Munich to discuss the possibility of imposing international regulations on CFCs. At this meeting:

> the British and French representatives referred to 'new developments'
> not yet reported in the scientific literature and given little credence at
> [a meeting of technical experts the previous week in Bonn]. ... If

European scientists had been more closely involved in assessment of fluorocarbon risks since 1974 Britain and France might not have felt so free to disregard the scientific consensus.[25]

Differing views about the science were thus making international co-operation much less likely.

Scientific research was also being undertaken under 'international' auspices during the 1970s. Although both the World Meteorological Organisation (WMO) and the International Council of Scientific Unions (ICSU) had been concerned with ozone for a number of years, the possibility of stratospheric ozone depletion had not been upon either's agenda before 1975. In that year, the WMO issued a statement on the issue calling for more data collection and research. Their contribution to this goal was the Global Ozone Research and Monitoring Project, which was established in 1976 in order to improve monitoring and data collection. The other important international body operating at the end of the 1970s was the 'Co-ordinating Committee on the Ozone Layer' (CCOL). Created after an international conference in Washington, DC in 1977, it met for the first time in Geneva in November of that same year. While it was recognised that the WMO would remain the primary international body conducting the 'science', the CCOL was expected to co-ordinate their efforts with other relevant national and international organisations.

At the end of the 1970s, many different views about the strength of the CFC–ozone layer hypothesis persisted. This, in turn, encouraged differences of opinion about how these concerns might be translated into policy. Although the ozone layer was an issue on the agendas of a number of states (because their leaders recognised that the depletion of stratospheric ozone had the potential to decrease levels of human welfare) and although discussions were taking place at the international level, the issue was seen (by many) to be one that required further scientific investigations. International co-operation, many decision-makers felt, was not justified by the state of knowledge.

Diminishing concern

As improvements in both the theoretical modelling and the data collection process continued during the late 1970s and early 1980s, scientists were able to recalculate their estimates of future ozone levels. As a consequence, the predictions for eventual ozone depletion were constantly being revised during the early 1980s. The estimates, however, were being revised *downwards*. Figure 2.1 presents a longitudinal comparison of the predictions of the two most influential scientific bodies – the CCOL and the US NAS – in which the downward trend is clearly evident.

Per Bakken argues that this trend had a significant impact upon the political process:

> This new information . . . reduced national concern about the whole issue. . . . The more or less annual reports from the CCOL became more diffuse and uncertainty became the dominant impression. Policy-makers were waiting for scientists to come up with a clear answer before further action was taken.[26]

Even within the United States, the country that had displayed by far the greatest interest (both scientific and political) about the issue, this trend served to diminish the level of concern. Anne Gorsuch, President Ronald Reagan's first head of the Environmental Protection Agency, said that the ozone theory was 'highly controversial', and that 'apparently there is a need for additional scientific data before the international scientific community would be willing to accept the ozone layer depletion theory as the basis for additional government action'.[27] Although her conservative disposition might have encouraged her to say something along these lines in any case, many felt that the data justified such a position. Lovelock caught the dominant perception during the first half of the 1980s when he said: 'Had we known in 1975 as much as we know now about atmospheric chemistry, it is doubtful if politicians could have been persuaded to legislate against the emission of CFCs.'[28]

As the sense of urgency receded, efforts to reach an international agreement likewise slowed. In 1982, the United Nations Environment Programme (UNEP) had initiated a process which, it was anticipated, would culminate in international agreements to halt and to reverse ozone layer depletion. The scientific findings from the early 1980s, however, meant that by 1985, ideas about a protocol had been put on the back-burner. Instead, representatives from twenty countries could only agree a framework convention. Although this document – the Vienna Convention for the Protection of the Ozone Layer – recognised the problem of ozone layer depletion and committed states, in principle, to its resolution, it

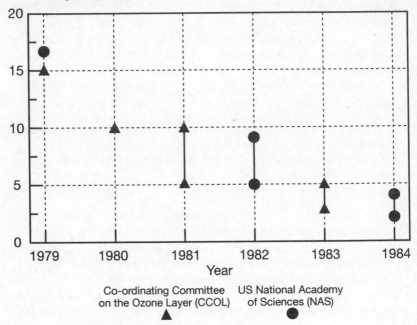

Figure 2.1 Estimates of projected ozone depletion by the CCOL and the US NAS, 1979–84

Sources: Robin Clarke and Lloyd Timberlake, *Stockholm Plus Ten: Promises, Promises?* (London, Earthscan, 1982), p. 44; Sharon L. Roan, *Ozone Crisis: the 15 Year Evolution of a Sudden Global Emergency* (Chichester, John Wiley & Sons, 1989); UNEP, *Annual Review* (Nairobi, UNEP, 1979), p. 30; UNEP, *Annual Review* (Nairobi, UNEP, 1981), p. 41; and UNEP, *Annual Report of the Executive Directory* (Nairobi, UNEP, 1983), p. 43.

stopped short of imposing any particular obligations upon its Parties. The science, many felt, simply did not justify any international policy co-ordination. European Communities opposition to any regulation, for example, was reinforced by then-recent findings that reported that the threat to the ozone layer from CFCs was 'distant' and 'that time can be allowed without risk for further scientific evaluation of theory'.[29] Yes, action might one day be needed, but only after 'further research and systematic observations to further develop scientific knowledge of the ozone layer and possible adverse effects resulting from its modification' had been undertaken.[30]

The ozone 'crater'

The entire debate, however, changed dramatically with the detection of a significant 'crater' in the ozone layer above the Antarctic continent by the British Antarctic Survey.[31] Publishing their results in May 1985, the group had discovered that ozone levels had dropped significantly – up to over 30 per cent – during the Antarctic spring. There had been discoveries of ozone depletion just a couple of years before. (In August 1980, NASA had, using satellite data, discovered a slight drop in global ozone levels.) The figure cited at that time of 0.5 per cent, however, paled in comparison to the significant depletion that the British team had detected. Indeed, what made it even more unexpected was that the US satellites that had been gathering data over the Antarctic since 1979 had not detected any significant change in ozone levels. The reason being, it was discerned later, was that the satellite's computers had been programmed to discard any data that were outside of an anticipated range. When the computers were reprogrammed, with this condition removed, they revealed the same pattern of spring-time depletion that had been discovered by the British ground-based stations.[32] As John Gribbin notes:

> The point is that in the late 1970s and early 1980s atmospheric scientists were increasingly confident that they understood, more or less, what was going on in the atmosphere. Both the chemistry and the dynamics of air movements were being analysed in more detail than ever before, and a coherent picture was emerging. But nowhere in that coherent picture was there even a hint that a dramatic change like the development of a huge hole in the ozone layer could occur.[33]

Ozone layer depletion was no longer just a theory.

Though the 'effect' was clearly evident, the 'cause' was still the subject of much debate. With the scientific community offering a variety of possible explanations for ozone layer depletion, politicians continued to encounter scientific disagreements.[34] Consequently, attempts to try to arrive at a consensual view were intensified.

As investigations continued after mid 1985, new data were collected that suggested not only that global ozone depletion had been far more severe than originally predicted, but also that an ozone crater could be forming over the Arctic as well. Indeed, the contents of a WMO report published in 1986 suggest that there was substantial consensus at this time that damage to the earth's ozone layer had in fact occurred.[35] Moreover, the findings from a gathering of atmospheric modellers in Wurzburg, West Germany in April 1987 showed that there was a further consensus growing that human activities could cause greater ozone layer depletion in the future.[36]

These developments – mounting empirical evidence, coupled with increasingly accepted ozone depletion projections – influenced the political process. After the Vienna Convention, representatives from various countries reconvened in 1986 to see if they could agree an international protocol. The scientific findings fed into their deliberations and gave their task a greater sense of urgency. The negotiation process culminated in the agreement by representatives from twenty-seven countries to sign the Montreal Protocol on Substances that Deplete the Ozone Layer in September 1987. The significance of this document is that it committed signatories to reduce their consumption of certain CFCs by 50 per cent of their 1986 level by 1999.

Nevertheless, one significant point of scientific contention still remained – namely, the question of causality. Although a research trip to the Antarctic continent by thirteen American scientists in August 1986 had narrowed the list of possible explanations, different interpretations of this group's findings sustained a variety of chemical and dynamical theories; moreover, the proponents of each were not willing to concede defeat. Therefore, in order to try to arrive at a scientific agreement over causality, there were calls for the creation of an international panel of atmospheric scientists.

In response to this, the Ozone Trends Panel was established in October 1986. The NASA-sponsored group had over a hundred scientists from ten countries. Wanting to encourage wide geographical participation, Robert Watson, a NASA scientist and one of the leaders of the investigation, invited scientists from around the world to participate on the Panel. Not only was the Panel cross-national, but it was also cross-sectoral, for the manufacturers' association played a key role. By casting his net so wide, Watson was hoping not only to ensure wide diffusion of the group's findings but also to pre-empt potential discontents.

The centrepiece of the Panel's efforts was a second trip to the Antarctic, which was called the Airborne Antarctic Ozone Experiment (AAOE). Preparations for this journey began soon after the Panel's formation, and in the Autumn of 1987, 150 scientists travelled to the south of Chile, from where they launched their experiments in the Antarctic. Their efforts were, in the end, rewarded, for they found the elusive 'smoking gun' that implicated CFCs in stratospheric ozone depletion – namely, they discovered an anticorrelation between chlorine monoxide and ozone levels. Thus, the journey's results demonstrated an undoubted chemical (and, consequently, human) cause in ozone layer depletion – that is, chlorine was leading to the destruction of stratospheric ozone.

These results were formalised on 15 March 1988, when the Ozone Trends Panel called a press conference to publicise their conclusions. The group's members found both evidence of ozone layer depletion *and* substantial proof of its cause.[37] Richard Benedick notes the impact that the weight of this evidence had: 'The panel's conclusions made headlines around the world. Ozone layer depletion was no longer a theory; at last it had been substantiated by hard evidence. And CFCs and halons were now implicated beyond reasonable doubt.'[38] With this pronouncement, the cause of stratospheric ozone depletion was no longer a major point of contention.

Continuing ozone depletion

The sequence of the major political and scientific events (that is, the opening for signature of the Montreal Protocol and the report of the Ozone Trends Panel, respectively), however, meant that just as the ink was drying on the former, the latter was suggesting that the agreed controls were not strong enough. More specifically, scientists believed that the Antarctic crater would not repair itself unless emission levels of controlled CFCs were reduced by at least 85 per cent (as compared to the longer-term 50 per cent reduction agreed in the Protocol). Moreover, they argued that other ozone-depleting substances, such as methyl chloroform, would also have to be regulated. In response, little of lasting substance could be done politically until the Protocol came into force (which, it was expected, would be in early 1989). In the meantime, though, scientific activity continued.

During the winter of 1988–89, a number of reports were published that speculated that significant reduction of stratospheric ozone over the Arctic was possible as well. Although a multinational investigation did not discover any ozone depletion, its members did detect conditions that suggested that Arctic ozone was primed for destruction. The sheer possibility of ozone depletion over the Arctic, which would have direct implications for the highly populated, northern latitudes, appeared to affect the policy positions of many industrialised states. Geoffrey Lean argues the consequences were not lost on some policy-makers at this time: 'Governments have been shaken by evidence disclosed last month that a new ozone hole may be opening up in the Arctic, over many northern countries.'[39]

Such views, though predominant, were not universal. Representatives from the Soviet Union, most significantly, challenged the conventional wisdom. At a conference in London in March 1989, they suggested that Arctic ozone depletion 'was primarily caused by weather and climate, and not by man's emission of gases'. Moreover, the leader of the Soviet delegation stressed that any moves to strengthen the Montreal Protocol needed to be based upon concrete scientific knowledge, thereby suggesting that he had yet to find any.[40] Although the Soviet delegation had changed its tune by the time of a meeting in Helsinki only two months later, others continued to challenge the consensual view. One observer writing in mid-1989 argued that natural sources of chlorine were significant and had been overlooked by most scientists. He remarked: 'Fortunately for mankind, Rowland's [CFC] theory has more holes than the ozone layer.'[41] Such people, however, formed only a tiny minority group.

With the Protocol coming into force in 1989, political meetings took place once again. At conferences in London in March 1989 and Helsinki in May 1989, concern about the increasingly astonishing scientific evidence led many policy-makers to push for controls that went beyond those embodied in the Montreal Protocol. Indeed, Michael Oppenheimer and Robert Boyle argue that 'the telltale signs of an ozone hole in the Arctic . . . prompted a change in the European Community's position [and] led to the May [1989] agreement in Helsinki to eliminate CFCs altogether'.[42] Presentations by scientists about their most recent findings on ozone layer depletion – in particular, the most likely scenario should a 'business-as-usual' situation prevail – had visible impacts upon government officials. So prompted, representatives from over eighty states expressed support for an early phase-out of a broad range of ozone-depleting chemicals.

The scientific assessment continued to dominate the discussions as they moved away from the limelight of the international, ministerial-level conference to the uncelebrated surroundings of the closed-door, working group – four of which were formed in May 1989 in order to recommend amendments to the Montreal Protocol. Richard Benedick reports:

> The discussions of the Open-Ended Working Group would prove to be dominated by the findings of the science panel. The scientists had become increasingly concerned about the inability of their models to predict accurately the actually measured depletion of the ozone layer. Their misgivings were heightened by the new elements in the science since Montreal: the unexpectedly large ozone losses measured over northern latitudes, the effects of the annual Antarctic ozone hole on southern populated latitudes, the potential for precipitous ozone depletion over the Arctic, and the ominous new factor of possible consequences from volcanic eruptions.[43]

Once the negotiations returned to the international stage (namely, at the Second Meeting of the Parties to the Montreal Protocol, which was held in London in June 1990), the urgent and consensual scientific view again informed the high-level political process. Indeed, the mounting scientific concern about ozone layer depletion was a significant force that pushed the Parties' representatives to agree, in London, to eliminate CFCs by the turn of the century.

After 1990, evidence continued to mount. On 22 October 1991, for example, the WMO and UNEP released the Executive Summary of their latest *Scientific Assessment of Stratospheric Ozone*. The report had substantial impact upon all governments, for it revealed a level of ozone layer destruction greater (and progressing at a faster rate) than predicted. So it continued into 1992. In January of that year, researchers discovered ozone losses of up to 20 per cent in the northern hemisphere, with a maximum depletion over Russia of 40–45 per cent below normal for a few days. These findings prompted the World Meteorological Organisation to issue the following statement: 'On the whole, the 1991–92 winter can be classified among those with the most negative deviation of systematic ozone observations, which started in the mid-1950s.'[44] Although, it was accepted that natural chlorine emissions – in particular, the volcanic eruption of Mount Pinatubo in the Philippines in June 1991 – would have also exacerbated the problem, there was still considerable concern about the extent of the damage.

By 1992, international negotiators had returned to the bargaining table in preparation for the Fourth Meeting of Parties in Copenhagen in November of that year. They had not only the most recent report of the Panel for Scientific Assessment in front of them (which had been published at the end of 1991)[45] but they were also conscious of other startling scientific revelations. Just prior to the Copenhagen meeting – in the middle of November 1992 – the World Meteorological Organisation reported that the Antarctic ozone 'crater' had lost up to 65 per cent of its ozone in the second half of September and early October.[46] Moreover, during the meeting itself, an article was published in *Nature*, which argued that if global warming were to occur, then the likelihood of an ozone crater in the Arctic would increase.[47]

These pieces of scientific information contributed to an agreement to make a number of changes to the terms of the Montreal Protocol: adjustments were made that tightened the control schedules on CFCs, methyl chloroform and carbon tetrachloride, and amendments were introduced that placed regulations upon future production and consumption of hydrochlorofluorocarbons. Though only one contributing factor to these decisions, the importance of scientific information to the officials' deliberations is suggested by the attention accorded the findings of the Panel for Scientific Assessment at the Copenhagen meeting. Indeed, throughout the history of the ozone layer debates, the Panel, which has had primary responsibility for undertaking and monitoring state of the art knowledge in the science of the ozone layer, has been treated with due reverence.[48]

Since the Copenhagen meeting, suggestions that ozone layer depletion has increased have themselves increased. NASA reported that levels in December 1992 and January 1993 were the lowest ever recorded by its Nimbus 7 satellite, even beyond what had been predicted. In April 1993, moreover, the British Meteorological Office noted that the lowest level of ozone ever recorded in either a February or a March had been uncovered earlier that year. Unfortunately, this trend continued unabated through the rest of 1993, for in the autumn of that year, the Antarctic ozone crater was found to be the 'deepest ever recorded'.[49]

Although there was recognition that the Montreal Protocol had made a substantial difference in the quest to slow and to halt ozone layer depletion,[50] scientists continued to urge further action. The UK's Stratospheric Ozone Review Group argued that 'until the amount of chlorine and bromine in the stratosphere have been stabilised, the downwards trend in ozone will continue and unpredictable natural events are likely to combine with this trend to produce new record amounts'. They went on to warn that 'the measurements confirm earlier scientific findings that in order to limit future ozone depletion there is a need to phase out these emissions as soon as possible'.[51] At the beginning of 1994, the consensual scientific opinion was that the problem of ozone layer depletion was not totally solved: with emissions of ozone-depleting substances continuing, many scientists maintained that more action had to be taken.

Notes

1   See, generally, John Gribbin, 'The ozone layer', *New Scientist*, 68 (2 October 1975), pp. 12–14.

2   Potential ozone layer depletion was by no means the only environmental concern arising from the development of the SST. Others included sonic booms and noise pollution more generally.

3   Lydia Dotto and Harold Schiff, *The Ozone War* (Garden City, Doubleday & Company, 1978), p. 48.

4   Ibid., p. 64.

5   Ibid., p. 61.

6   Johnston believes that without the attention drawn to the issue by himself and other scientists, politicians would not have pursued the issue. He stated that: 'The [Department of Transport] said they had planned even back in 1970 to make a study but Congress turned them down in 1970 and probably would have turned them down again in 1971' (quoted in Dotto and Schiff, p. 67.)

7   Climate Impact Assessment Program, *Report of Findings. The Effects of Stratospheric Pollution by Aircraft* (Washington, DC, Department of Transport, DOT-TST-75–50, 1974).

8   Allen L. Hammond, 'Public credibility on ozone', *Science*, 187 (28 March 1975), p. 1182.

9   Noted in Climate Impact Assessment Program, *Report of Findings*.

10   By 1977, NASA had gathered sufficient evidence to conclude that the effect upon the ozone layer of sixty shuttle launches a year would be negligible (NASA, *Chlorofluoromethanes and the Stratosphere* (Greenbelt, NASA Reference Publication 1010, 1977)), a conclusion which was independently supported by the US National Academy of Sciences.

11   Sharon L. Roan, *Ozone Crisis: the 15 Year Evolution of a Sudden Global Emergency* (Chichester, John Wiley & Sons, 1989), p. 18.

12   Mario J. Molina and F. S. Rowland, 'Stratospheric sink for chloro-fluoromethanes: chlorine atom-catalysed destruction of ozone', *Nature*, 249 (28 June 1974), pp. 810–12.

13   Dotto and Schiff, *The Ozone War*, p. 206.

14   The National Academy of Sciences is a private, non-profit society, which is mandated to advise the US federal government on scientific and technical matters.

15   Dotto and Schiff, *The Ozone War*, p. 198.

16   Committee on Impacts of Stratospheric Change, *Halocarbons: Environmental Effects of Chlorofluoromethane Release* (Washington, DC, National Academy of Sciences, 1976).

17   Panel on Stratospheric Chemistry and Transport, *Stratospheric Ozone Depletion by Halocarbons: Chemistry and Transport* (Washington, DC, National Academy of Sciences, 1979).

18   Roan, *Ozone Crisis*, p. 96.

19   Peter Haas argues that 'atmospheric research was predominantly an American activity . . .' (Peter M. Haas, 'Banning chlorofluorocarbons: epistemic community efforts to protect stratospheric ozone', *International Organization*, 46:1 (Winter 1992), p. 193). Even in a consciously 'international' ozone assessment effort during the early 1990s, US-based scientists still accounted for just under one-half of all participants (author's calculations from Daniel Albritton and Robert T. Watson (eds), *Scientific Assessment of Ozone Depletion: 1991* (Geneva, WMO, Global Ozone Research and Monitoring Project – Report No. 25, 1991)).

20   Department of the Environment, Central Unit on Environmental Pollution, *Chlorofluorocarbons and Their Effect on Stratospheric Ozone* (London, HMSO, Pollution Paper No. 5, 1976).

21   Quoted in 'Mixed response to aerosol propellants', *New Scientist*, 76 (15 December 1977), p. 685. Emphasis added.

22   Department of the Environment, Central Directorate on Environmental Protection, *Chlorofluorocarbons and Their Effect on Stratospheric Ozone (Second Report)* (London, HMSO, Pollution Paper No. 15, 1979), p. 209.

23   Quoted in John Gribbin, 'Ozone passion cooled by the breath of sweet reason', *New Scientist*, 80 (12 October 1978), p. 94.

24   John Gribbin, 'Disappearing threat to ozone', *New Scientist*, 81 (15 February 1979), p. 474.

25   Thomas Stoel, 'Fluorocarbons as a global environmental case study', *New Scientist*, 81 (18 January 1979), pp. 166–7.

26   Per M. Bakken, 'Science and politics in the protection of the ozone layer', in Steinar Andresen and Willy Ostreng (eds), *International Resource Management: the Role of Science and Politics* (London, Belhaven, 1989), p. 200.

27   Quoted in David Dickson, 'Congress faces decision on CFC', *Nature*,

293 (3 September 1981), p. 4.

28 James E. Lovelock, 'Report on reports: *Causes and Effects of Changes in Stratospheric Ozone: Update 1983'*, *Environment*, 26:10 (December 1984), p. 26.

29 Report of a study by two Belgian scientists: Guy Brasseur and A. de Rudder (Anna Lubinska, 'Europe takes a cheerful view', *Nature*, 313 (28 February 1985), p. 727).

30 The quotation is taken from the *Vienna Convention for the Protection of the Ozone Layer*.

31 J.C. Farman *et al.*, 'Large losses of total ozone in Antarctica reveal seasonal CLO_x /NO_x interaction', *Nature*, 315 (16 May 1985), pp. 207–10.

32 This has subsequently been denied by NASA officials (Friedrich Pukelsheim, 'Robustness of statistical gossip and the Antarctic ozone hole', *The IMS Bulletin*, 19:4 (1990), pp. 540–2.) Regardless, NASA officials had not suspected that such extensive amounts of stratospheric ozone depletion were taking place.

33 John Gribbin, *The Hole in the Sky: Man's Threat to the Ozone Layer* (London, Corgi Books, 1988), p. 95.

34 One commentator reported that: 'Theorists are offering explanations, almost as many as there are workers in the field' (Richard A. Kerr, 'Antarctic ozone hole is still deepening', *Science*, 232 (27 June 1986), p. 1602). In fact, most of these were derived from one of three contending theories – the CFC or chemical theory, the natural or dynamic theory, and the solar cycle or 'odd-nitrogen' theory. Only the first of these suggested human causes.

35 World Meteorological Organisation, *Atmospheric Ozone 1985* (Geneva, WMO, Global Ozone Research and Monitoring Project – Report No. 16, 1986).

36 UNEP, '*Ad hoc* scientific meeting to compare model-generated assessments of ozone layer change for various strategies for CFC control, Wurzburg, 9–10 April 1987' (UNEP/WG.167/Inf.1).

37 Robert T. Watson, F. Sherwood Rowland and John Gille, *Ozone Trends Panel: Executive Summary* (Washington, DC, NASA, 1988).

38 Richard Elliot Benedick, *Ozone Diplomacy: New Directions in Safeguarding the Planet* (London, Harvard University Press, 1991), p. 110.

39 Geoffrey Lean, 'Ozone: UN acts to tighten controls', the *Observer* (London) (5 March 1989), p. 2.

40 John Ardill and Tim Radford, 'EEC official pledges to speed up ozone fight', *Guardian* (London) (6 March 1989), p. 1.

41 Rogelio Maduro, 'CFCs are not depleting the ozone layer', *EIR* (9 June 1989), p. 19.

42 Michael Oppenheimer and Robert Boyle, *Dead Heat: the Race Against the Greenhouse Effect* (London, I.B. Tauris & Co. 1990), p. 160.

43 Benedick, *Ozone Diplomacy*, p. 129.

44   World Meteorological Organisation, 'On the State of the Ozone Layer 1992' (UNEP/OzL.Pro.4/Inf.2), pt. 6.

45   Albritton and Watson, *Scientific Assessment*.

46   WMO, 'On the State of the Ozone Layer 1992', pt. 11.

47   John Austin, Neal Butchart and Keith P. Shine, 'Possibility of an Arctic ozone hole in a doubled-CO_2 climate', *Nature*, 360 (19 November 1992), pp. 221–5.

48   Edward Parson reports:

> These panels have provided a channel for science to feed directly into the negotiation process from a forum with the stamp of international objectivity and authoritativeness. All was not sweetness and light in the creation of the panels; many participants describe them as having a U.S. bias, and some report a systematic program of excluding employees of producer industries from the Technology Panel. But even the critics acknowledge that the science and technology reports were of high quality and that the leaders of the process 'played fair'.

(Edward A. Parson, 'Protecting the ozone layer', in Peter M. Haas, Robert O. Keohane and Marc A. Levy (eds), *Institutions for the Earth: Sources of Effective International Environmental Protection* (London, The MIT Press, 1993), p. 61.)

49   Meteorological conditions may have contributed to ozone depletion as well. See Gabrielle Walker, 'Weather contributes to record ozone loss', *Nature*, 365 (21 October 1993), p. 683.

50   See, for example, 'More protection for the ozone layer', *Our Planet*, 5:6 (1993), p. 17.

51   Stratospheric Ozone Review Group, *Stratospheric Ozone* 1993 (London, HMSO, 1994), quoted in 'Ozone levels hit record lows', *ENDS Report*, 228 (January 1994), p. 13.

3

Science and climate change

The weather is important. The amount of sunshine, precipitation and so on that an area receives is critical, for it determines, to a significant extent, the range and intensity of activities that can be sustained upon it. In this way, many human decisions must take climatic factors into consideration. This requirement has long been recognised, and references to the relationship between climate and society are in evidence through much of recorded history – even as far back as the ancient Egyptians and Greeks.[1]

Energy is also important. In fact, energy is necessary for human survival. However, energy is something of a two-edged sword, producing both goods and bads. Societies have recognised the harmful potential of energy production for at least two thousand years, with coal, in particular, singled out as a potentially damaging source of energy. James Lodge, for example, notes that the 'Romans complained of the foul air of Rome, possibly recording the first documentation of the problem'.[2] By the second millennium, words were being followed by actions. In 1273, the city of London passed the world's first air pollution law, with the aim of countering the nuisance of smoke from domestic fires.[3] Nevertheless, the problem persisted. In 1661, for example, John Evelyn described how human health and well-being, as well as plants, buildings, monuments and waters, were being ruined by coal smoke.[4] Attention, however, focused exclusively upon the local environmental impacts of energy production. Any potential global ramifications – more specifically, the impact of fossil fuel combustion upon climate – had yet to be identified. That had to wait until the nineteenth century.

Initial theories about climate change

In 1827, French mathematician Baron Jean-Baptiste Fourier set out the analogy between the behaviour of heat in the atmosphere and its behaviour in a greenhouse, suggesting therefore that the sun's warmth was able to enter the atmosphere, but not to escape it.[5] Thirty-eight years later, John Tyndall built upon these ideas by further developing the concept of the 'atmospheric envelope' and adding the notion that particular atmospheric gases – water vapour and carbon dioxide – were responsible for the retention of radiation heat.[6] He did not suggest, however, that the strength of the greenhouse could change. This was left to Svante Arrhenius, a Swedish scientist, who in 1896 argued that rising concentrations of atmospheric carbon dioxide would increase this effect and lead to global warming. He postulated that an effective doubling of the amount of carbon dioxide in the atmosphere would cause the average global temperature to rise by 5°C.[7] Despite the facts that Arrhenius was a well-respected scientist (he won a Nobel Prize in chemistry in 1903) and that subsequent investigations in the area effectively bore out his conclusions, his work was largely ignored for over fifty years. Instead, the conventional wisdom throughout the first half of the twentieth century was that climate is essentially constant, apart from some short-term fluctuations.[8]

Two important challenges to this consensus were issued during the 1950s. First, Roger Revelle and Hans E. Suess of the Scripps Institute of Oceanography questioned the accepted view that the oceans, which have a large capacity to store carbon, would harmlessly absorb almost all of the carbon dioxide that was being emitted by human activities. In 1957, they found that the oceans had not absorbed as much carbon dioxide as previously assumed. The implications, they maintained, were that:

> human beings are now carrying out a large scale geophysical experiment of a kind that could not have happened in the past nor be reproduced in the future. Within a few centuries we are returning to the atmosphere and oceans the concentrated organic carbon stored in the sedimentary rocks over hundreds of millions of years. This experiment, if adequately documented, may yield a far-reaching insight into the processes determining weather and climate.[9]

The impact of the second challenge, meanwhile, was not as immediate; nonetheless, it would prove to be highly influential in the future debate. Also occurring in 1957, an atmospheric carbon dioxide measuring station was established at the Mauna Loa Observatory in Hawaii. Situated at an elevation of 11,000 feet, far from any human-made sources of pollution, this was the first major attempt to construct a longitudinal record of measurements of background carbon dioxide concentrations.

By the early 1960s, the Mauna Loa Observatory was recording a modest, yet steady, increase in carbon dioxide concentrations. Revelle and Suess's findings, meanwhile, meant that this might have significant ramifications for climate. Further studies were thus encouraged. William Kellogg reports that one of the first reports on possible global warming was by an American non-governmental organisation:

> In 1963, the Conservation Foundation sponsored a meeting, and its report stated the situation more succinctly than anyone had before: 'It is estimated that a doubling of the carbon dioxide content of the atmosphere would produce a temperature rise of 3.8 degrees [Celsius]' – the timescale involved is left unspecified, however.[10]

The United States Government soon followed suit. In 1964–65, Roger Revelle led a White House study into the relationship between the burning of fossil fuels and climate change. The members of Revelle's task force concluded that the expected 25 per cent increase in carbon dioxide concentrations by the year 2000 might be 'sufficient to produce measurable and perhaps marked changes in climate, in the temperature and other properties of the stratosphere'. Such shifts, they concluded, could be 'deleterious from the point of view of human beings', and they therefore called for exploring 'the *possibilities of bringing about countervailing climatic changes*'.[11] The significance of this report, Kellogg argues, is that it was the 'first public recognition in a United States government document that climate change could be caused by human activities and that this would have important consequences for the world'.[12]

This report was not only the first US government document to address climate change, but it was also the only one of note before 1970. One explanation for this relative inattention is that much of the science remained unexplored. During the late 1960s, only a few scientists were working on climatic issues, and no computer model of climate or climatic change yet existed. Without sufficient understanding of carbon dioxide–atmosphere interactions, scientists were in a relatively weak position to suggest the consequences that continued human activities might have upon the climate. Consequently, the climate change issue remained largely void of political dimensions during this period.

Global cooling, global warming or climatic stability?

During the early 1970s, climate change surfaced on a number of political agendas. This was prompted, at least in part, by the widespread feeling that something was 'going wrong with the weather'.[13] Changes in the Indian monsoons, along with more general variations in the temperatures and rainfalls of the middle latitudes of both hemispheres, gave rise to worldwide droughts during the early 1970s. As a consequence, global food supplies fell to dangerously low levels. With welfare levels thus being threatened by changes in both weather and climate, politicians were prompted to take greater notice. They, in turn, looked for answers from the scientific community.

In July 1970, a conference on 'The Study of Critical Environmental Problems' was convened at the Massachusetts Institute of Technology (MIT). The participants concluded that the likelihood of climatic change during the twentieth century was small. Nevertheless, they did stress that 'the long-term potential consequences of CO_2 effects on the climate or of societal reaction to such threats are so serious that much more must be learned about future trends of climate change', and they therefore called for more data collection.[14] Reflective of the predominantly dismissive attitude at the time, however, an observer, commenting upon the MIT report, argued that the greenhouse effect had been a greatly exaggerated topic for anxiety: 'In short, half a degree by the end of the century (by which time nuclear power should have taken the load off the fossil fuels) is much more than sober men should worry about.'[15]

The debate about climate during the early 1970s was not restricted to the prospect of a CO_2-induced global warming. Indeed, many scientists and decision-makers – if interested in climatic change at all – were exploring the likelihood of a global cooling. Average global temperatures had decreased from 1945 to 1970, and this had initiated a spell of investigations into the prospects of a coming ice-age. During this period, publications with titles like 'In the Grip of a New Ice Age', 'Brace Yourself for Another Ice Age' and 'Are We

Headed for a New Ice Age?' were in circulation.[16] In 1971, for example, Ichtiaque Rasool and Stephen Schneider, two prominent climatologists, were arguing that, in spite of the

> obvious uncertainties in estimating and predicting the effects of carbon dioxide and aerosols in the atmosphere, it seems that, on balance, *man's continued pollution is likely to lead to a reduction rather than an increase in global temperature*. Thus, far from there being a melting of the ice caps, it is [their] view that the triggering of an ice age is more likely.[17]

Thus, there was by no means any consensus about the direction that any climate change would take, let alone if it would even occur.

The debate had another dimension at this time. Both global warming and global cooling were concerned with the uncalculated and undesired impacts that human activities and/or natural variations might have upon the climate. Others, however, were interested in weather modification and climate change as a purposeful activity – with either military or civilian intentions. In fact, the first investigation into climate change during the 1970s had relatively little to say about either carbon dioxide accumulation, global warming or global cooling. Instead, its primary concern was with deliberate weather and climate modification.[18] The political debate about weather and climate change had many different elements.

An investigation to study explicitly the causes and consequences of carbon dioxide accumulation was launched by the US National Academy of Sciences (NAS) in 1975. Under the joint chairmanship of W. Lawrence Gates and Yale Mintz, it produced a report which highlighted the need for more research – in both data collection and theoretical modelling. Although the Panel's members placed their primary emphasis upon the need to improve the science, they also argued that climatic change could have potentially major economic and social impacts.[19]

Another NAS report, prepared by a committee headed by Roger Revelle, was published in July 1977. Like their predecessors, the members of this committee called for more research to try to 'address some of the major unknowns in the climatic models and measurements on which the projections are based'. Nevertheless, despite the uncertainties and the qualifications, the committee's members made it clear that 'if use of fossil fuels continues to increase at present rates, average global temperature could rise by about

6[°C] over the next 200 years, with potentially dire consequences for agriculture and fisheries'. They also argued that 'the implications warrant prompt action'.[20] This report is symptomatic of a broader trend during the late 1970s – namely, that in the debate between the ice-age prophets and those who saw global warming as being more important in the medium-term, the latter were slowly coming to dominate.

Subsequent reports published in the United States in 1979, 1982 and 1983[21] confirmed the hypotheses that global warming could occur, over some period, and that it could have significant impacts for human societies. Though this was agreed, there was continued disagreement about the implications of these suppositions. Authors of reports published by the NAS and the EPA in 1983, for example, reached different conclusions from similar findings – the former noting that the 'CO_2 issue [was] reason for concern, but not panic . . .'; while the latter adopting a much more anxious tone, arguing that the projected 'temperature increases are likely to . . . [disrupt] environmental and economic systems, and [stress] political institutions'.[22] Politicians were therefore presented with two reports that had significantly different recommendations. In light of this, George Keyworth, US President Reagan's science adviser, chose to endorse the NAS report. The EPA study, he felt, was 'unnecessarily alarmist'.[23]

As was the case in Chapter 2, the focus of this section has been upon scientific research that was being conducted in the United States. The reason for this initial concentration is, once again, that the majority of atmospheric science was being undertaken in this country.[24] But as in the ozone layer case, this should not be taken to suggest that the US was the location of *all* studies into climate change.

Beyond the US borders, the first major international meeting of scientists to examine climate change was held in Wijk, Sweden in July 1971. The participants' aim was to produce an authoritative assessment of the state of scientific understanding of the possible impacts of humankind's activities upon regional and global climates. (This would then serve as the major background paper for the discussion of climate change at the 1972 UN Conference on the Human Environment in Stockholm.) However, they could not reach agreement about many of the projected effects of climatic change. At this time, there were 'just too many honest differences of opinion and not enough facts at hand to resolve them'.[25]

Apart from the United States National Academy of Sciences, the most important body undertaking, co-ordinating and summarising research into climate change was the World Meteorological Organisation (WMO). The WMO had been concerned, at least nominally, with the issue since the creation of its predecessor, the International Meteorological Organisation (IMO), in 1873. Although some work took place during the 1960s, the WMO's first major foray into the climate change issue took place in 1974, when its Executive Council agreed to initiate an international programme on climate. In the following year, the WMO made one of its first major contributions to the debate. In co-operation with the International Association of Meteorology and Atmospheric Physics, it sponsored an 'International Symposium on Long-Term Climate Fluctuations' in Norwich, England. The findings from this meeting effectively challenged the viability of the global cooling hypothesis and, according to one observer, left greenhouse warming 'to dominate the stage'.[26] Additionally, the WMO convened a panel of experts and issued periodic statements on the issue during the 1970s.

The most significant international gathering on climate change, to that date, was the First World Climate Conference, which the WMO convened in Geneva in February 1979. The final declaration from this meeting agreed that:

> We can say with some confidence that the burning of fossil fuels, deforestation, and changes of land use have increased the amount of carbon dioxide in the atmosphere . . . and it appears plausible that [this] can contribute to a gradual warming of the lower atmosphere, especially at high latitudes. . . . It is possible that some effects on a regional and global scale may . . . become significant before the middle of the next century.[27]

In such international fora, however, the issue was being discussed primarily by scientists. Kenneth Hare notes that at the time of the First World Climate Conference, the response was 'little or none from politicians'.[28]

Nevertheless, scientific activity continued, and in the wake of this conference, the Eighth World Meterological Conference created the World Climate Programme (WCP). The first major initiative to result from the establishment of the WCP was an international conference on climate change, held in Villach, Austria, from 17 to 22

November 1980. Under the chairmanship of Professor Bert Bolin of the University of Stockholm, the delegates issued a warning that the accumulation of greenhouse gases posed a great risk to the earth's natural equilibria; they declared that the issue consequently had to be addressed with some urgency. Although their pronouncement drew some attention, its political impact was negligible.

In addition to the US Government and the WMO, investigations were also being carried out by organisations in Europe during this period. Although the reports from different groups were highlighting the fact that global warming could become significant during the twenty-first century, they did not inspire any significant parallel enquiries by European governments.[29] Thus, the climate change issue did not occupy a prominent position upon political agendas in Europe at this time.

During the first half of the 1980s, a number of scientific uncertainties about global climate change – particularly with respect to theoretical modelling and data coverage – remained unresolved. Although the potential socioeconomic impacts of global warming were being discussed by scientists in national and international fora, it was generally accepted that the time-horizons associated with global warming safely provided ample opportunity for further scientific investigations. Decision-makers' consideration of climate questions could therefore wait until further advances had been made in the science. Consequently, climate change was not a highly political issue at this time.

The debate heats up

Scientific investigations into the global warming issue continued during the second half of the 1980s. In October 1985, and as part of the ongoing WCP, the WMO hosted another meeting in Villach, Austria. Scientists from twenty-nine countries reviewed the state of understanding about the greenhouse effect. The participants at this meeting agreed that human activity was causing increases in atmospheric concentrations of greenhouse gases which, in turn, would raise global mean surface temperatures. In light of this consensus about the scientific aspects of global warming, the participants at this meeting also recommended a 'start on policy analysis to identify the widest possible range of social responses for limiting or adapting to climatic changes'.[30]

The gravity attributed to the issue by some members of the international scientific community is not only revealed by the declaration coming from this particular conference but also by the fact that they felt it necessary to increase the frequency of their meetings. Thus, instead of next gathering in 1990 (as the original WCP plans had dictated), two further workshops were held in Villach and Bellagio, Italy in 1987. Stewart Boyle and John Ardill argue that the 'Villach-Bellagio workshops were significant for two main reasons. Not only were global warming trends confirmed, but, for the first time, policies to respond to climatic change were discussed in detail and agreed.'[31] From these meetings, another multinational agreement about climate change emerged. Although many aspects of the debate were still enveloped in uncertainties, these scientists maintained that ongoing human activities would cause substantial changes in the natural environment and, consequently, in the social environment as well.

By 1988, the findings of the climatologists were filtering into the political process more directly. One of the most significant statements in this regard was delivered on 23 June 1988. On this day, James Hansen, of NASA's Goddard Institute for Space Studies in New York, appeared before the US Senate Energy and Natural Resources Committee. He declared that he was 99 per cent certain that the warming already experienced during the 1980s had not been a chance event, but was indeed evidence of global warming.[32] Hansen went on to argue that it was time to stop stalling on the basis of scientific uncertainty and time to start taking action to address global warming. This statement attracted widespread attention, illuminated the importance of the issue and proclaimed a causal link.

Beyond the testimonies of the 'experts', events in the 'real world' were seeming to support the view that global warming was taking place. In North America, the summer of 1988 was one of the hottest and driest for decades. The drought conditions, although not necessarily manifestations of global warming, galvanised interest in the issue for both policy-makers and the general public. At this time, a writer for the scientific journal *Nature* noted that:

> [US] congressional attitudes about chlorofluorocarbons (CFCs) and carbon dioxide emissions are influenced far more by the fact that the corn in most of Iowa is nowhere near as high as an elephant's eye, and that outside the House and Senate chambers it has been stiflingly hot, than any number of scientific treatises on the subject.[33]

Moreover, events in the United Kingdom – particularly the hurricanes of 1987 and 1988 – did much to increase speculation in that country that the climate was somehow changing. More generally, the 1980s was also proving to be one of the hottest decades of the century (at the end of the decade, it was calculated that six of the ten warmest years during the twentieth century had occurred during the 1980s). In these ways, some empirical evidence was being gathered which, at least superficially, appeared to support the scientific case advancing global warming. With the potential severity of the issue being illuminated so brightly, decision-makers began to take greater notice.

Global warming first appeared on the international political agenda as a significant issue in 1988. In June of that year, over 300 individuals from forty-six countries attended a conference on 'The Changing Atmosphere: Implications for Global Security' in Toronto. With a mandate to 'consider the threats posed by the changing global atmosphere and how they might be addressed', this conference was the first major international political gathering to have global warming as one of its principal foci. Indeed, when in the planning stages, the organisers did not think that it would attract significant international attention. Its timing, however, was impeccable, for the June heat in North America proved to be one of the conference's best selling points. In the end, its final statement attracted considerable attention, and its conference goal of a 20 per cent reduction of carbon dioxide levels by the year 2005 has become commonly known as the 'Toronto target'.

Notwithstanding empirical evidence, expert testimony and the attention of international decision-makers, a universal scientific consensus about global warming remained elusive in 1988. A number of highly-respected atmospheric scientists in the United States challenged Hansen's remarks. Given the various scientific uncertainties that remained, they argued that there was no conclusive link between the observed changes in the weather and any larger global climatic shift.[34] Consequently, there was no agreement among members of the scientific community about what the ramifications of 'business-as-usual' would hold for the earth's natural systems.

Nevertheless, with such devastating predictions of both natural changes and their impacts upon socioeconomic systems being voiced, the issue continued to be a concern of politicians. Given the divergent scientific predictions, however, decision-makers were finding it difficult to formulate policy. Martin Parry, of Birmingham University, noted that the politicians were saying to the scientists: 'You have to come clean. Is the greenhouse effect happening or not?'[35] Thus, demands for a clearer scientific picture were being made in an increasingly urgent manner.

In response, the Intergovernmental Panel on Climate Change (IPCC) was formed. First proposed in 1987 and subsequently endorsed by UNEP and WMO bodies in 1988, this Panel brought together most of the world's pre-eminent climatologists, as appointed by their national governments. It was charged by the UN General Assembly with the task of preparing a comprehensive review of options and recommendations in response to global warming. For our purposes, the most important of the IPCC's three Working Groups was the one that investigated the science (IPCC I). Its Terms of Reference were that it should consider:

> factors affecting climate change, including greenhouse gases, responses to these factors of the atmosphere–ocean–land–ice system, assessment of current capabilities of modeling global and regional climate change and their predictability, past climate record and presently observed climate anomalies, projections of future climate and sea level and the timing of changes. The reports should identify the range of projections and their regional variations, gaps and uncertainties. The Working Group should reduce the uncertainties. A peer review should be incorporated in the preparation of the reports.

The aim was to discover whether a consensual scientific view on global warming existed.

Heeding the lesson of, among other past episodes, the ozone layer experience, there was a conscious effort to include scientists from as many different countries as possible. Particular effort was expended in order to ensure the active involvement of representatives from the developing world.[36] To further this objective, a Special Committee on the Participation of Developing Countries was created in 1989 in order to try to ensure that participation would be as universal as possible. By this means, the international group, under the chairmanship of John Houghton of the United Kingdom, began its deliberations in Geneva in November 1988 on the science of global warming.

While the scientific jury was out – the IPCC did not present its report until 1990 – scientific consensus remained elusive. This, in turn, provided justification for policy inaction, for many actors publicly proclaimed that more needed to be learnt about global warming before any decisions could be taken. Some explicitly cited the IPCC's deliberations, arguing that they would postpone political actions until its report was published. Others, meanwhile, simply cited the 'lack of science' rationale without explicitly anticipating the IPCC report.

The state of the scientific deliberations played a particularly important role in policy-justification, if not actual policy-making, in the United States. During this period, US President George Bush often pointed to the gaps in the scientific knowledge as a rationale for advocating an intensive scientific response (i.e. more research), coupled with a cautious political response (i.e. do little or nothing). Moreover, once when there was no science available to provide justification, the Bush Administration simply 'rewrote the science' in order to ensure that their policy-rationale appeared to remain defensible. More specifically, on 8 May 1989, the Office of Management and Budget confirmed that it had altered the Congressional testimony of NASA's James Hansen, thereby weakening his conclusion that enough was known about the phenomenon to justify immediate action. The White House defended this action by claiming that it wanted to avoid the appearance of policy disagreements within the Administration.[37] The political fallout from this episode was considerable, not only within the United States but also internationally.

The US Administration brought its scientific scepticism to the international negotiations later that same year. At a ministerial conference in the Netherlands in November of 1989, the Americans claimed that there was insufficient scientific evidence to know by how much the emissions of greenhouse gases needed to be cut. They therefore successfully blocked the inclusion of any timetables for the stabilisation of greenhouse gas emissions, preferring a statement that maintained that such stabilisation should be achieved 'as soon as possible'.[38]

Scientific uncertainties continued to justify US policy inaction at a conference in April 1990. Following President Bush's election promise to implement the 'White House Effect', the President gathered international decision-makers for 'The White House Conference on Science and Economics Research Related to Global Change'. Bush opened the seventeen-nation conference by saying: 'What we need are facts, the stuff that science is made of.'[39] He continued to emphasise scientific differences, citing a recent television interview in which scientists disagreed on the extent of temperature change: ' "Two scientists, two diametrically opposed points of view", Bush said. "Now where does that leave us?" '[40] 'Without enough information to justify policy responses', according to Bush, so he called for further study and proposed a 60 per cent increase in spending for climate change research.

The United States was not alone in following this tack, however. During the IPCC's deliberations, officials from the United Kingdom and the Soviet Union were also known to cite gaps in the scientific knowledge, and use this to explain their inaction.[41] Additionally, and perhaps most stridently, a number of representatives from the fossil fuels industry were articulating the need for a better scientific understanding before the conclusion of any international agreements. Unlike the ozone layer issue, however, industry representatives did not have sufficient scientific expertise to undertake their own studies. Consequently, their participation in the scientific discussions was less influential, and generally more limited.[42]

On the other side of the debate, however, some had accepted the scientific case for global warming and consequently argued that action therefore needed to be taken. Officials from the Netherlands and West Germany were putting this view forward most emphatically. Indeed, the Dutch were the first to take policy action on global warming, setting a target in 1989 to stabilise carbon dioxide emissions at the 1989/90 level by the year 2000 at the latest.

These differing opinions about the authenticity of global warming first clashed at the Noordwijk conference in November 1989. Though leading to some disagreements over future action, the level of confrontation in the Netherlands was low compared to that experienced at the subsequent White House Conference in April 1990. At this time, European representatives were frustrated by the US dependence on scientific scepticism. German environmental minister Klaus Topfer articulated the view of a number of states' decision-makers by noting that 'gaps in information should not be used as an excuse for worldwide inaction'.[43] They felt that there was sufficient scientific evidence to warrant serious policy consideration.

Meanwhile, the presence of a variety of views regarding the persuasiveness of the collected evidence seemed to hamper what could be agreed in international declarations on global warming, for only cautious and tentative statements about the state of the science were passed at this time.[44] Until the middle of 1990, national leaders were able to use the presence of scientific non-consensus in a palatable manner by referring to the then-imminent report of the IPCC science working group. In other words, some members of international society viewed it as 'acceptable' to delay further decisions until this scientific report had been tabled.

Consensus without certainty

The IPCC's first Working Group released its interim report in May 1990, finalised its report at a meeting in Sundsvall, Sweden in August 1990 and presented its findings to the Second World Climate Conference in Geneva in November 1990. The group's members were particularly eager to stress the fact that their findings represented the prevailing international scientific consensus on global warming:

> In the preparation of the main Assessment most of the active scientists working in the field have been involved. One hundred and seventy scientists from 25 countries have contributed to it, either through participation in the twelve international workshops organised specially for the purpose or through written contributions. A further 200 scientists have been involved in the peer review of the draft report. Although, as in any developing scientific topic, there is a minority of opinions which we have not been able to accommodate, the peer review has helped to ensure a high degree of consensus amongst authors and reviewers regarding the results presented. Thus the Assessment is an authoritative statement of the views of the international scientific community at this time.[45]

The Group was able to report that it was certain that:

> emissions resulting from human activities are substantially increasing the atmospheric concentrations of the greenhouse gases: carbon dioxide, methane, chlorofluorocarbons (CFCs) and nitrous oxide. These increases will enhance the greenhouse effect, resulting on average in an additional warming of the Earth's surface. The main greenhouse gas, water vapour, will increase in response to global warming and further enhance it.[46]

Additionally, the group's members were able to highlight some of the consequences of ongoing human activities:

> a rate of increase of global mean temperature during the next century

of about 0.3 [°C] per decade (with an uncertainty range of 0.2 [°C] to 0.5 [°C] per decade); this is greater than that seen over the past 10,000 years. This will result in a likely increase in global mean temperature of about 1 [°C] above the present value by 2025 and 3 [°C] before the end of the next century. The rise will not be steady because of the influence of other factors.[47]

With this report, it appeared that a substantial level of consensus had been achieved among members of the worldwide community of atmospheric scientists.[48]

The report was greeted with trepidation by some, for the scientists predicted, to the best of their abilities, global climatic change of unprecedented rates. The United Kingdom government was quick to respond to the interim report's publication, and in May 1990, its officials changed their position on the science – most notably for the first time at a conference in Bergen, Norway – and thereby separated its policy position from that of its close ally, the United States. More generally, between May and December 1990, fourteen of the OECD's twenty-four member-states initiated policies to stabilise or reduce emission levels of greenhouse gases. Additionally, three other states had already done so, and five other states, though not proclaiming unilateral goals, nevertheless endorsed the European Communities' target of the stabilisation of carbon dioxide emissions at the 1990 level by the year 2000.

Members of the IPCC also, however, acknowledged that a number of uncertainties remained. This fact, coupled with the absence of any unqualified proof that greenhouse-induced global warming was happening, left the door open for politicians and others to continue to cite conflicting scientific advice as a reason for a cautious political programme. American officials were one such group to adopt this tactic. At the conference in Sundsvall, Sweden in August 1990, the US delegation proposed a number of amendments that claimed that the scientists' forecasts of global warming were still highly uncertain. Although most of these were successfully opposed, some American changes were adopted, including one:

saying there were formidable difficulties for policy-makers in drawing up a response to climate change and that information available for sound policy analysis was inadequate. It emphasised what it termed the remaining scientific uncertainties and also uncertainty about the costs. . . . However, the amendment was countered with an Australian amendment underlining the wide scientific consensus on climate change.[49]

More generally, the United States' officials avoided use of the term 'global warming', instead favouring the more innocuous 'climate change'. Though more isolated in Sundsvall, some others still supported their scientific scepticism. The Soviet Union's delegates, for example, questioned the findings and 'complained that some of the figures were "fictional" '.[50]

United States' representatives continued to question the consensual view during the lead-up to the Second World Climate Conference in Geneva in November 1990. Just one week before the meeting began, US President George Bush was asked about the validity of the IPCC's report. He was reported to have replied: 'My scientists are telling me something very different.'[51] He was referring to a report from the George C. Marshall Institute in Washington, DC, which argued that other natural factors would offset global warming by cooling the earth's atmosphere.[52] Although most climatologists dismissed the report's validity,[53] its existence reveals that some continued to question the scientific consensus on the issue. Furthermore, its covert endorsement by President Bush also helps to explain the subsequent position advanced by the Americans at the Second World Climate Conference: 'The draft US ministerial resolution [for this conference said] that human action "may" be altering the atmosphere but "the state of our knowledge is imperfect – many important uncertainties remain".'[54] Responding to this position, one environmental campaigner complained: 'Instead of the politicians working according to the answers they have been given by the scientists, they are moving the goalposts.'[55]

Despite mounting evidence that appeared to confirm the consensual scientific position during 1991 – an NAS report in the US went so far as to argue that 'even given the considerable uncertainties in our knowledge of the relevant phenomena, greenhouse warming poses a potential threat sufficient *to merit prompt responses*'[56] – the Americans continued to highlight the remaining uncertainties in the international negotiations. Moreover, they continued to use this as a justification for refusing to introduce any specific targets for stabilising or reducing greenhouse gas emissions.

Disagreements about the extent of possible climate change, and, indeed, the sheer validity of the global warming hypothesis endured during 1992 and 1993. Although US rhetoric in the formal negotiations subsided with the ascendency of the Clinton Administration, challenges were still forthcoming from a variety of quarters. Richard Lindzen, for example, a prominent scientist at the Massachusetts Institute of Technology, maintained that too much faith was being put on computer models that not only overestimated both present and future carbon dioxide levels but also in fact got most of the crucial physical processes wrong.[57] Fred Singer from the University of Virginia advanced similar arguments.[58] Their challenges were given greater weight by measurements of both temperatures and carbon dioxide. Around the world, 1992 and 1993 were cooler years, with particularly harsh winters in North America. Additionally, readings taken at the Mauna Loa Observatory in 1993 revealed a decline, a plateau and then another decline in carbon dioxide concentrations during the previous four years.[59] Finally, the more cautious tone of the IPCC's 1992 updated report suggested that there may have been more uncertainties than initially believed.[60]

Nevertheless, the authors of the 1992 IPCC Report – again, representing the majority of scientists working in this area – stood by their original estimate of future average warming, a figure of 0.3°C per decade. Moreover, at the ninth meeting of the Intergovernmental Negotiating Committee, in February 1994, IPCC Chairman Professor Bert Bolin reiterated the Panel's view that the original commitments in the Convention did not go nearly far enough. He argued that 'even *stabilizing the total global emissions would not stabilize atmospheric concentrations for several hundred years*'.[61] Thus, at the beginning of 1994, the consensual scientific opinion was that the global warming challenge was both real and serious. With emissions of greenhouse gases continuing, scientists argued that significant changes in everyday activities had to be forthcoming. A Special Report on the science of climate change was scheduled to be released by the IPCC towards the end of 1994 (in preparation for the First Conference of the Parties), while their fuller Second Assessment Report was intended to be published in late 1995.

Notes

1   The first climate model, according to one report, was 'that of the Egyptian scribe who said, around 3000 BC, "the Sun warms the Earth" ' (T.M.L. Wigley and P. Brimblecombe, 'What is climatology?', *Nature*, 276

(16 November 1978), p. 214). Additionally, Theophrastus and others in classical Greece wrote about the possibility of widespread artificially-induced climate change (J.D. Hughes, 'Theophrastus as ecologist', *Environmental Review*, 4, (1985), pp. 296–307, cited in Richard Grove, 'Threatened islands, threatened earth; early professional science and the historical origins of global environmental concerns', in David J.R. Angell, Justyn D. Comer and Matthew L.N. Wilkinson (eds), *Sustaining Earth: Response to the Environmental Threat* (Basingstoke, Macmillan, 1990), p. 15).

2   James P. Lodge, *The Smoake of London: two Prophecies* (Elmsford, Maxwell Reprint Co., 1969), pp. ix–x.

3   Matthew Wilkinson and Sarah Woodin, 'Acid precipitation', in Angell *et al.*, *Sustaining Earth*, p. 43.

4   John Evelyn, *Fumifugium: the Incovenience of the Aer, and the Smoake of London Dissipated*, reprinted in Lodge, *The Smoake of London*.

5   Jean-Baptiste Fourier, 'Les temperatures du globe terrestre et des espaces planétaires', *Mémoires de L'Académie Royale des Sciences de L'Institut de France*, 7 (1824), pp. 569–604.

6   J. Tyndall, 'On radiation through the earth's atmosphere', *Philosophical Magazine*, 4 (1863), pp. 200–7.

7   Svante Arrhenius, 'On the influence of carbonic acid in the air upon the temperature on the ground', *Philosophical Magazine*, 41 (April 1896), pp. 237–76.

8   One (unsuccessful) challenge to this conventional wisdom is worth noting. In 1938, G.D. Callendar, a British meteorologist, having gathered temperature records from over 200 weather stations around the world, discovered that a global warming had occurred between the 1880s and the 1930s. He tried to persuade the members of the Royal Society in London that this was the result of increasing carbon dioxide levels in the atmosphere. His argument, however, was greeted with much scepticism. (G.D. Callendar, 'The artificial production of carbon dioxide and its influence on temperature', *Quarterly Journal of the Royal Meteorological Society*, 64 (1938), pp. 223–40.)

9   R. Revelle and H. E. Suess, 'Carbon dioxide exchange between atmosphere and ocean and the question of an increase of atmospheric CO_2 during the past decades', *Tellus* 9 (1957), pp. 18–27.

10   The report is entitled *Implications of Rising Carbon Dioxide Content of the Atmosphere* (New York, The Conservation Foundation, 1963); while the quotation is from William W. Kellogg, 'Theory of climate: transition from academic challenge to global imperative', in Terrell J. Minger (ed.), *Greenhouse Glasnost: the Crisis of Global Warming* (New York, The Ecco Press, 1990), p. 99.

11   President's Science Advisory Committee, *Restoring the Quality of Our Environment: Report of the Environmental Pollution Panel* (Washington, DC, The White House, 1965), pp. 126–7. Emphasis added.

12   William W. Kellogg, 'Mankind's impact on climate: the evolution of awareness', *Climatic Change*, 10 (1987), p. 117.

13   John Gribbin, 'Weather warning: you are now experiencing a climatic change', *Nature*, 252 (15 November 1974), p. 182.

14   *Man's Impact on the Global Environment: Report of the Study of Critical Environmental Problems* (London, The MIT Press, 1970), p. 12.

15   'The great greenhouse scare', *Nature*, 229 (19 February 1971), p. 514.

16   See the examples gathered in Anna J. Bray, 'The ice age cometh: remembering the scare of global cooling', *Policy Review*, 58 (Fall 1991), pp. 82–4.

17   'CO_2 versus aerosols', *Nature*, 232 (23 July 1971), p. 225. Emphasis added.

18   Committee on Atmospheric Sciences, National Research Council, *Weather and Climate Modification: Problems and Progress* (Washington, DC, National Academy of Sciences, 1973), p. 155.

19   Committee for the Global Atmospheric Research Program, National Research Council, *Understanding Climate Change: a Program for Action* (Washington, DC, National Academy of Sciences, 1975).

20   Panel on Energy and Climate, Geophysics Study Committee, Assembly of Mathematical and Physical Sciences, National Research Council, *Energy and Climate* (Washington, DC, National Academy of Sciences, 1977). See, also, National Academy of Sciences, *Climate, Climatic Change, and Water Supply* (Washington, DC, National Academy Press, 1977).

21   National Academy of Sciences, *Carbon Dioxide and Climate: a Scientific Assessment* (Washington, DC, National Academy of Sciences, Climate Research Board, 1979); National Academy of Sciences, *Carbon Dioxide and Climate: a Second Assessment* (Washington, DC, National Academy Press, 1982); National Academy of Sciences, *Changing Climate: Report of the Carbon Dioxide Assessment Committee* (Washington, DC, National Academy Press, 1983); and Stephen Seidel and Dale Keyes, *Can We Delay a Greenhouse Warming?: the Effectiveness and Feasibility of Options to Slow a Build-Up of Carbon Dioxide in the Atmosphere* (Washington, DC, Office of Policy and Resources Management, US EPA, September 1983).

22   Ibid., p. i.

23   Peter David, 'Two views on whether more means doom', *Nature*, 305 (27 October 1983), p. 751.

24   Moreover, in 1993, it was noted that '[w]ith an annual budget for climate-research in the neighbourhood of [US]\$1 billion (up to [US]\$1.4 billion in fiscal year 1993), the United States was providing about half the world's climate research . . .' (R.A. Reinstein, 'Climate negotiations', *The Washington Quarterly*, 16:1 (Winter 1993), p. 82). Even in a consciously

'international' climate assessment effort in 1990, US-based scientists still accounted for over one-third of all participants (author's calculations from J.T. Houghton, G.J. Jenkins and J.J. Ephraums (eds), *Climate Change: the IPCC Scientific Assessment* (Cambridge: Cambridge University Press, 1990)).

25   Kellogg, 'Mankind's impact on climate', p. 122. The report is *Inadvertent Climate Modification: Report of the Study of Man's Impact on Climate* (London, The MIT Press, 1971).

26   Kellogg, 'Mankind's impact on climate', p. 122. See, also, World Meteorological Organisation, *Proceedings of the WMO/IAMAP Symposium on Long-term Climatic Fluctuations: Norwich 18–23 August 1975* (Geneva, WMO, No. 42, 1975).

27   Cited in W.W. Kellogg, 'Prediction of a global cooling', *Nature*, 280 (16 August 1979), p. 615.

28   F. Kenneth Hare, 'The global greenhouse effect', in *The Changing Atmosphere: Implications for Global Security, Conference Proceedings* (Geneva, WMO, No. 710), p. 60.

29   Although in 1984, for example, a United Kingdom Royal Commission did consider the global warming question, its only recommendation was 'that all necessary steps should be taken to ensure that there is the best chance of an early resolution of the uncertainties surrounding the effects of increasing concentrations of carbon dioxide in the atmosphere' (Royal Commission on Environmental Pollution (Chairman: Sir Richard Southwood), Tenth Report, *Tackling Pollution – Experience and Prospects* (London, HMSO, February 1984), Chapter 5.130, p. 160).

30   World Climate Programme, *Developing Policies for Responding to Climatic Change* (Geneva, WMO and UNEP, WCIP-1, WMO/TD-No. 225, April 1988), p. 2.

31   Stewart Boyle and John Ardill, *The Greenhouse Effect: a Practical Guide to the World's Changing Climate* (Sevenoaks, New English Library, 1989), p. 41.

32   He said: 'The probability of a chance warming of that magnitude is about 1 percent. So, with 99 percent confidence, we can state that the warming during this time period [the past 30 years] is a real warming trend' (Statement of Dr James Hansen, Director, NASA Goddard Institute for Space Studies, *Greenhouse Effect and Global Climate Change (Hearing Before the Committee on Energy and Natural Resources, United States Senate, One Hundredth Congress, First Session on the Greenhouse Effect and Global Climate Change, Part 2)* (S.Hrg 100–461 Pt. 2, 23 June 1988)).

33   'Summer heat fires policy hares', *Nature*, 334 (11 August 1988), p. 457.

34   For two sceptical views of the science of global warming that received much attention at the time of their respective publication and transmission, see Warren T. Brookes, 'The global warming panic', *Forbes*, 144:14 (25

December 1989), pp. 96–102; and *The Greenhouse Conspiracy: an Edited Transcript* (London, Channel 4 Television, 1990).

35   Quoted in Amit Roy, 'Hot news from the Pacific', *The Sunday Times* (London) (12 February 1989).

36   Bert Bolin argued in 1987–88 that: 'Right now, many countries, especially developing countries, simply don't trust assessments in which their scientists and policy-makers have not participated' (quoted in Stephen Schneider, 'Three reports of the intergovernmental panel on climate change', *Environment*, 33:1 (January 1991)). Of course, the difficulties associated with advancing developing world scientific expertise have long been recognised. In response, a Committee on Science and Technology in Developing Countries (COSTED) was established in 1966 by the eleventh General Assembly of ICSU (held in Bombay), for the encouragement of science and technology in developing countries. With similar aims, the Third World Academy of Sciences was founded in 1983. See, also, Ivan Head, 'North/South dangers', *Foreign Affairs*, 68:3 (Summer 1989), pp. 80–2.

37   'Opposition to global warming convention', *Environmental Policy and Law*, 19:3/4 (July 1989), p. 116.

38   Robert E. Morrison, *Global Climate Change*, CRS Issue Brief (Washington, DC, Congressional Research Service, Library of Congress, 5 January 1990), p. 13.

39   The White House, Office of the Press Secretary, 'Remarks by the President in the opening address to the White House conference on science and economics research related to global change' (Washington, DC, 17 April 1990).

40   Michael Weisskopf, 'Bush says more data on warming needed', *Washington Post* (18 April 1990), p. A1.

41   Indeed, Soviet climatologist Mikhail Budyko – though not challenging the fundamental hypothesis – claimed (contrary to general opinion) that areas such as the Sahara desert would thrive with global warming, and therefore encouraged greater fossil fuel emissions (Jack Miller and Fred Pearce, 'Soviet climatologist predicts greenhouse "paradise" ', *New Scientist*, 123 (26 August 1989), p. 24).

42   Lunde argues that industry proposals forwarded by the fossil fuel lobbies 'either point to the vaguest statements in the background material as suggestions for inclusion in the executive summary, or propose genuinely new statements shrouded in the same "language of uncertainty" ' (Leiv Lunde, *Science or Politics in the Global Greenhouse?: the Developments Towards Scientific Consensus on Climate Change* (Oslo, Energy, Environment and Development Publication No. 8, 1991), p. 93). Moreover, John Gribbin relays an interesting piece of gossip: '. . . last month, when members of the George C. Marshall Institute, a privately funded think tank based in Washington DC, were flown in to present their maverick views on climate change, it came as no surprise to find that the room at the Hyde Park Hotel in

which they gave their talks, ... had actually been booked by British Coal' (John Gribbin, 'Why caution is wrong on global warming', *New Scientist*, 127 (28 July 1990), p. 18).

43   Quoted in Weisskopf, 'Bush says more data on warming needed', p. A1.

44   See, for example, the resolution of the fifteenth UNEP Governing Council from the summer of 1989, which notes that 'further scientific studies are needed' (reprinted in *Environmental Policy and Law*, 19:3/4 (July 1989), p. 118).

45   Houghton, Jenkins and Ephraums, *Climate Change*, p. iii.

46   Ibid., p. xi.

47   Ibid., p. xi.

48   The consensus was not universal. Indeed, some were critical of the IPCC, arguing that they did not treat opposing views with sufficient concern: 'IPCC's failure to discuss dissenting opinions, perhaps to dismiss them, was a mistake' ('Next steps on global warming', *Nature*, 348 (15 November 1990), p. 182).

49   John Hunt, 'US stand on global warming attacked', the *Financial Times* (London) (30 August 1990).

50   Ibid.

51   Quoted in David Nicholson-Lord, 'Bush defies alert on global warming', *Independent on Sunday* (London) (4 November 1990), p. 6.

52   *Scientific Perspectives on the Greenhouse Problem* (Washington, DC, George C. Marshall Institute, 1989).

53   See the critique in John Gribbin, 'An assault on the climate consensus', *New Scientist*, 128 (15 December 1990), pp. 26–31.

54   Nicholson-Lord, 'Bush defies alert'. Further, at a 'private briefing last month, Robert Reinstein, a senior official at the US Department of State, complained that Continental European countries tended "to make the political commitment first, then gather the information". Anglo-Saxons, he said, did things the other way round.' *Independent on Sunday* (London) (4 November 1990).

55   Steve Elsworth, Greenpeace's atmosphere campaigner, ibid., p. 6.

56   Committee on Science, Engineering, and Public Policy, *Policy Implications of Greenhouse Warming – Synthesis Panel* (Washington, DC, National Academy Press for the National Academy of Sciences, National Academy of Engineering and the National Institute of Medicine, 1991), quoted in Robert Pool, 'NAS on global warming: "insurance needed" ', *Nature*, 350 (11 April 1991), p. 449. Emphasis added.

57   See, for example, Richard S. Lindzen, 'Palaeoclimate sensitivity', *Nature*, 363 (6 May 1993), pp. 25–6.

58   See, for example, S. Fred Singer, 'Benefits of global warming', *Society*, 29:3 (March/April 1992), pp. 33–40; and 'Warming theories need warming label', *Bulletin of the Atomic Scientists*, 48:5 (1992), pp. 34–9.

59 These phenomena may have been accounted for by the 1991 Mount Pinatubo explosion (Kristin Leutwyler, 'No global warming?', *Scientific American* (February 1994), pp. 12–13).

60 J.T. Houghton, B.A. Callander and S.K. Varney (eds), *Climate Change 1992, the Supplementary Report to the IPCC Scientific Assessment* (Cambridge, Cambridge University Press, 1992). The uncertainty most usually highlighted by critics of the global warming hypothesis was the question of where 20–25 per cent of all emitted carbon actually goes. Additionally, the IPCC Report admits that 'the unequivocal detection of the enhanced greenhouse effect from observations is not likely for a decade or more'.

61 Bert Bolin, 'Report to the ninth session of the INC/FCCC' (Geneva, IPCC, 7 February 1994), p. 2. Emphasis in original.

4

Science and global environmental politics

Science is important in politics. Belief in this assertion led me to propose my first hypothesis – namely, that a consensus regarding the problem's causal relations is necessary for international co-operation. The experience on the issues of global atmospheric change, as outlined in Chapters 2 and 3, has delivered mixed results with respect to this hypothesis. Let me consider each of the two issues in turn.

On the ozone layer issue, the degree of correlation between the evolution of consensual scientific knowledge and international co-operation is moderate to high. Laboratory hypotheses during the late 1960s and early 1970s placed the problem of stratospheric ozone depletion upon the scientific agenda. The recognition that human activities could exacerbate the effect subsequently prompted its appearance upon political agendas as well. While scientific activity intensified, however, different groups of scientists proposed different explanations for ozone layer depletion. By 1985, only a general statement of principles could be agreed internationally in the Vienna Convention. Although the discovery of the ozone crater over Antarctica later that same year magnified the urgency of the issue, an agreed causal explanation remained elusive. One was finally found during the 1987 AAOE trip to the Antarctic, for CFCs were implicated in stratospheric ozone destruction. With the publication of these findings by the Ozone Trends Panel early the following year, international political efforts to tighten the terms of Montreal Protocol snowballed. Revisions in both 1990 and 1992 were prompted by findings from the Protocol's Panel for Scientific Assessment. Indeed, the simple fact that the Parties to the Montreal Protocol created and institutionalised a body made up of international scientific experts suggests the importance placed upon scientific knowledge.[1]

One striking refutation of my hypothesis, however, exists. Note the timing of the publication of the Ozone Trends Panel Report and the agreement of the Montreal Protocol. While my hypothesis would lead to the assertion that the former is a precondition for the latter, it was indeed the politicians who made the first move: they signed the agreement in September 1987, while the scientists did not publish their report until March 1988. If the negotiators in Montreal had been responding solely to the scientific information at their disposal, then they would have agreed only to step up monitoring activities. That they went beyond this is an effective challenge to my first hypothesis.

On the climate change issue, the degree of correlation is moderate. Although speculation about anthropogenic-induced climate change had been evident for decades, significant scientific activity on the issue did not begin until the 1970s, when erratic variations in the weather encouraged such investigations. Throughout the late 1970s and early 1980s, feelings grew not only that a global warming was more likely than a global cooling, but that a 'business-as-usual' policy could bring about significant climatic changes. In response to this speculation, the members of international society formed a multinational panel of experts to investigate further the phenomenon. Their report, published in 1990, confirmed that ongoing human activities would bring about enhanced global warming. It represented a significant worldwide scientific consensus on the issue, and did prompt some national and international responses. More specifically, fourteen of the OECD's twenty-four member-states initiated policies to stabilise or reduce levels of greenhouse gas emissions in the wake of these findings. Substantive international co-operation, however, was not forthcoming: two years later, only a relatively weak agreement could be reached. Nevertheless, scientific knowledge was also formalised and institutionalised in this document (namely, the Climate Change Convention).[2] The relative marginalisation of the IPCC by the INC, however, suggests that the politicians regarded any consensual scientific knowledge as but one of many inputs.[3]

Although the correlation in each instance is not exact, these results nevertheless suggest that it would be unwise to overlook the role that science plays in the quest for international co-operation on issues of global atmospheric change. The ways in which actors receive, process and interpret new information is important. Disregard of them would be ill-advised, for without study of such factors, a full understanding of the politics of ozone layer depletion and climate change would not be possible.

Still, *how* do science and politics relate? More specifically for this chapter's purposes, *how* does scientific knowledge affect the prospects for international co-operation on issues of global environmental politics? Within the existing literature (and as reflected in my first hypothesis), it is usually assumed that some degree of scientific consensus must be in place before international co-operation on environmental issues can be possible. Seyom Brown and colleagues, for example, argue that all participants must agree that the raw data being collected is accurate and that the analysis (that is, the method of interpretation) is acceptable in order to achieve a co-operative agreement.[4] Additionally, Per Bakken maintains that as 'a basis for any international environmental treaty there has to be a scientific cause–effect relationship. ... without agreement at least in influential parts of the scientific community, the chances of reaching international agreement are small'.[5] Most scholars, however, do not undertake any further exploration of the science–politics relationship.

Conclusion of the investigation at this point would indicate subconscious acceptance of the notion that 'if we get the science right, then we will be that much closer to our goal of international co-operation'. In other words, a linear conceptualisation of the relationship between science and politics – an understanding that is dominant in much of the literature – would thus be sanctioned.[6] At this point, it is useful to recall Helga Nowotny's description of one particular view of the world: '[Science offers] advice held to be clean from political considerations, free from values and mere opinions, from interests and control over its later applications. Science was disinterested and neutral, committed solely to its own impartial and context-independent conception of Truth.'[7] Similarly, Ernst Haas and colleagues identify another commonly held portrayal: 'Politicians and lay publics disagree and argue over values. Scientists discover facts.'[8] The suggestion is that once science has 'discovered' the 'answer', politics will use these 'facts' to make policy. Finding the 'answer', meanwhile, may be taxing, but implicit in this view is that it is achievable: if enough resources are committed, then answers will be discovered.

Such an understanding of the science–politics relationship is still, in some ways, helpful – for reasons that are explained below – but it is by no means comprehensive. Those who searched only for the presence of a scientific consensus would overlook many elements that are vital for a fuller understanding of international co-operation. There are a number of reasons why this linear view of the science–politics relationship is no longer sufficient.

First, resources for investigating scientific problems are not endless, and therefore decisions to support one individual, one institute, or one technique, in lieu of another, are themselves political. Harvey Brooks noted this over thirty years ago when he distinguished 'science in policy' from 'policy for science'. The first relates to this traditional understanding of the science–politics relationship. The second, however, directs attention to 'the development of politics for the management and support of the national scientific enterprise and with the selection and evaluation of substantive scientific programs'.[9] Lynton Caldwell adds to this by recognising that '[g]overnment investment in science, almost everywhere, is influenced heavily by particular interests and with little effort to assess relative benefits to society'.[10] Indeed, a comparison of the two issues of global atmospheric change reveals an interesting difference that can be best explained by the increasing politicisation of science.

Scientific investigations on the ozone layer were carried out by, for the most part, bodies that were independent of government. Groups like the CCOL were self-selected, had few links with governments and were funded largely by the UN Environment Programme and non-governmental groups. By contrast, the lead body investigating climate change science was made up of government representatives, for they successfully seized the lead from UNEP and WMO and formed the Intergovernmental Panel on Climate Change (IPCC; note what the 'I' stands for). Consequently, the decision of 'where' to conduct the science was political, and it had implications for the subsequent international politics.

Second, scientists may be active in the political process. Given the linear nature of the traditional model, the output of science becomes the input of politics. In reality, however, the relationship is much more intertwined than this. Peter Haas's recent work on 'epistemic communities' has done much to advance the notion that scientists can play a pro-active role in the policy-making process.[11] For much

longer, others have shown how the legal and institutional relationships in particular countries (especially the United States)
encourage 'activism' among scientists.[12] Indeed, many point to a
singular event predating most of these studies: with the explosion of
an atomic bomb over Hiroshima in 1945, scientists could no longer
remain detached from the uses of their knowledge. On issues of
global atmospheric change, there has been an intimacy between
scientists and politicians, perhaps best exemplified by the participation of various expert bodies' in the international negotiations
(noted in the opening paragraphs of this chapter).

Third, the world is not as 'simple' as this traditional model of
science–politics would lead us to believe. More specifically, the
Newtonian view that all cause–effect relationships can necessarily be
'discovered' – that is, 'facts' will, if sufficient effort is exerted, be
'found' – is no longer indisputable. Physicists came to realise this in
the nineteenth century: with advances in quantum physics and
relativity, universal simplicity flew out the window. As a consequence, when complex systems, such as the global atmosphere, are
being examined, complete certainty may necessarily be elusive. Traditional ideas about linearity and predictability have to be supplemented with notions of chaos and uncertainty. In such circumstances, 'facts' are hard to find.

But under such conditions, how might science be used? Michael
Thompson argues that: 'In all of those situations in which the true
state of the world is not entirely certain . . . people will choose those
certitudes that best support their social constructions of reality.'[13]
Speculation about how this reality might be constructed yields a few
thoughts.

First of all, the presence of non-scientific pressures may cause
different scientists working within different organisations to hold
dissimilar views. Ernst Haas argues that scientists are 'subject to
personal and social constraints derived from the institutional
pressures on their careers, which may result in deviations from
stipulated norms of behavior in the production of knowledge'.[14]
Steve Breyman reminds us that bureaucratic politics can be just as
evident in scientific organisations as in other bodies: 'Further
damage is done to the model [of linearity] when the veil concealing
the internal dynamics of scientific enterprise is lifted to reveal operations similar to other large institutions: competition for funding and
honors, bureaucratic strife and turf battles, fraud and egoism.'[15]

On global atmospheric issues, scientific research was undertaken by international organisations, governments, universities, environmental pressure groups, industrial and business interests and associations, along with a host of other organisations. Chapters 2 and 3 have revealed how business interests may have encouraged scientists working for chemical companies and fossil-fuel-dependent industries to emphasise certain findings and downplay others. Scientists working for environmental groups, meanwhile, may have had analogous pressures placed upon them.

Recognise also that scientists come from different countries. As a consequence, Ernst Haas argues that scientific terms may be contested, because they are embodied in specific (mainly Western) cultures and because each particular society 'decodes' them in a different way.[16] Similarly, Brian Wynne and Sue Mayer argue that: 'What becomes institutionalised as "good science" is therefore a product of culture as well as intellectual principles.'[17] Consequently, in different states, scientists may pose different questions, employ different 'methods' and undertake different data search patterns, which may well lead to divergent scientific conclusions. Indeed, comparing experiences on either side of the Atlantic Ocean, Raymond Vernon reports:

> The contrast between European and U.S. practices is especially evident in how scientific opinion is amassed. In the United States, the government formally relies on the testimony of qualified experts that is accumulated largely through overt adversarial procedures – a process that usually generates a disparate set of conclusions, all purportedly supported by scientific authority and objectivity. In contrast, Europe's administrators garner their evidence, to the extent that it contributes to their decisions, from scientific sources largely of their own choosing.[18]

Experience from the two issues of global atmospheric change, moreover, serves to support these conclusions. Recall on the ozone layer issue, for example, that similar findings during the late 1970s prompted different conclusions from British and American scientists. Kiki Warr maintains that there was 'an attitude prevalent among British scientists that the US was overreacting in the urgency of its response'.[19] While James Maxwell and Sanford Weiner argue that the 'reports differed in their approach to scientific uncertainties'.[20] Implicit in each of these conclusions is a belief that recognition of cultural differences can help to make sense of divergent conclusions.

Variations across countries may hinder the chances for international co-operation, particularly if decision-makers base their decisions upon the advice of their 'own' scientists. This may well be the case, for Helge Ole Bergesen notes that: 'All too often we have seen in the area of resource management that scientific results produced by institutions in one particular country involved in the political process are not recognised as valid by other countries.'[21] Peter Haas arrives at a similar conclusion – looking explicitly at the differences between the North and the South in this regard.[22] Indeed, this provided the motivation for the leaders of various panels of experts on issues of global atmospheric change to gather as 'international' a team as possible.

In summary, then, the traditional linear model of science–politics can no longer tell the whole story. In particular, three conclusions derived from it can no longer be sustained. First, do not assume that a single scientific consensus is necessarily achievable. Given the complexity of many of the planet's systems, certainty may be impossible. Second, do not assume that any apparent scientific consensus is necessarily stable. Because of the aforementioned uncertainty, what is thought today to be a highly unlikely outcome, may tomorrow be considered to have a much greater probability. And finally, do not assume that just because a scientific consensus has apparently been achieved, that it is necessarily either 'good' or 'just'. Recognise that the evolution of any scientific consensus may be manipulated by a hegemonic power in order to further its own goals (in either a Gramscian interpretation of 'hegemony', whereby the language, ideas and other cultural elements are the key variables; or the more-popular [at least in international relations] sense of hegemony as military or economic power, as discussed by HST in Chapter 1). Further, look to the actors who shape the scientific agenda. Those who decide, for example, the type of research questions that are legitimate, will wield significant influence in the broader debate.

Given this fragmentation of the traditional relationship between science and politics, is my first hypothesis totally discredited? Not at all. It has already been recognised that Chapters 2 and 3 showed that the correlation between scientific consensus and international co-operation is moderate to high, and moderate. More specifically, the experience on the issues of global atmospheric change reveals that the perception that political decisions must be based upon 'hard' and 'consensual' scientific evidence is deep-rooted: US Presidents demand 'facts';[23] internationally esteemed scientists declare that they are in the business of providing impartial assessments;[24] respected journals applaud the objective communication of scientific information;[25] and established academics call for more of it.[26] Indeed, progress on the ozone layer issue was possible because of the presence of an indisputable 'fact' (that is, the discovery of, first, the ozone crater and, second, the anti-correlation between chlorine monoxide and ozone levels), while the climate change issue did not benefit from such a 'simple' demonstration.[27] The prospects for international co-operation will continue to increase whenever there is a consensus regarding the problem's causal relations. Still, while being an important part of the story, it is nevertheless not the complete story.

In spite of the disillusionment that many feel for 'science',[28] its role in the broader 'sustainable development' debate was consolidated at the 1992 Earth Summit. Principle 9 of the Rio Declaration declares that:

> States should cooperate to strengthen endogenous capacity-building for sustainable development by improving scientific understanding through exchanges of scientific and technological knowledge, and by enhancing the development, adaptation, diffusion and transfer of technologies, including new and innovative technologies.

Chapters 31 and 35 of Agenda 21, moreover, give further prominence to the role of scientists. Indeed, many have argued that 'scientific management' is an integral part of the 'mainstream of sustainable development'. Consequently, scholars striving to understand global environmental politics are well advised to examine the role of science therein. However, they should also be aware of the increasing interactions between the two.

Notes

1   Article 6 of the Montreal Protocol, 'Assessment and review of control measures'.

2   Article 9 of the Climate Change Convention, 'Subsidiary body for scientific and technological advice'.

3   Though meeting for the first time in February 1991, the INC did not make a specific request to the IPCC for information until March 1993

(Daniel Bodansky, 'The United Nations Framework Convention on Climate Change', *Yale Journal of International Law*, 18:2 (Summer 1993), p. 536, n. 506).

4   Seyom Brown *et al.*, *Regimes for the Ocean, Outer Space, and Weather* (Washington, DC, The Brookings Institution, 1977), pp. 234–5.

5   Per M. Bakken, 'Science and politics in the protection of the ozone layer', Steinar Andresen and Willy Ostreng (eds), *International Resource Management: the Role of Science and Politics* (London, Belhaven, 1989), p. 198.

6   In her study of the relationship between science and public policy, Sheila Jasanoff reports that 'there is an unspoken presumption in many of the aforementioned works that better scientific characterization of a problem will lead to better policy' (Sheila Jasanoff, *The Fifth Branch: Science Advisors as Policymakers* (London, Harvard University Press, 1990), p. 7).

7   Helga Nowotny, 'A new branch of science, inc.', in Harvey Brooks and Chester L. Cooper (eds), *Science for Public Policy* (Oxford, Pergamon Press, 1987), p. 62.

8   Ernst B. Haas, Mary Pat Williams and Don Babai, *Scientists and World Order: the Uses of Technical Knowledge in International Organizations* (London, University of California Press, 1977), p. 27.

9   Harvey Brooks, 'The scientific adviser', in Robert Gilpin and Christopher Wright (eds), *Scientists and National Policy-Making* (New York, Columbia University Press, 1964), p. 76.

10   Lynton Keith Caldwell, *Between Two Worlds: Science, the Environmental Movement, and Policy Choice* (Cambridge, Cambridge University Press, 1990), p. 26.

11   See, for example, Peter M. Haas, 'Introduction: epistemic communities and international policy coordination', *International Organization*, 46:1 (Winter 1992), pp. 1–35.

12   'In this adversarial setting, participating scientists often appear as advocates of particular regulatory outcomes rather than as disinterested experts. When scientists testifying before the agencies espouse positions that can be clearly identified as "pro-" or "anti-" regulation, their contribution tends to merge with that of overtly political interests, such as industry, labor, and environmental groups' (Ronald Brickman, Sheila Jasanoff and Thomas Ilgen, *Controlling Chemicals: the Politics of Regulation in Europe and the United States* (London, Cornell University Press, 1985), p. 309).

13   Michael Thompson, 'Good science for public policy', *Journal of International Development*, 5:6 (November–December 1993), p. 674.

14   Ernst Haas, *When Knowledge Is Power: Three Models of Change in International Organizations* (Oxford, University of California Press, 1990), p. 41.

15   Steve Breyman, 'Knowledge as power: ecology movements and global environmental problems', in Ronnie D. Lipschutz and Ken Conca (eds), *The State and Social Power in Global Environmental Politics* (New

York, Columbia University Press, 1993), pp. 132–3.

16 Ernst Haas, *When Knowledge Is Power*, p. 47.

17 Brian Wynne and Sue Mayer, 'How science fails the environment', *New Scientist*, 138 (5 June 1993), p. 33.

18 Raymond Vernon, 'Behind the scenes: how policymaking in the European Community, Japan and the United States affects global negotiations', *Environment*, 35:5 (June 1993), p. 35.

19 Kiki Warr, 'Ozone: the burden of proof', *New Scientist*, 128 (27 October 1990), p. 37.

20 James H. Maxwell and Sanford L. Weiner, 'Green consciousness or dollar diplomacy?: The British response to the threat of ozone depletion', *International Environmental Affairs*, 5:1 (Winter 1993), p. 22.

21 Helge Ole Bergesen, 'The credibility of science in international resource management', in Andresen and Ostreng, *International Resource Management*, p. 126. This may not always be the case, however. Despite contributing the largest number of scientists to Working Group I of the IPCC, the Bush Administration still used scientific questions to justify a cautious policy position.

22 Peter M. Haas, *Saving the Mediterranean: the Politics of International Environmental Cooperation* (New York, Columbia University Press, 1990), p. 209.

23 See note 39 and accompanying text in Chapter 3.

24 'The scientific/technical assessments should be clearly distinguished from the judgements and political negotiations that will be required in order to develop international and national strategies for adaptation and mitigation' (Bert Bolin, 'Report to the ninth session of the INC/FCCC' (Geneva, IPCC, 7 February 1994), p. 7).

25 'The real news in all this, perhaps, is that some scientists have learnt how to talk to politicians. The breakthrough was the ozone treaty. . . . In the ozone debate, scientists learnt to unite, and to tell politicians their side of the story. They decided what they agreed upon, and estimated the range of their disagreement in terms that the politicians could understand' ('The warmth of unity', *New Scientist*, 120 (19 November 1988), p. 17).

26 Marc Levy and colleagues argue that knowledge creation is important, and that institutions should have a key role therein:

Such a process would require regular scientific monitoring of the environment. The universal circulation of information should be encouraged. Such science should be nonpartisan and untainted by national concerns, to offset suspicions that monitoring activities constitute political control by another means, or are a disingenuous way to promote the economic advantages of selected groups. Monitoring should be done in laboratories, through direct contracts with international organizations, to guarantee its insulation from national policy agendas. But actual work should be done by national scientists, since governments typically pay closer attention to the findings of their own nationals . . .

(Marc A. Levy, Robert O. Keohane and Peter M. Haas, 'Improving the effectiveness of international environmental institutions', in Peter M. Haas, Robert O. Keohane and Marc A. Levy (eds), *Institutions for the Earth: Sources of Effective International Environmental Protection* (London, The MIT Press, 1993), p. 411.)

27   See, also, the discussion of 'issue tangibility' in Part V.

28   'One reason why the UNCED process attracted so much political energy was the public's growing sense of technological disquiet – thus science and technology are seen by many as part of the problem. The role of the Working Group is to show that science and technology can be part of the solution' (quoted in 'Commission on Sustainable Development: report on the intersessional *ad hoc* open-ended working groups', *Earth Negotiations Bulletin*, 5:14 (10 March 1994), p. 2).

III
Interests

5

Interests and ozone layer depletion

Once ozone layer depletion became the subject of political debate, decision-makers attempted to evaluate the relative merits of different courses of action. Although no one wished for the destruction of stratospheric ozone, its preservation would not be cost-free. Many, therefore, wanted to know how the costs compared to the benefits. As has been revealed in Chapter 2, the ozone layer issue did not acquire a significant international dimension until the CFC debate arose during the mid 1970s. Nevertheless, the period before 1974 is still noteworthy, for actors' perceived economic interests in the debate about the supersonic transport (SST) were crucial.

In addition to the environmental consequences of SST operation, opponents also highlighted its huge costs. A sizeable contingent within the US Government believed that if the SST project was worth doing at all, then it was worthwhile for the private sector (that is, Boeing, along with General Electric) to fund it. If they were not prepared to fund it, then it was obviously not worth doing. By 1971, over US$1 billion of taxpayers' money had been spent on the project, and there was little to show for it. The March 1971 Senate decision to stop financial support for the SST thus had considerable economic motivation. Consequently, one of the reasons why the ozone layer was spared significant damage by SSTs was because the project was deemed to be uneconomical. The threat posed to the ozone layer by CFCs, however, suffered from the opposite fate: the action that was destroying stratospheric ozone was initially seen to have more monetary benefits than monetary costs, while any action involving regulation was seen to have more monetary costs than monetary benefits.

The 'can ban' debate

If Molina and Rowland were right about the impact of CFCs upon the ozone layer, then something would have to be done. Within the United States, that 'something' was thought most likely to be some kind of restriction upon the use of CFCs. In order, therefore, to determine the potential impact of restrictions upon CFCs, a number of studies were commissioned during the mid-1970s.[1] Although there were significant variations among the details of the different studies, most agreed that regulatory action would have a detrimental effect upon the American economy in the short term. This damage was usually presented in terms of money and jobs. A study by the US Department of Commerce's Domestic and International Business Administration, for example, 'calculated that a ban on the use of [CFCs] from 1978 could cost billions of [US] dollars and adversely affect the jobs of millions of workers'.[2]

There was another point of consensus among these different studies – namely, that the magnitude of the economic impact would be primarily determined by whether or not substitutes existed for the regulated ozone-depleting chemicals. If restrictions were implemented upon uses that did not have available substitutes, then there would be a huge price to pay, because many important goods and processes would have to be eliminated. But if appropriate substitutes did exist, then the cost of switching over to alternatives, although still significant (because new plants would have to be constructed and existing production facilities would have to be redesigned and retooled), would pale in comparison to the first scenario outlined.

In 1973, the US Department of Commerce had estimated that most CFCs in the United States were used as either aerosol propellants or refrigerants, with the former accounting for 49 per cent of all CFC use and the latter 28 per cent.[3] In the refrigeration industry, CFCs were irreplaceable, for no other chemicals were feasible. This was not the case, however, in the aerosol industry. When Molina and Rowland published their hypothesis, only one-half of all aerosol products in the US were propelled by CFCs. Because of the availability of substitutes (for example, carbon dioxide, hydrocarbons or simple mechanical pressure), manufacturers were able to respond to the consumer pressure that arose after 1974. Three years later, the share of aerosols propelled by CFCs had fallen to 29 per cent. Outside the aerosol industry, meanwhile, neither replacement chemicals nor alternative technologies were available for CFCs. Therefore, if CFC emissions had to be reduced, then a ban on their use in aerosol sprays appeared to be the least costly means of achieving immediate reductions.

Before action would be taken, however, the promise of future benefits would have to be clearly illustrated. Otherwise, a *laissez-faire* policy would be preferable to one that brought about economic costs, no matter how small. Demonstrating the size and indeed the sheer existence of benefits was contingent upon the scientific estimations of eventual stratospheric ozone depletion.[4] Because the scientific debate was plagued by uncertainties (as has been outlined in Chapter 2), the size of any potential benefits was also subject to much uncertainty.

One group that had a particular interest in the issue was the members of the chemical industry. Before anyone had speculated about possible ozone layer depletion, CFCs had been hailed as 'wonder chemicals'. In 1930, their inventor, Thomas Midgely of General Motors, demonstrated their non-toxic and non-flammable nature by inhaling CFCs and blowing out a candle. Few probably thought about the environmental implications beyond that particular gathering.

By the early 1970s, CFCs had become profitable components of the major chemical companies' operations, and their use was increasing at over 10 per cent a year. CFC regulation would obviously threaten such continued growth. Industry representatives were therefore initially sceptical about the wisdom of any kind of restrictions upon production. Officials from Du Pont, the world's largest CFC manufacturer, maintained that more facts were needed before 'a valuable industry is hypothesized out of existence'.[5] The science was too uncertain, industry representatives argued, to justify burdening the United States with the substantial economic costs of regulation.

However, it was not only the potential costs of action that were evident; so too were the potential costs of inaction. In particular, the publication of the National Academy of Sciences' 1976 report, estimating that eventual ozone layer depletion would most likely be 7 per cent, gave strength to the feeling that something had to be done. As was reported in Chapter 2, something was done – namely, legislation was introduced in the United States in 1978. This legislation, however, stopped short of a total prohibition of CFCs; only CFCs in 'non-essential' aerosols were banned. US policy-makers had, in this way, made a distinction between non-essential aerosols and all other uses of CFCs. It appears that the cost of regulating the former was acceptable, but any regulation of the latter could not be justified.

In this chapter, attention has initially been devoted to the United States for two reasons: not only was the US the world's largest producer of CFCs (with approximately 44 per cent of the 1974 world share; see Figure 5.1), but the debate during the 1970s about potential regulation was also the most spirited in the US. Nevertheless, the CFC issue still attracted attention in other countries as well. Some – like Sweden in 1979, Norway in 1979 and Canada in 1980 – followed the US lead by implementing 'can bans'. Others – including most of the world's other large CFC producers – did not follow the US lead. It is to some of these countries that I now turn.

Apart from the United States, the most significant producers of CFCs were in Western Europe, a region which accounted for approximately one-third of worldwide production in 1974 (see Figure 5.1). During the 1970s, the West Europeans did not see the benefits to be as large as the Americans did. As in the United States, industry representatives, particularly in the United Kingdom and France, highlighted the scientific uncertainties associated with the CFC–ozone layer hypothesis. In 1978, for example, a report published by the British Aerosol Manufacturers Association noted that there was much scientific confusion, and therefore 'there is no hazard in waiting for more definite scientific conclusions, nor any reason to restrict manufacturers' choice of propellants for aerosol cans'.[6] Coupled with this, however, and making the situation in Western Europe distinct from that in the United States, was the fact that government-sponsored research was also stressing the uncertainties and challenging the validity of some of the suggested catastrophic ramifications of eventual ozone layer depletion (as Chapter 2 has revealed). Accordingly, the magnitude of the benefits as perceived in Western Europe were not as large as they were in the United States.

In addition, the costs of regulation for West Europeans were seen to be higher for three reasons. First, the aerosol industry was the main customer for the West European CFC producers. Compared with the US, the aerosol industry was larger in not only relative terms (in 1973, approximately three-quarters of all CFCs used in Western Europe went into aerosols, while in the US, the figure was just under

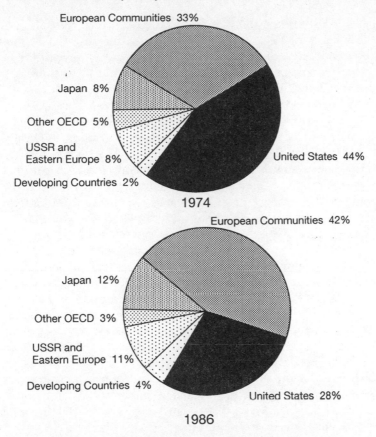

Figure 5.1   Global CFC production by region, 1974 and 1986

Note: All calculations by weight. Figures for 1974 are for CFC-11 and CFC-12 only. Figures for 1986 are for all CFCs.

Sources: Author's calculations based upon the following sources: UNEP, 'The reporting of data by the Parties to the Montreal Protocol on Substances that Deplete the Ozone Layer' (UNEP/OzL.Pro.5/5, 24 August 1993); P.H. Gamlen, B.C. Lane, P.M. Midgley and J.M. Steed, 'The production and release to the atmosphere of CCl_3F and CCl_2F_2 (Chlorofluorocarbons CFC-11 and CFC-12)'. *Atmospheric Environment*, 20:6 (1986), pp. 1077–85; OECD, *Fluococarbons: An Assessment of Worldwide Production, Use and Environmental Issues, First Interim Report* (Paris, OECD Environment Directorate, 1976); and Grant Thornton, *1989 Production and Sales of Chlorofluorocarbons 11 & 12* (Washington, Chemical Manufacturers Association, Fluorocarbon Program Panel, 1990).

one-half) but also in absolute terms (in 1973, more aerosol units were filled with CFCs).[7] An EC ban upon the use of CFCs in non-essential aerosols would therefore affect a greater proportion of its industry, and could thereby be more economically disruptive in Europe than it had been in the United States. Consider, for example, the unilateral action taken by a large multinational company in 1975. At that time, Johnson Wax decided to replace the CFCs in its aerosol products with other propellants. This decision, however, applied to its products in the US, not in the UK. This uneven application of policy may have been partially 'connected with national differences, both in product formulation and in public reaction to the ozone scare'.[8] However, because this policy change affected less than 5 per cent of the company's American aerosol business, while 20 per cent of Johnson Wax's British aerosol business was CFC-propelled, the motivation may also have been, at least partially, economic.

Second, the international trade in CFCs was very lucrative for a number of European states during the 1970s. Compared with the US, the West Europeans exported a greater proportion of the CFCs than they produced. The British, for example, had exports valued at [UK]£70 million in 1975. Thus, if the EC states were to restrict production, then substantial export markets might have to be forsaken. Explicitly citing this as a rationale for its *laissez-faire* policy on CFCs, the UK Minister of State for the Environment, Denis Howell, said in 1975 that an aerosol ban could cause 'a considerable loss to our balance of payments' and have 'far-reaching repercussions on the aerosol industry'.[9]

Finally, the British and French envisaged further costs of CFC regulation. As noted above, the Americans' SST programme had been cancelled during the early 1970s. The British and the French, meanwhile, were continuing to develop, albeit on a limited scale, an SST – namely, the Concorde. Consequently, technological superiority in this strategic industry was perceived to be slowly drifting eastward across the Atlantic Ocean. Some in Britain and France, therefore, suspected that US policy on ozone layer protection was being motivated by a fear of European dominance in supersonic flight. In this view, the re-opening of the ozone layer debate, ostensibly by the CFC route, was seen to be a circuitous method to sabotage the Concorde project, whose demise would damage the British and French economies.

Such concerns help to explain why the EC response was more

hesitant than some other countries'. Although the Commission of the European Communities encouraged member-states to increase the search for CFC substitutes, to halt the leakage of CFCs, and to restrict production of CFCs to 1975 levels, no regulation of any sort was adopted during the 1970s. Some EC members were pushing for strong regulation, specifically the West Germans (particularly towards the end of the decade), but British and French efforts effectively thwarted any significant action. These two states' representatives 'opposed a wider negotiation mandate for the Commission. . . . As the Council had to decide unanimously, these countries determined the EC's position.'[10] The costs of regulating CFCs were simply perceived to be unjustifiably large.

Winds of change in the United States

The 1979 report of the National Academy of Sciences, which estimated eventual ozone depletion to be 16.5 per cent, gave support to the view that regulation upon CFCs should be extended. In the United States, the Environmental Protection Agency (EPA) was investigating the possibility of broadening the restrictions upon CFCs to cover non-aerosol uses such as refrigerants, foaming agents and solvents.

Industry representatives, however, continued to oppose restrictions, demanding 'clear scientific evidence' that CFCs posed a threat to humans and the environment. This position was being articulated most directly by a coalition called The Alliance for Responsible CFC Policy ('the Alliance'). Formed in September 1980 by representatives of CFC user and producer industries in the United States, its prime purpose was, initially, to fight the EPA's proposals for further restrictions. Although the debate in the first half of the 1980s seemingly appeared to be the same as that of the late 1970s, changes in the ways in which costs and benefits were perceived had taken place in the United States.

The perceived value of the future benefits was declining, because it was being predicted that eventual ozone layer depletion would be lower than originally envisaged. Two developments led decision-makers to reach this conclusion. First, the international scientific group that was studying the issue was steadily revising its calculation of ozone depletion – downward (see Figure 2.1). Because a good 'rule of thumb' suggested that for every 1 per cent decrease in stratospheric ozone levels there would be a 2 per cent increase in carcinogenic ultraviolet radiation, the estimated cost of future health-care for skin cancer victims was therefore also falling.

Second, primarily because of the US 'can ban', the use of CFCs was declining worldwide. With fewer CFCs being discharged into the atmosphere, the level of eventual ozone depletion was thought to be decreasing, and accordingly, the value of the perceived benefits of further regulation was also diminishing. Although the influence of declining production levels is being partially double-counted in this kind of analysis (because they were also being accounted for by the scientists in their predictions), it nevertheless did help to diminish the magnitude of the perceived benefits. More specifically, because the revised depletion estimates were generally perceived to be separate from the downward trend in CFC use, the latter seemed to strengthen independently the view that the problem of ozone layer depletion was quickly receding. In this way, policy-makers perceived benefits to be falling more rapidly than the scientific evidence and the statistics justified.

Not only were the future levels of the benefits declining but also their present values were depreciating even more substantially. With the election of Ronald Reagan as US President in 1980, a new era of public sentiment became formally institutionalised in the United States. The 1980s was, in many ways, a period during which the importance of the individual was emphasised, and the importance of others – fellow citizens or future generations – was downplayed. Accordingly, 'discount rates' were increasing, causing the present-day value of future benefits to decrease.

Further, the benefits of further regulatory action were being aired less persuasively during the early 1980s for two reasons. First, the US EPA, whose members had done so much to argue the value of regulatory action during the 1970s, adopted a different position. Owing to staffing changes in the organisation – not least of which was the appointment of Anne Gorsuch as its head – the EPA did not pursue the issue vigorously, with Gorsuch dismissing ozone layer depletion as just another environmental scare.[11]

Second, as a consequence of President Reagan's Executive Order 12291, signed shortly after he took office, all new major regulations had to undergo benefit–cost analysis.[12] It was, however, quite difficult to quantify the benefits of further CFC regulation. For the general case, Charles Caccia observes that proponents of regulation must 'search desperately for an assessment of the true cost to the economy of not taking action. Data are often not available and such costs are not easily calculated.'[13] More specific to the ozone layer issue, Anil Markandya reports that, at this time, 'there were no studies showing how the damage attributable to these chemicals compared to the costs of limiting their use'.[14] Advocates stressing the benefits of regulatory action to preserve the ozone layer could thus only substantiate their case with 'soft', qualitative evidence; whatever 'hard', quantitative evidence existed appeared to highlight seemingly peripheral matters (for example, the price of replacing plastics damaged by increased ultraviolet radiation). For a variety of reasons, therefore, the perceived benefits of regulatory action were falling during the early 1980s.

Moreover, the perceived costs of regulation were also increasing in the United States. Members of the Alliance were highlighting these shifts, stressing the immediate economic costs of further legislative action. The theme of the members' arguments was not new; industrial interests had issued similar dire warnings in the campaign against the aerosol ban during the second half of the 1970s. This time, however, the arguments seemed to have greater persuasive effect, primarily for three reasons.

First, the Reagan Administration was instinctively averse to any kind of regulation, instead preferring to take government out of the homes and workplaces of the nation. Second, the White House was keen to protect the interests of business. By claiming that 260,000 businesses, most of them small, used CFCs, the Alliance struck a receptive chord with the Administration.[15] Finally, these predictions of potentially dire economic straits, should further regulation be pursued, were being made against the backdrop of a global economic recession. Hence, any policy that would cause layoffs and economic disturbance was held to possess a higher marginal cost (both economically and politically) at this time than had been the case during more buoyant periods.

In order to examine further an important element of the government–industry relationship, a brief tangent is required. Within a free market, we are told that products are always made in the manner which is most cost-efficient. Alternative ways of producing output will usually be more expensive (or else they would be adopted and therefore would not be 'alternative' in the first place). Nevertheless, companies will sometimes investigate alternatives to existing modes of production, primarily for one of two reasons. First, these other methods may hold particular promise, or second, the cost of the existing method may be increasing, or be expected to increase. Let us consider further this second reason.

Elementary economic theory teaches us that the cost of any good will rise with scarcity or the expectation of scarcity. Scarcity, in turn, can come about when either the good is being depleted or a regulatory body is threatening its future supply – for example, an announcement that it will be banned, or its production restricted, by legislation. Thus, one condition that accelerates the development of alternatives is the prospect of government regulation. Our brief aside ends here; we return to the ozone layer issue in order to explore the implications of these observations.[16]

The threat and implementation of regulations during the 1970s prompted the major chemical companies in the West to undertake research and development into new, ozone-benign substances. By 1979, a number of different possible substitute chemicals had been identified. Although none could be produced as cheaply as the most widely used CFCs, advances in research and development were nevertheless reducing the anticipated market price of the new chemicals.

As the 1970s ended and the 1980s began, toxicological and environmental tests were being carried out on these chemicals as part of the seven-to-ten-year process of bringing a new product on to the market. Although costs were mounting, company officials were anticipating (though certainly not encouraging) further regulation on ozone-depleting substances and thus substantial future markets for the new chemicals. These expectations justified the short-term expense.

The situation, however, changed dramatically during the early 1980s. For the reasons outlined above, the likelihood of regulation receded. Consequently, the prospects for future markets for the alternative chemicals also diminished. Because industry could no longer be certain that it would recoup its research and development costs, continued expenditure into the substances could no longer be justified. (And a significant further commitment would have had to be made, for further studies of the substitutes would have required major investments in new plants in order to undertake trial production-runs.) All of the major chemical companies, therefore, abandoned their investigations into CFC alternatives. Donald Strobach, director of Du Pont's Environmental Division, asked: 'No matter how good a material is, if no one will buy it, what good is it? . . . The (research) program came to an end because there wasn't enough interest.'[17] Similarly, Imperial Chemical Industry's (ICI) Chief Executive told the UK House of Commons Environment Committee that had ICI continued its research programme during the early 1980s, it 'would have been doing so in a complete commercial vacuum'.[18] Resources would have been diverted from other areas, which might have given competitors an advantage. Therefore, with research programmes stagnating, the potential cost of substitute chemicals ceased falling during the early 1980s. Thus, in the United States, a combination of decreasing benefits and increasing costs contributed to decision-makers' resistance to impose further regulatory controls.

During the first half of the 1980s, the West Europeans maintained the position that they had adopted during the 1970s. Granted, the EC did adopt a very loose regulatory 'production cap' in 1980, which, on paper, may have appeared to have had a restrictive effect.[19] Richard Benedick, however, argues that their commitment to a 30 per cent cutback in CFC aerosol use from 1976 levels was really only 'a trivial target, since European sales of CFCs for aerosols had already declined by over 28 per cent from their 1976 peak, mainly as a result of West German actions'.[20] Instead, the interests of both the West European states' chemical companies and the same states' economic well-being overrode any perceived benefits that might have been obtained. Thus, during the early 1980s, there was agreement that further regulatory action was too costly to justify.

Trans-Atlantic disputes

As was revealed in Chapter 2, the issue entered a new dimension with the discovery of an ozone crater above Antarctica in 1985. In the immediate aftermath, however, industry's position did not change. Instead, the representatives of the major chemical companies greeted it with a fair measure of scepticism. Although the ozone crater did accelerate the feeling that something needed to be done, there had been so many contradictory findings in the past that no one in the industry wanted to react in a 'knee-jerk' manner. Caution was thus the order of the day.

Cost–benefit analyses continued to inform the policy positions of the major states' representatives during late 1985 and early 1986. The inability to resolve the debate about the availability of substitutes, a key economic determinant, prompted the convening of a series of workshops. At the first of these, held in Rome in late May 1986, seventy-five participants examined a wide range of issues. Differences across nations about the perceived costs and benefits were plain to see.

The US and their allies (known collectively as the 'Toronto Group')[21] advocated global control of CFC usage in aerosols. Having implemented such bans during the late 1970s, this option was their economically most-preferable route for two important reasons. First, because they had already undertaken such a ban, no further regulation would be necessary. And second, because their industries had already been required to eliminate CFCs from aerosols, they were well-advanced in developing alternative technologies and substitute chemicals. Hence, a global ban could open up lucrative export markets for this group's (primarily American) chemical companies.

Meanwhile, on the other side of the Atlantic, the EC was still only willing to discuss a potential cap on production, because its representatives argued that any ban on particular end uses would only be a temporary remedy. In addition, however, they also continued to place a high value upon the interests of their domestic chemical industries, for they recognised that an aerosol ban would allow the Americans, for the reasons outlined above, to capitalise upon an important comparative advantage. Moreover, an aerosol ban would not only sacrifice important export markets for CFCs but could also force EC countries to increase their levels of imports, in order to satisfy domestic demand for alternative chemicals. Obviously, this would be a double-blow to the countries' trade balances. The Europeans, therefore, were resistant to the American-led 'can ban plan'.

Within the United States, however, the economic calculation shifted dramatically during the second half of 1986. Perceived costs decreased and perceived benefits increased for American industry representatives at this time. This change was so great that a threshold was crossed, and the American chemical industry found it in its interest to support some sort of regulation for the first time. This shift in perception was manifested in a significant change in Alliance policy. On 16 September 1986, Alliance President Richard Barnett announced support for a 'reasonable global limit' on CFC growth. Large increases in CFC emissions, declared Barnett, would be 'unacceptable to future generations'. He cited the mounting scientific evidence of stratospheric ozone depletion – particularly NASA's recent estimates and the continuing Antarctic mystery – as the reasons for the change in policy.[22] Although the public declaration was that the policy shift was inspired by scientific evidence, the impacts of these changes upon the economic analysis may have also made a powerful contribution to the decision.

The benefits of regulatory action were seen to be increasing on two fronts. First, in 1986, a draft study by the EPA estimated that the incidence of skin cancer could increase significantly if CFC emissions were to continue unabated.[23] Although this was not new, such health reports were starting to enter industry's future planning in a more tangible way. Lawsuits were beginning to be brought against cigarette manufacturers, holding them responsible for lung-cancer cases. Seeing this, chemical companies' representatives wondered if lawsuits might, one day, also be brought against their organisations, holding them responsible for skin-cancer cases. Because the prospect of future legal action has a particularly persuasive influence in the American corporate boardroom, this potentiality was not dismissed lightly.

Second, the major chemical companies in the United States were concerned about the damage that CFC production was doing to their corporate images, for they wanted to present themselves as good citizens in a community which was becoming increasingly concerned about the global environment. Although CFCs were but one facet of a large business for most of these organisations (perhaps 2 to 3 per cent of total sales), negative press about their CFC activities could cast a shadow over their entire operations. Therefore, the restriction of CFC production was perceived to be a small price to pay in return for avoiding potentially disastrous consumer boycotts. (Du Pont, for one, responded to the Antarctic ozone discovery by taking the CFC issue out of the Freon Division's hands and turning it over to senior corporate management. Sharon Roan argues that at this level of the company, 'the issue would be looked at in a broader manner'.)[24]

On the other side of the calculation, the perceived costs of regulatory action were, once again, starting to fall. Du Pont and the other major chemical producers, in light of both the scientific discoveries and the renewed political activity at the international level, had resurrected their research and development programmes to investigate substitute chemicals. Although, owing to the requirements of intra-industry secrecy, it is difficult to discover the exact direction that the companies' programmes were taking, clues that progress was being made in this area had been revealed earlier in the year. Most notably, during one meeting early in 1986, Du Pont officials conceded that substitute chemicals for CFCs as refrigerants and in other applications could be manufactured, if the company was given sufficient incentive to do so.[25] Thus, as during the late 1970s, ongoing work was once again lowering the costs of alternatives and thereby lowering the costs of regulation.

Representatives of American industry recognised, however, that the status quo, with respect to policy, was now almost completely precluded. The Natural Resources Defense Council, an American non-governmental organisation, had launched a court order against the US Environmental Protection Agency, forcing them to promulgate regulations to control CFC emissions. Given this, many observers believed that some sort of regulatory action by the US Government was inevitable. Consequently, the main alternative policies being examined by US industry officials (and by US policy-makers) were no longer the costs and benefits of certain forms of further regulation versus the costs and benefits of no further regulation. Rather, they were the costs and benefits of certain forms of further regulation in isolation versus the costs and benefits of certain forms of further regulation in concert with the other major countries of the world. Because the latter would allow the maintenance (and perhaps expansion) of US markets (for the US would be able to 'assist' others to achieve CFC reductions), it was preferred by both American industry representatives and policy-makers alike.

In light of this, the European reaction was cautious. Benedick argues that:

> Some European industrialists had suspected all along that the United States was using the ozone scare to cloak commercial motivations. They now believed that American companies had endorsed CFC controls in order to enter the profitable EC export markets with substitute products that they had secretly developed.[26]

Nevertheless, perceptions of costs and benefits among EC decision-makers themselves were also changing. First, they recognised the potential costs associated with retarding the Toronto Group's efforts to forge an international agreement. More specifically, as the formal international negotiations on the Protocol started up in late 1986 and early 1987, EC officials realised that if they did not contribute constructively to these discussions, then the United States could well follow up their threat to take unilateral action and impose trade sanctions.

The EC members also recognised that the Americans were at a competitive disadvantage because of the unilateral action that they had taken during the 1970s. Banning non-essential aerosols, as is argued above, is the economically least painful way of reducing CFC consumption. Hence, if some sort of uniform percentage reduction in CFC usage were agreed by the international community, then it would be more easily achieved by the EC for two reasons. First, the West Europeans would be able to cut back in the most cost-painless sector – namely, aerosol usage – while the Americans would have to achieve reductions in applications that had fewer and less favourable substitution possibilities. And second, the West Europeans continued to use a higher percentage of CFC-propelled aerosols than even the pre-ban Americans. Thus, even if the cutbacks were relatively high, all of the gains could be made in this type of usage. At a second workshop (in Leesburg, VA in early September 1986), it was clear that the discussion was moving towards a focus on a cap on global emissions, rather than on the restriction of particular end uses. This delighted the EC delegations, and with this barrier removed, the states outside of the Toronto Group were no longer preoccupied with the American-market-share-conspiracy argument. Although international co-operation would not necessarily be economically benign, the economic costs of regulation were certainly decreasing.

Nevertheless, the West Europeans remained reluctant to impose ambitious targets, like those being advanced by the Toronto Group, and the EC position did not shift significantly until the summer of 1987, at which time Britain and France changed their policy stances. Although the reasons for the United Kingdom's *volte-face* are unclear, it is probable that the economic factor played a major part in the policy decision. As Markus Jachtenfuchs notes, '[o]nly after ICI, the UK's biggest producer, had lifted its total opposition to further reductions did the British government soften its position within the Council, thus following the policy of ICI'.[27]

The focus, thus far, has been upon the US and the members of the

European Community, because they were the major CFC-producing states of the world. (In fact, by the late 1980s, six American and European chemical companies – Du Pont, Atochem, Allied Signals, ICI, Hoechst and Montesfluos – controlled over 80 per cent of the world CFC production capacity.[28] See Figure 5.1.) By the mid-1980s, however, other industrialised states were starting to take greater interest in the progress of the discussions. The Japanese became particularly concerned with the negotiations during the end of 1986 and the beginning of 1987. This was because the chemical CFC-113, used as a solvent in the electronics industry, became one of the objects of proposed regulations (that is, in addition to CFC-11 and CFC-12). The importance of the electronics industry to their economy no doubt helped to arouse Japanese interest in the ozone layer. The Soviet Union, another major producer of CFCs, was also starting to take a more active part in the negotiations. As is noted in the next section, however, these countries' concerns about the potential costs of regulation were eventually addressed.

The demise of CFCs

The Montreal Protocol on Substances that Deplete the Ozone Layer was opened for signature on 16 September 1987. This path-breaking document is remarkable for many reasons. In this chapter, I consider those elements that reflect its balancing of environmental protection and economic development.

First, the Americans wanted to ensure that mechanisms designed to encourage compliance were included. Without broad international compliance, foreign companies would be free to continue producing CFCs and potential export markets for ozone-benign chemicals would thus fail to materialise. (Hence, some argue that this was to guarantee the protection of not only the ozone layer but also US industry.) Article 4 (entitled, 'Control of Trade with Non-Parties') was drafted in response to this concern. It declared that those nations that did not participate would be penalised with trade restrictions. The potential efficacy of these measures was generally assessed favourably. One commentator, for example, argued that: 'Faced with the loss of major U.S. markets, it is inconceivable that other countries will decline to [comply], . . . a step [which has] trivial economic and political costs in comparison.'[29]

Second, the EC representatives were concerned about the impact of regulation upon their lucrative export markets. In response to this anxiety, the most restrictive measures were placed upon consumption, which was calculated to be the level of production minus exports plus imports. Because some additional production was permitted if it were to be exported, the controls were not as tight as they otherwise could have been.

Third, officials from the Soviet Union insisted that they be allowed to complete two CFC plants that were then under construction (as part of their 1986–90 five-year plan). Though not explicitly mentioning the Soviet Union, it is clear that Article 2.6 was included in the Montreal Protocol to meet this demand. It allows any (non-Article 5) country that has facilities under construction to add the future production from these plants to its 1986 (base-year) production levels (so long as it did not increase per capita consumption above 0.5 kg).

Finally, eager to protect its interests in the continued use of CFC-113, Japanese representatives insisted upon a degree of flexibility in the terms of the Protocol. By introducing 'ozone-depleting potentials', index numbers representing the degree to which a particular chemical destroyed stratospheric ozone, countries received some freedom to pursue the reduction path that their decision-makers thought best. Consequently, Japan would be able to make most of the required reductions in CFC-11 and CFC-12.[30] In these ways, it appears that some attention had to be given to the potential costs and benefits for each of the major states.

After the Protocol was opened for signature, CFC substitutes began to appear on the market. A number of such chemicals were first displayed at a large chemical trade fair in Washington, DC in early 1988. One of the most significant was unveiled by A T & T: their representatives announced that they had, with the assistance of Petroferm, Inc., developed an environmentally safe substitute for CFC-113. Eileen Claussen, director of the US EPA's CFC programme, called the development a 'major breakthrough', because many countries (especially Japan) were concerned that substitution would be particularly difficult for this chemical.[31]

Also significant was the announcement, in January 1988, that thirteen chemical companies from seven nations were joining together to spend US$8 million on the testing of alternative, less-damaging compounds. Such a move was unprecedented among the major chemical companies, for they usually conduct research independently in order to preserve competitive advantage. This type of co-operation would likely speed the development process and thereby bring forward the date that additional alternatives would appear on the market.

Although the original Montreal Protocol did not nail the coffin shut on the CFC industry (for reasons that are elaborated in Chapter 8), any expectations that CFCs would undergo a major resurrection in the North soon disappeared. Du Pont officials – in spite of resistance to further restrictions on CFCs right up until the middle of March 1988 – announced, in late March 1988, that their goal was 'an orderly phaseout of fully halogenated CFC production'. Citing the recently released report of the Ozone Trends Panel, Du Pont officials noted that 'new scientific evidence suggested more rapid global ozone change than previously reported, as well as the likely involvement of fully halogenated CFCs in that change'.[32]

In addition to this public justification based upon scientific evidence, an exploration of the company's perceived costs and benefits might offer additional insight into the motivation for this policy shift. First, it was becoming clear that the costs of adopting such a position were falling – most significantly, as noted above, development of alternatives was progressing rapidly. Additionally, the benefits of eliminating CFCs were also increasing. Not only was the scientific evidence that was implicating the chemicals in future wrongs contributing to the calculation but also the importance of cultivating a 'green corporate image' was perceived to be not only beneficial, but even vital. Finally, the profits that could be made from the international marketing of CFC substitutes were not overlooked by the company's officials.

Du Pont's announcement had a profound ripple effect, and the race for substitutes was soon proceeding at top speed. Calls for a full 100 per cent phase-out sparked investigations into replacement chemicals and technologies for *all* usages of CFCs. In this way, although substitutes were not yet available for every CFC application, it was anticipated that they would soon appear on the market.

Other ozone-depleting substances

During the rest of 1988 and the beginning of 1989, the cost of substitute chemicals continued to fall at an appreciable rate. While costs were falling, however, scientific findings were prompting calls for tighter controls upon ozone-depleting substances (that is, beyond the terms of the original Montreal Protocol). Thus, the potential costs and benefits of further regulations were being examined.

By this time, however, an explicit examination of the economic costs of regulation was being undertaken at the international level. Under the terms of the Montreal Protocol, a Panel for Technical Assessment – consisting of experts from governments, industry and research institutions – had been established. It was charged with the task of monitoring the development of substitute chemicals and technologies. This information was to be made available to policy-makers, when they were considering changes to the Protocol's terms.

The Panel for Technical Assessment reported on the state of development of alternative substances and technologies at the First Meeting of the Protocol's Parties in Helsinki in May 1989. They noted that the technology to eliminate all CFCs was not yet available, with the adaptation of industrial refrigeration being particularly difficult because of the large capital costs involved. Nevertheless, the Panel concluded that it was at least 'technically feasible' to phase out completely some of the chemicals by the turn of the century. Policy-makers responded to this information by agreeing a non-binding resolution to 'phase out the production and the consumption of CFCs, controlled by the Montreal Protocol as soon as possible but not later than the year 2000'. This commitment was not extended to halons, primarily because of the continued unavailability of prospective substitutes for these ozone-depleting chemicals. Instead, only an agreement to phase out 'as soon as feasible' could be agreed.[33]

The Helsinki Declaration also committed the Parties to 'control and reduce other ozone-depleting substances which contribute significantly to ozone depletion as soon as feasible'.[34] Of the many possible ozone-depleting substances, one in particular was becoming of increasing concern in 1989 – namely, hydrochlorofluorocarbons (HCFCs). HCFCs were identified as potential substitutes for up to 30 per cent of the controlled CFCs. Although more ozone-benign than CFCs, they are by no means 'wonder chemicals', for they still destroy some stratospheric ozone.[35] In light of this fact, pressure mounted during the first half of 1990 to impose restrictions upon their use at the Second Meeting of the Parties in London in June of that year.

Industry officials resisted this pressure. They maintained that society's primary goal must be to eliminate CFCs as quickly as possible. Although there are problems associated with the use of HCFCs, they were perceived to be the most attractive alternative. Thus, the argument continued, it is better to use the lesser of two evils while more appropriate alternatives are being developed and tested – in this instance, therefore, the ends justify the means.

This view eventually prevailed. Although some low-producing chemical countries – like Norway, Sweden, Australia and New Zealand – called for a phase-out date for HCFCs between 2010 and 2020, they were thwarted by representatives from chemical producing countries, who insisted that no firm date be set.[36] Thus, in London, signatory nations could only call for 'producers to use [HCFCs] responsibly, and work towards eliminating them by 2040'.[37]

The debate about HCFCs continued following the conclusion of the London meeting. It gathered steam two years later, during the lead-up to, and proceedings of, the Fourth Meeting of the Parties in Copenhagen. Industry representatives continued to maintain that an immediate ban upon HCFCs would destroy the commercial incentives both for producers to make the chemicals and for manufacturers to utilise them. They claimed that a slower phase-out was appropriate, so that businesses would be able to recoup their research, development and capital investments. Without this, companies would continue to use ozone-damaging CFCs while waiting for more suitable alternatives. Moreover, they argued that the case supporting the existing alternatives was not strong: hydrofluorocarbons (HFCs, a family of chlorine-free substitutes) are strong global warming gases, and the more traditional chemicals (for example, ammonia, butane and pentane) have problems with either toxicity and/or flammability.

Others challenged this position, for they argued that suitable alternatives to CFCs and HCFCs did exist. To support this claim, they pointed to the fact that a refrigerator using a mixture of propane and butane (two ozone-benign substances) had been developed by DKK Scharfenstein in Germany.[38] Moreover, they argued that international regulation would both encourage the scientific development of suitable substances and add to the commercial attractiveness of such alternatives. Indeed, the experience in CFCs suggests that this may be the case. They further noted, however, that the corollary also holds: that is, that 'the development of technologies that do not use either controlled or transitional substances can be inhibited because the prospect of technology using transitional substances discourages investment in technology that would only be profitable if transitional substances were not acceptable'.[39] The motivations for industry's position, they argued, were to secure and to protect its established markets.

In the end, the negotiators agreed to cap consumption of HCFCs in January 1996 at a level equal to the sum of their consumption in 1989 plus 3.1 per cent of the level of consumption of CFCs in 1989.[40] Subsequent to that, Parties agreed to reduce their consumption of HCFCs by 35 per cent by 2004, by 65 per cent by 2010, by 90 per cent by 2015, by 99.5 per cent by 2020 and by 100 per cent by 2030. The fact that the relatively late date of 2030 was accepted for the final phase-out can be at least partially explained by the political clout of those who were supporting the arguments cited above – namely, industry and the United States. Industry's interest has already been identified, and their representatives were out in force in Copenhagen.

The Americans also had a particular interest in securing this timetable, for they would be particularly hindered by a more imminent phase-out of HCFCs. The largest pieces of equipment that use HCFCs are the air conditioners that cool office buildings. The country that makes the most use of these large chillers is the United States. Because they have economic lifetimes of up to forty years, business people want to ensure that they will be able to keep these chillers operational throughout this period. The 'tail' – that is, the 0.5 per cent usage between 2020 and 2030, which the Americans demanded and received – ensures this.[41] Although the history of the ozone layer debate suggests that the phase-out dates for HCFCs will be brought forward (indeed, many at the conference thought that the 'writing was on the wall' for these chemicals), it may be that the Americans (and others) will be able to qualify such uses of HCFCs as 'essential' in the future. Regardless, HCFC controls will likely be reviewed at some point, and further amendments could well be introduced in 1995.

At the beginning of 1994, not every human activity with the potential to destroy stratospheric ozone was covered by the terms of Montreal Protocol.[42] Consequently, debate about the regulation of further activities was set to persist. Bodies established under the terms of the Protocol – in particular the Panel for Technical Assessment and the Panel for Economic Assessment – were thus well-poised to continue to play vital roles in future efforts to strengthen international co-operation.

Notes

1   A review of these studies can be found in The Department of Economic and Social Affairs, 'Protection of the ozone layer – some economic and social implications of a possible ban on the use of fluorocarbons', in Asit K. Biswas (ed.), *The Ozone Layer* (Oxford, Pergamon, 1983), pp. 141–67.

2   'Fluorocarbons and national economics', *New Scientist*, 68 (2 October 1975), pp. 17–18.

3   Cited in OECD, *Fluorocarbons: an Assessment of Worldwide Production, Use and Environmental Issues, First Interim Report* (Paris, OECD Environment Directorate, 1976), p. 14.

4   Recall that the primary benefits of regulatory action would be the value of the costs that would have been caused by a thinner ozone layer.

5   From a Du Pont advertisement in *Science*, 190 (3 October 1975), pp. 8–9.

6   Cited in 'Verdict still open on fluorocarbons', *New Scientist*, 79 (21 September 1978), p. 830.

7   Data from: Frudolf J. Engelmann, 'A look at some issues before an ozone convention', *Environmental Policy and Law*, 8 (1982), p. 53; Patricia L. Layman, 'Aerosols back on road to success', *Chemical and Engineering News* (28 April 1986), p. 42; and OECD, *Fluorocarbons: an Assessment*, p. 14.

8   Martin Sherwood, 'Johnson waxes eloquent – in US but not UK', *New Scientist*, 67 (3 July 1975), p. 34.

9   Quoted in 'MP calls for British fluorocarbon ban', *New Scientist*, 67 (7 August 1975), p. 336.

10   Markus Jachtenfuchs, 'The European Community and the protection of the ozone layer', *Journal of Common Market Studies*, 28:3 (March 1990), p. 265.

11   See note 27 and accompanying text in Chapter 2.

12   V. Kerry Smith, 'Environmental policy making under Executive Order 12291: an introduction', in V. Kerry Smith (ed.), *Environmental Policy Under Reagan's Executive Order: The Role of Cost–Benefit Analysis* (London, University of North Carolina Press, 1984), p. 4.

13   Charles Caccia, 'OECD nations and sustainable development', in David J.R. Angell, Justyn D. Colmer and Matthew L.N. Wilkinson (eds), *Sustaining Earth: Response to the Environmental Threats* (Basingstoke, Macmillan, 1990), p. 125.

14   Anil Markandya, 'Economics and the ozone layer', in David Pearce (ed.), *Blueprint 2: Greening the World Economy* (London, Earthscan,

1991), p. 64.

15   The price of substitute chemicals was higher than the price of CFCs. Recall that any further regulation in the US at this time would have to be imposed upon applications other than aerosol propellants. This would prove to be quite difficult, for studies undertaken during the late 1970s and the early 1980s suggested that potential substitutes remained elusive for many CFC applications.

16   See, more generally, Eugene B. Skolnikoff, *The Elusive Transformation: Science, Technology and the Evolution of International Politics* (Princeton, Princeton University Press, 1993).

17   Quoted in Sharon L. Roan, *Ozone Crisis: the 15 Year Evolution of a Sudden Global Emergency* (Chichester, John Wiley & Sons, 1989), p. 100.

18   United Kingdom House of Commons Environment Committee, First Report, *Air Pollution, Volume 1 (Report and Appendices Together with the Proceedings of the Committee Relating to the Report)* (London, HMSO, 25 May 1988).

19   'Decision concerning chlorofluorocarbons in the environment' (80/372/EEC).

20   Richard Elliot Benedick, *Ozone Diplomacy: New Directions in Safeguarding the Planet* (London, Harvard University Press, 1991), p. 25.

21   This group also included Canada, Switzerland and the Scandinavian countries.

22   'Statement of Richard Barnett, Chairman, The Alliance for Responsible CFC Policy, September 16, 1986, National Press Club, Washington, DC', pp. I–1 to I–2.

23   The final report, released in 1987, was the most detailed assessment of costs and benefits of policy action and inaction undertaken to that point (Environmental Protection Agency, *Regulatory Impact Analysis: Protection of Stratospheric Ozone, 3 Volumes* (Washington, DC, EPA, 1987)).

24   Roan, *Ozone Crisis*, p. 193.

25   Michael Oppenheimer and Robert Boyle, *Dead Heat: The Race Against the Greenhouse Effect* (London, I.B. Tauris & Co., 1990), p. 46.

26   Benedick, *Ozone Diplomacy*, p. 123. Benedick goes on to note that: '. . . this suspicion was unfounded: to the dismay of environmentalists, Du Pont had admitted in 1986 that it had ceased research on chlorofluorocarbon alternatives in 1981' (p. 123).

27   Jachtenfuchs, 'The European Community', p. 268. See, also, James H. Maxwell and Sanford L. Weiner, 'Green consciousness or dollar diplomacy?: The British response to the threat of ozone depletion', *International Environmental Affairs*, 5:1 (Winter 1993), pp. 19–41.

28   Chemical Economics Handbook, 'Marketing research report on fluorocarbons' (Stanford, SRI International, 1990), cited in Mohan Munasinghe and Kenneth King, 'Accelerating ozone layer protection in developing countries', *World Development*, 20:4 (1992), p. 610.

29   David Wirth, quoted in Annette M. Capretta, 'The future's so bright, I gotta wear shades: future impacts of the Montreal Protocol on Substances that Deplete the Ozone Layer', *Virginia Journal of International Law*, 29 (1989), p. 231, n. 135.

30   The Japanese had also called for a transition period, so that the 'initial costs of converting equipment' would not be intolerable (Lois R. Ember *et al.*, 'Tending the global commons', *Chemical and Engineering News* (24 November 1986), pp. 50–1).

31   Margaret E. Somerset, 'An attempt to stop the sky from falling: the Montreal Protocol to protect against atmospheric ozone reduction', *Syracuse Journal of International Law and Commerce*, 15:3 (Spring 1989), p. 414.

32   'Summary of the Chairman's remarks (27 April 1988)', *Du Pont: First Quarter Report* (1988), p. 4.

33   'Helsinki Declaration on the Protection of the Ozone Layer', reprinted in *Environmental Policy and Law*, 19:3/4 (July 1989), p. 137.

34   Ibid., p. 137.

35   Because it has a shorter atmospheric lifetime, one HCFC molecule will destroy a much smaller amount of stratospheric ozone than one CFC molecule. This shorter lifetime, however, means that the HCFC's destruction of ozone will also take place much sooner. Opponents of HCFCs, therefore, point to its relatively high 5-year ozone-depleting potential (which is 0.51 and 0.19 for HCFC-123 and HCFC-22 respectively), while supporters of the chemical highlight its low 500-year ozone-depleting potential (which is 0.02 and 0.05 for HCFC-123 and HCFC-22 respectively). (Susan Solomon and Daniel L. Albritton, 'Time-dependent ozone depletion potentials for short- and long-term forecasts', *Nature*, 357 (7 May 1992), pp. 33–7.)

36   Nicholas Schoon, 'Deal to save ozone layer agreed', *Independent* (London) (30 June 1990), p. 1.

37   Ibid., p. 1.

38   See, for example, John Vidal, 'Second front: the big chill', *Guardian* (19 November 1992), p. T2.

39   *Report of the Technology and Economic Assessment Panel* (Nairobi, UNEP, December 1991), pp. 3–6.

40   This formula acknowledges both the considerable existing uses of HCFCs and their role as transition substitutes for CFCs.

41   The Americans were not the only ones who were pleased with this outcome. Any possible opposition to relatively lax HCFC controls by the EC was thwarted by French resistance. The French government, reportedly working in the interests of one of its assets (namely, the French chemical company, Atochem, which is the world's largest producer of HCFCs) opposed both a lower figure for the 1996 cap and an advancement of the initial phasedown date for HCFCs. Because the EC had competence in this

area (compared with, for example, questions about the international funding mechanism, where EC states could formulate positions independently), the Commission could not offer a strong common position in response to the US one.

42   In this regard, it is instructive to note that when the members of the Protocol's Panel were charged with the task of determining ozone-depleting potentials for HCFCs and HBFCs (hydrobromofluorocarbons), they were expected to return with about 30 figures. However, because these substances have many different isomers, they returned to the 1992 Copenhagen meeting with some five hundred values. (UNEP/OzL.Pro/WG.1/8/L.1, p. 10, Pt. 53 (NASA's Robert Watson quoted in that document).) Additionally, debates about the possible damage caused to the ozone layer by airplanes also continued.

6

Interests and climate change

With the prospect of climate change near the top of political agendas by the late 1980s, decision-makers were attempting to assess the wisdom of alternative sets of policies. The goal of any policy that aimed to avoid a warmer future was, usually, the stabilisation of atmospheric concentrations of greenhouse gases.[1] To achieve this end, many alternative suggestions were being tossed around in the public debate. Some challenged the imagination. One proposal, for example, involved the dumping of iron filings into the world's oceans, so that algae would be encouraged to grow. These algae would, in turn, absorb excess greenhouse gases. Proposals like this, however, were the extreme. The vast majority focused upon emissions of greenhouse gases resulting from human activities, in order to discover how they might be reduced.

The major anthropogenic greenhouse gases are carbon dioxide, methane, CFCs and nitrous oxides. Addressing the global warming problem, therefore, could concern any or all of these gases. The debate in the North, however, focused upon carbon dioxide. Not only was it the most culpable but also because most carbon dioxide was produced as a by-product of fossil fuel combustion, it would also be the easiest greenhouse gas to monitor.[2]

However, the notion that carbon dioxide emissions arising from fossil fuel combustion would have to be curtailed was not greeted passively. With the burning of coal, oil and gas being so central to the everyday activities of industrialised society, some considered such recommendations to be drastic, if not revolutionary. Informing this position was a deep-rooted belief that pollution was an undesirable, yet necessary, by-product of economic growth. I begin this chapter by considering further this traditional view of the world.

Delinking production and pollution

A country's welfare (or, at least, its 'economic performance') is, in many cases, measured by the value of all the goods and services that are produced by its inhabitants during one year – in other words, its Gross Domestic Product (GDP). In order to create a good or a service of some value, an input of at least a minimal quantity of energy is required. For reasons of cost efficiency, the most attractive means of producing that energy have been, since the Industrial Revolution, the burning of fossil fuels (coal, oil and gas). Fossil fuels, however, contain carbon, which is released in the form of carbon dioxide when burned. Logic therefore suggests that if a reduction in carbon dioxide emissions is required, then the incidence of combustion should be reduced, which in turn means that fewer fossil fuels should be burned. With fewer fossil fuels being burned, however, less energy will be produced, which in turn suggests that fewer goods and services will be provided. The country that burns fewer fossil fuels will consequently have a lower GDP and an associated lower level of welfare. Although extremely rudimentary, this deductive cycle has a certain power to it. Moreover, such reasoning appeared to be given greater confirmation by the more general post-Second World War debate about the relationship between economic growth and pollution. Perhaps most celebrated by the 1972 *Limits to Growth* report,[3] it appeared that huge computers, prestigious universities and distinguished thinkers were also suggesting that continued growth would have devastating environmental effects. Consequently, the view that growth and pollution necessarily went hand-in-hand was further ingrained into the consciousness of industrialised society. William Reilly, former United States Environmental Protection Agency Administrator, recalls an incident that effectively illustrates this position:

> Twenty years ago, when the original Clean Air Act was being debated in the House of Representatives, one of the bill's opponents took the floor to insist that pollution control is incompatible with economic growth. The congressman quoted a constituent, a small-town mayor, as saying: 'If you want this town to grow, it has got to stink.'[4]

For many, any suggestion to reduce pollution was automatically perceived to be a prescription for zero economic growth.

Though the preceding view was dominant, it was by no means without critics. The notion that environmental protection and economic growth could, indeed, be compatible had been evident in the international debate since the 1960s. It did not, however, manage to challenge the conventional wisdom vigorously until the 1980s. The single most important document to advance this opinion was the 1987 report of the World Commission on Environment and Development (WCED), which was entitled *Our Common Future*.[5] In this report, the WCED's members argued for 'a new era of economic growth – growth that is forceful and at the same time socially and environmentally sustainable'.[6] The Report's impact was substantial, and its popularisation did much to erode the automatic tendency to equate 'protection of the environment' with 'stagnation of the economy'. Instead, its focus on 'sustainable development' brought the idea of economic growth that was compatible with environmental preservation to the attention of decision-makers.

Therefore, two understandings about the relationship between economic well-being and pollution comprised the debate by the late 1980s. Each subsequently led to a different policy recommendation on climate change. On the one hand, those who viewed economic growth and environmental degradation as complementary considered suggestions to reduce greenhouse gas emissions as being prescriptions for the reduction of industrial growth, and thus unacceptable. On the other hand, those who considered true 'sustainable development' to be a possibility judged those same suggestions to be not only tolerable but also desirable. In the rest of this chapter, I consider more closely the case of two of the world's largest industrialised countries, each of which adopted a different attitude with regard to policy action on global warming. (See Figure 6.1 for energy-related CO_2 emissions of all OECD countries.) I begin with an investigation of Germany – the country that espoused the most ambitious goal for reduction of carbon dioxide emissions[7] – and follow this with an investigation of the United States – a country that set, among OECD countries, one of the least stringent targets.[8]

The case of Germany: experience of efficiency

By the late 1980s, experience had led many German industrialists to challenge the traditional view that growth and pollution necessarily

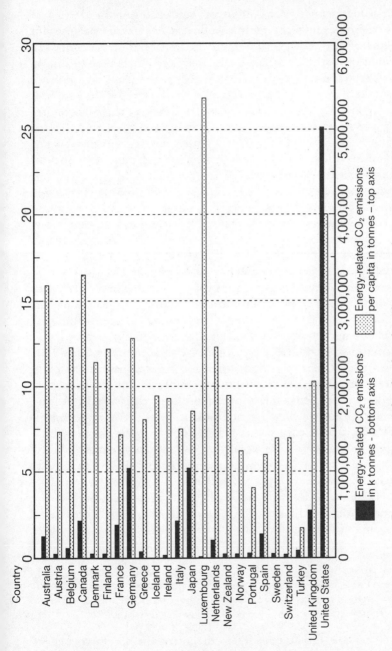

Figure 6.1 Energy-related carbon dioxide emissions for OECD countries, 1990

Source: IEA, *Climate Change Policy Initiatives* (Paris, OECD, 1992), p. 28.

went hand in hand.[9] When oil prices went up during the 1970s and early 1980s, overall energy use went down (though coal use did increase). This, however, did not bring about a reduction in economic growth. Instead, Germans used their energy more efficiently – the country's energy intensity decreased significantly during the 1970s and 1980s, from 2.97 TCE/GNP in 1970 to 2.12 TCE/GNP in 1990 (an improvement of 29 per cent).[10] Therefore, when policies designed to reduce carbon dioxide emissions were proposed during the late 1980s, German business people did not reject them out of hand. Instead, they viewed them as potential stimuli to efficiency and productivity.

Additionally, a number of Germans also felt that such policies might bring about benefits; benefits, that is, beyond the fact that the world would avoid a warmer fate.[11] If carbon dioxide emissions were reduced, then those other pollutants that are produced in the same processes would also be reduced (for example, nitrous oxides, sulphur dioxide, carbon monoxide and particulates). As a consequence, other environmental problems – for example, acid precipitation and urban pollution – would inadvertently be addressed. In an oft-cited study of Norway, Glomsrod and colleagues find that reduction of carbon dioxide emissions would also lessen local environmental damage.[12] Given Germany's traditional concern with many kinds of environmental problems, the country's inhabitants regarded these sorts of side-effects favourably as well.[13]

Other so-called 'secondary' or 'spin-off' benefits would also be forthcoming after the implementation of policies that were primarily intended to reduce carbon dioxide emissions. These would include health improvements from reduced emissions of pollutants, reduced corrosion, reduced traffic accidents, reduced traffic congestion, reduced road damage and reduced noise.[14] Again, every industrialised society – Germany included – viewed these favourably.

Benefits could also stretch beyond a country's national borders. As the histories of various environmental issues have shown, the:

> greenest countries, indeed, can expect an added bonus. Their firms have to meet tough regimes at home, so they will be well poised to clean up (in both senses) when dirtier countries see the light. . . . The country that pioneers the taxes and charges that make polluters pay will enjoy a boom as purveyor of greenness to a dirty world.[15]

This proposal – that benefits from potentially lucrative export markets are also possible – has already been given support by the findings from Chapter 5's study of the politics of the ozone layer. Not only did research into alternatives and substitutes for environmentally destructive products and practices increase when the prospects of regulation increased but also the desire for international markets subsequently motivated US policy-makers to press for stringent international controls on CFCs. The same could come true on the global warming issue: nationally imposed greenhouse gas regulations could serve as incentives for industries to develop technologies and substitutes that could help to reduce emission levels; moreover, the company that manufactures new products successfully could subsequently have access to vast foreign markets.[16]

In 1990, the worldwide pollution protection and prevention market was valued at approximately US$200 billion annually, and it was expected to rise to US$300 billion by the turn of the century. Moreover, Germany was at the forefront of this surge. In 1992, the Federation of German Industries reported that the value of this market in western Germany was approximately DM40 billion (about US$24 billion) a year, with a growth rate of 6 to 8 per cent annually. Consequently, they concluded that 'the environmental protection market is well on the way to becoming a major sector in German industry'.[17] A combination of bearable costs and considerable benefits, therefore, suggests that German interests would be served by international co-operation on global warming. Though potentially seductive, these elements formed only part of the calculation.

The reduction of carbon dioxide emissions in Germany would not necessarily have brought joy to all. Germany is a major coal-producing country. In 1990, coal satisfied about one-third of the country's primary energy requirements.[18] Because coal is the 'dirtiest' fossil fuel, it would be the first to be targeted in an effort to achieve reductions in carbon dioxide emissions. One study suggests that the proposed EU carbon-energy tax,[19] for example, would reduce coal output by over 40 per cent between 1990 and 2050.[20] Although closure of German pits would have made good sense economically, the perceived political costs could have rapidly become the most dominant factor for German policy-makers. More specifically, the state has traditionally played a major role in the German coal industry, providing subsidies of upwards of 7 billion marks (US\$4.2 billion) a year. The removal of subsidies would have been met with fierce resistance by the coal constituency, and no German government would have voluntarily incurred their wrath.

Moreover, notwithstanding their recognition of the value of environmental protection, the feelings of German industrialists still fell well short of unreserved enthusiasm. A statement from the Federation of German Industries identifies its priorities on the climate change issue: 'voluntary, efficient and economically sound measures in keeping with competition and free-market principles, instead of . . . regulatory and fiscal regimentation'.[21] Business, even in Germany, had its limits.

In addition, some Germans might well have enjoyed a warmer world. Higher temperatures would mean lower heating bills, savings that would easily exceed the increased cost of air conditioning. Beyond changes in surface temperatures, global warming would primarily manifest itself in the form of higher sea levels and shifting climatic zones. With respect to the former, only about one-sixth of the country borders on the sea, and therefore its inhabitants would not have needed to construct vast sea defences, to relocate numerous people and industry or to safeguard many fresh water supplies against salt-water intrusion. While, with respect to the latter, it is noted above that German agriculture and forestry activities were relatively small contributors to national GDP. Consequently, a number of elements in the German calculation suggest that international co-operation would have brought considerable costs and relatively insignificant benefits.

The clean, the coastal and the consumer-conscious

Although the focus here is, thus far, upon Germany, I can explore the perceived interests of other 'progressive' countries. First, in light of the argument above about energy efficiency, I can speculate that any country that had been able to make gains in efficiency might have been more receptive to agreements to limit greenhouse gas emissions. Among G7 countries, France came second to (western) Germany in energy/GNP gains between 1979 and 1989.[22] Moreover, if we measure efficiency not in terms of energy used per economic unit produced, but instead in terms of carbon dioxide emitted per economic unit produced, France's improvement was even more dramatic. The reason for this is that France met most of its electricity needs by nuclear power, a form of generation which produces no carbon dioxide. Overcapacity in nuclear-generated electricity helps to explain the French government's belief that the EU should have been pursuing a 'carbon tax', rather than the originally proposed carbon-energy version.

Consider, as well, the potential impact of global warming. Recognition of possible sea-level rises leads me to speculate that coastal states would have supported co-operative measures on global warming. In fact, this was the case, for the country that had the second most ambitious target for limitations on greenhouse gas emissions was the Netherlands.[23] The coastline accounts for about half of the country's borders, and the historical battle that the Dutch have had with the sea is well-known. Denmark and New Zealand's pro-active approaches may also be partially explained by concerns about sea-level rises in a warmer world.

Finally, what about secondary benefits of an international variety? Again building upon the arguments laid out above, I can suggest that any country that had a highly developed technological base may have been tempted by potential gains in international trade to support co-operative efforts. Consider the case of Japan. In October 1990, the Japanese government set a target of stabilisation of 1990 per capita emission levels by 2000. This was, according to a representative of the Association for the Conservation of Energy, a 'signal that consensus between the Japanese industry and government has been reached, and *that they do not feel that setting this target is something they cannot cope with economically*'.[24] As well, Japanese eyes may have been on potential overseas markets: during the early 1990s, its government and industries made significant moves into environmental technology, establishing an International Center for Environmental Technology and a Research Institute of Innovative Technology.[25] Believing that a technological fix to the climate change problem was possible, Japan felt well-poised to help the rest of the world meet the challenges.[26]

The case of the United States: energy enthusiasts

While some countries were actively promoting co-operative initiatives, others were not nearly as eager. Among OECD countries, none was less enthused than the United States. During the late 1980s and the early 1990s, the United States did not support international co-operative efforts on the global warming issue. Chapter 3 has already revealed the Bush Administration's scepticism for much of the scientific work on the issue. Legitimation for the 'go-slow' approach was, however, not only based upon considerations of science; economics also had an important public role to play.

A study by the Council of Economic Advisors was particularly influential in the US decision-making process. Released in 1990, it estimates the cost to cut America's carbon emissions by 20 per cent by the year 2100 to be between US$800 billion and US$3.6 trillion. Given this figure, the report concludes that the 'highest priority in the near term should be to improve understanding in order to build a foundation for sound policy decisions. Until such a foundation is in place, there is no justification for imposing major costs on the economy in order to slow the growth of greenhouse gas emissions.'[27] US officials often referred to this figure in order to justify their policy position not only within the national debate but also internationally.

In August 1990, for example, the Intergovernmental Panel on Climate Change's three working groups released their final reports. The Americans had chaired the IPCC's third Working Group, which was charged with the task of exploring possible response strategies. This group's final report was widely criticised, for its proposals were judged to be much too cautious and unimaginative. Many believed that the Americans had made full use of their position as chair to ensure that measures that would have far-reaching economic ramifications were kept off the agenda.

In spite of criticism launched against them, officials from the United States remained unbending. At the Second World Climate Conference in Geneva in November 1990, they expressed concern that 'actions we agree to take do not unduly curtail economic growth', and, as has been outlined in Chapter 3, ensured that scientific uncertainties were highlighted. This theme remained a central part of the US position during the intergovernmental negotiations towards a climate treaty. If anything, their steadfastness increased during the six months immediately prior to the UN Conference on Environment and Development in June 1992.

During this period, US President George Bush made it clear that if a climate convention containing specific commitments was agreed, then he would not attend the Earth Summit. In the end, his determination prevailed, for the Climate Change Convention does not place obligations upon its signatories. Although Article 2 does have a strong objective (namely, 'stabilization of greenhouse gas concentrations in the atmosphere at a level that would prevent dangerous anthropogenic interference with the climate system'), Article 4.2 does not, in strict terms, oblige any Party to take any particular reduction or stabilisation action. The Americans' desire to avoid any specific co-operative action was thus realised.

At the beginning of this chapter, it was suggested that the degree to which a country might have been receptive to action on global warming is directly proportional to the degree to which a country had been able to delink economic well-being from pollution. Although the United States took some action in light of the oil crises of the 1970s and 1980s, it was relatively trivial in comparison to other OECD countries – energy prices remained low, and efficiency standards were not raised significantly. For example, the 1985 figure for energy intensity in the country was 0.61 TOE/US$1000, placing it nineteenth of the twenty-one IEA nations.[28] Consequently, the traditional view of the production–pollution relationship remained as deep-rooted as ever. Effectively reflecting this attitude, William Fulkerson of the US Energy Department's Oak Ridge National Laboratory noted in 1990: 'My overall view is that [reducing carbon dioxide emissions] will be very difficult and very expensive . . . It's not any accident that the world depends on fossil fuel. We're still hooked on fossil fuel because it is marvellous.'[29] This energy-dependence suggested that it would be difficult to break society's addiction.

In light of this, some American decision-makers believed that policies aiming to cut carbon dioxide emissions – for example, taxes on energy consumption – would damage the economy. First of all, they thought that higher energy costs would result in higher overall costs, which would be passed on in higher prices. Thus, inflation would be fuelled. Numerous studies document this, speculating that an internationally-uniform carbon tax would cause greater increases in end-use prices of energy in the United States than, for example, in Germany and Japan.[30]

Second, they also believed that action to curb greenhouse gas emissions would cause American jobs in the manufacturing industries to be lost, primarily for two reasons. First, jobs would go to those countries that remained outside of any co-operative arrangement (the so-called 'pollution-haven' hypothesis).[31] And second, jobs would also be lost to those countries within the co-operative arrangement that were able to keep cost increases, in light of higher energy costs, under greater control. Given the point about inflation above, American manufacturing might consequently relocate in any of a large number of other countries.

In addition, employment levels would also fall in the US energy sector. It is an oft-overlooked fact that the US was a significant energy producer, with about 35 per cent of that being in the form of coal. Just as in the German case, 'dirty' coal would have been one of the first energy sources to be cut back in any carbon dioxide reduction programme. One study, for example, found that a phased-in carbon tax of US$30 per ton would have eventually raised coal prices by 78 per cent, while oil and gas prices would have risen by only 19 per cent each.[32] Such a price rise would have obviously put the future of American coal workers at risk. Thus, unemployment would be increased.[33]

Given these possibilities, might international co-operative action on global warming not be a prescription for economic depression in the United States? As noted above, the report by the US Council of Economic Advisors was suggesting that it would, and subsequent studies laid out the implications more explicitly. Though there were significant variations among details, there was general agreement that the costs of achieving a 2 per cent reduction of baseline emissions annually would be about 2 per cent of GDP.[34] Although the United States was not unique among industrialised countries in that it found that greenhouse gas emission reductions would have a price, the cost to most other OECD countries was not as high as it was to the United States. Moreover, most other OECD countries could find at least one policy alternative that would result in some economic benefit – for example, a 1990 OECD report that cites a study comparing the effects of four different policies to reduce emissions by 50 per cent over 1990–2030 concludes that both Japan and the EC member-states would be better off if national consumption taxes were the policy instruments chosen. By contrast, the report finds that North America would be the only region to be worse off in *every* scenario.[35]

Beyond these economic costs, there were also potential political costs. Americans did not have a particular affection for regulation in general, or taxes in particular. Therefore, any Administration which was seen to be agreeing to new controls might have to accept significant political costs as a by-product. Moreover, in light of the Americans' special relationship with their automobiles (and the reliance, in such a vast country, upon road transportation more generally), a tax upon motoring could have been like shooting oneself in the proverbial political foot.[36]

Further, powerful industrial interests – particularly, energy producers and users – perceived significant costs associated with reductions in carbon dioxide emissions. Although the ozone layer experience might lead to the belief that any initial opposition would eventually give way to industry co-operation, significant differences between the two issues of global atmospheric change challenge this. Recall that, on the ozone layer issue, the large chemical companies eventually supported CFC regulation, because their representatives realised that they would be the ones that would manufacture the substitute chemicals. The collapse of one market, therefore, would be compensated by the emergence of another. In contrast, substitution would not occur to the same extent on the global warming issue. Notwithstanding the alternative use of lower-carbon or non-carbon fuels, the primary prescriptions to combat global warming did not involve replacement (as in the CFC case), but rather reduction. Energy producers therefore did not anticipate 'different' business, but rather 'dissipating' business.

In the United States, industrial interests organised in order to fight against policies that would require reductions in greenhouse gas emissions. Most significantly, representatives from sixty US corporations and interest groups came together in 1989 to form the Global Climate Coalition, a group that aimed 'to provide the business perspective' on the global warming issue. During, and after, the negotiations towards the Climate Change Convention, this group pressed its position. At the Earth Summit, for example, the Coalition's Executive Director, John Shlaes, maintained that some of the proposals being mooted could have a US$95 billion impact on the US economy and could result in the loss of 550,000 jobs.[37] They, therefore, fully supported President Bush's cautious approach on the issue.

As with the investigation of Germany, however, the analysis should not be restricted to perceived costs; perceived benefits should be explored as well. These, as has already been noted, could come in a variety of shapes and sizes. The primary ones would arise from slowing global warming – namely, the costs associated with a warmer world that would be avoided. I have already recognised that arriving at some estimate of such benefits may be plagued with difficulties. Frances Cairncross elaborates:

> Calculations of the costs of curbing carbon dioxide may be difficult,
> but they are easy compared with the task of estimating the benefits.
> Here language can be muddling: a benefit of curbing greenhouse gases
> may take the form of avoiding some of the costs of adapting to a hotter
> world. Thus, while building sea walls is a cost of adapting to the rise in
> sea levels that global warming may bring, avoiding the need for the
> expense of building sea walls appears in the arithmetic as a benefit.[38]

Not surprisingly, therefore, little was known during the late 1980s
and the early 1990s, about how to form credible estimates of the
benefits arising from abatement. Instead, those that did appear
tended to be only qualitative or to be confined to individual effects
rather than a comprehensive evaluation.[39]

There was, however, one study from this period that attempted to
present a more comprehensive analysis, striving to quantify the
damage to the United States of global warming. William Nordhaus,
an economist from Yale, concludes that the damage would not have
been significant:

> In sum, the economic impact upon the U.S. economy of the climatic
> changes induced by a doubling of CO_2 concentrations is likely to be
> small. The point estimate today is that the impact, in terms of
> variables that have been quantified, is likely to be around one-fourth
> of 1 percent of national income.[40]

Consequently, Nordhaus's prescription for policy was relatively
modest – substantial reductions in CFC emissions, but only 'steps to
slow the growth of uneconomic use of fossil fuels'.[41] Given the
dearth of systematic studies of the benefits from action to slow global
warming, his verdict against co-operative action commanded
significant respect and currency in the US debate.

What about, however, the secondary or spin-off benefits? The first
to consider are those other environmental benefits that might have
resulted from action to slow global warming. Although it was
accepted that emissions of sulphur dioxide and nitrogen oxides
would fall with any reduction in carbon dioxide emissions, the sheer
physical size (and hence absorptive capacity) of the United States
meant that these benefits were not as highly valued as they were in,
for example, any small country.

Secondary benefits at the international level were also con-
spicuously absent. During the 1980s, the United States cut back

much of its research and development into energy conservation and alternative energy sources. Michael Oppenheimer and Robert Boyle expand:

> Funding subsequently dried up when the Reagan Administration slashed the Department of Energy's efficiency-research budget by half and outlays for renewable energy by 82 percent. For example, federal support for photovoltaics dropped from [US]$160 million in 1981 to [US]$35 million in 1988, while most of the tax credits for renewable-energy systems were terminated in 1985.[42]

The US lost its competitive position in the manufacturing and marketing of such products. Although many in business recognised that there was money to be made in cleaning up the environment, the evidence suggested that those helping to reduce greenhouse gas emissions in the US would be, among others, the Germans and the Japanese.[43] This, combined with the fact that higher energy prices would make US goods less competitive on global markets, suggested that policies to curb greenhouse gas emissions would have additional costs for the country's trade balance.[44] Consequently, a number of elements – reflecting both perceived costs and benefits – suggest that international co-operation might not have been in the US interest.

As with the German case, however, there is also a flip side. First of all, other studies during this period suggested that the economic costs of reductions in greenhouse gas emissions – in terms of dollars, cents and jobs – would not be significant. In fact, there might not even be costs at all, but instead economic 'gains'. Responding to the claims of the Global Climate Coalition, a study by the Alliance to Save Energy and others concluded that US carbon emissions could be cut by 25 per cent by 2005 and 70 per cent by 2030 at a net cost savings of US$2.3 trillion over 40 years.[45] The 1991 Report of the National Academy of Sciences, moreover, suggested that: 'The United States could reduce its greenhouse gas emissions by between 10 and 40 percent of the 1990 levels at low cost, or perhaps some net savings, if proper policies were implemented.'[46]

Why were these conclusions in such apparent contradiction with the findings of previously mentioned studies? Those arguing that economic analyses yielded results that supported policy action maintained that these other models were flawed in three important respects. First, many overlooked the potential for cost-effective efficiency-investment opportunities. The reasons why improvements in energy efficiency had yet to be achieved were not economic – for they would generate positive economic returns – but were, instead, social and political. If these social and political barriers – for example, institutional constraints, transaction costs, regulatory barriers, restrictions on information and limited access to capital – were eliminated (presumably by government intervention), then reductions in energy demand could be made at no cost. Many of the models that suggested that losses in American GDP would necessarily occur ignored these possibilities. William Cline argues that it was the engineers' 'bottom-up' models (rather than the economists' 'top-down' models) that directed attention to such possible savings.[47]

Second, the potential for technological innovation, some argued, was underestimated in most of the macroeconomic models. Roger Dower and Mary Beth Zimmerman, for example, note that although most models considered some technological improvements, they were usually based solely upon historical trends; they found only one that 'factors in the potential impact of price changes on technological change'. However, in *all* models, they continue, specific technological options do not change as a result of the introduction of a carbon tax. Therefore, by underestimating the potential for technological innovation, these models were overestimating the cost of implementing co-operative policies.[48]

Third, different discount rates were used by different modellers. Lawrence Summers, when Chief Economist at the World Bank, argued that a rate of at least 8 per cent should be used in studies on global warming. William Cline, alternatively, maintained that about 2 per cent a year in real terms was correct. John Broome, finally, held that a zero discount rate should be used.[49] While all agreed that some nod to the future was necessary, the operationalisation of that particular principle took different forms. A seemingly insignificant difference of a few percentage points has spectacular ramifications when future values are being brought forward by one hundred or even fifty years.[50]

By correcting these flaws, a number of alternative studies suggested that it was in the US interest to adopt pro-active policy measures. William Cline's, published in 1992, was the most influential. In one of the first significant challenges to Nordhaus's findings, Cline found that the economic damages in the US from climate change might be closer to US$60 billion annually, or 1 per cent of GDP, rather than the 0.25 per cent figure that Nordhaus calculated. Moreover, if intangible costs, such as species loss and human disamenity, are also included, then the figure almost doubles – to US$117 billion or close to 2 per cent of US GDP. Cline also explores the potential costs beyond the standard policy benchmark of a doubling of carbon dioxide equivalent. He finds that the associated nonlinear damage in the very long term means that the tangible costs of global warming could reach 6 per cent annually.[51] The benefits to the United States of policy action, therefore, might be significant.

Others, meanwhile, proposed a variety of secondary or spin-off benefits. There might be some other environmental benefits, though they would probably not be as great in the United States as they would be in smaller countries. At the international level, meanwhile, benefits might come in a variety of forms. Some studies, for example, suggested that the level of imported oil would decrease. Not only would a lower oil bill help the American trade balance, but it would also increase American security. In fact, one study estimates the national security benefits of a carbon tax at US$40 per ton to be approximately US$18.1 billion.[52] More generally, some were suggesting that American competitiveness might not be as poor as many had suggested, for the country's productivity had been increasing during the preceding years.[53] The country might therefore respond positively to the new competition engendered by international co-operative agreements. Finally, some were suggesting that there were intangible political benefits associated with action – among them, the benefits accruing from taking on a leadership role at the international level. An alternative calculation of US costs and benefits, therefore, suggests that it would have been in the country's interest to support co-operative action.

And with the significant change in the national political scene on 3 November 1992, expectations were high that US policy on climate change would respond to these kinds of calculations. The Clinton/Gore Administration soon sprang into action. On 21 April 1993 (Earth Day), US President Bill Clinton committed the United States to reducing emissions of greenhouse gases to their 1990 levels by the year 2000. With this proclamation, a US President agreed to a specific 'target' for the first time.

Although this was a significant step, it would be foolish to conclude that US policy had changed radically. First, note the use of the word 'reduce' in the pledge. By avoiding the alternative word, 'stabilise', no commitment beyond 2000 was made. Second, 'greenhouse gases', rather than 'carbon dioxide', remained the objects being regulated. Third, the Administration's modest (though, in retrospect, ambitious) BTU tax failed to become law. In the face of Congressional opposition, it had to be scrapped in favour of a small gasoline tax. Finally, the Administration's (delayed) 'Climate Change Action Plan' was restrained. Therefore, although the rhetoric changed dramatically, policy did not shift to a comparable extent.[54]

The filthy and the fuelhardy

Although attention has been focused thus far upon the United States, I can explore the perceived interests of other countries that took conservative positions on the global warming issue. In light of the above observations, I can speculate that any country that had either inefficient industry or high carbon dioxide emissions might find regulatory action on global warming too costly to justify. The case of the United Kingdom appears to substantiate this hypothesis.

With respect to energy efficiency, the United Kingdom sat in the middle of the OECD league-table, ranking twelfth of twenty-four. When the index changes to CO_2-efficiency, the UK falls to sixteenth, reflecting a substantial use of oil and coal, in particular.[55] During international negotiations, meanwhile, the United Kingdom adopted a relatively cautious approach. Although they put some distance between themselves and the United States after 1990, British officials nevertheless continued to advocate passive policies. In discussions about possible EU policies during 1993, for example, the British (in alliance with, primarily, the Spaniards) worked to ensure that no carbon-energy tax was implemented. In public, the hesitancy to take further action was justified by British decision-makers with reference to the possibility of inflation, job losses (particularly in the coal industry) and other economic factors (for example, the disturbance that any stricter targets might have upon the privatisation of the UK electricity industry). The mind set and priority of British policy-makers are usefully captured by the comments of the then UK Environment Minister, David Trippier, who said in 1990: 'We could go for [stabilisation in] 2000, if we wanted to close down half of the coal mines in Britain and go for no economic growth.'[56] The fact that the UK would be hard hit by sea level rises did not seem to override the concerns about the perceived economic costs of policy to combat global warming. Among OECD countries, meanwhile, the EU's 'southern members' (particularly Greece, Portugal and Spain), Ireland, Turkey, Canada and Australia were other relatively energy-inefficient countries. Many of them, moreover, did not follow the lead of those states calling for substantial international co-operative commitments.

Just as the analysis of the United States revealed that energy producers and users *within* a country may oppose co-operative measures, I can speculate that energy exporters would have little interest in regulatory action. To explore this further, the natural place to start is with the Arab states, for they were responsible for 26 per cent of global oil production, and 43 per cent of global oil exports.[57] Oil producers would not necessarily be worse off after the introduction of a carbon tax, for their welfare would be determined by the location whereby the tax was imposed. A study by John Whalley and Randall Wigle reveals this most graphically. If a carbon tax were slapped on at the well-head, then the major oil exporting states would experience a GDP increase of 4.5 per cent over a forty-year period (because the effect of the tax would be similar to a price rise). If, on the other hand, a tax were placed on consumption, then these countries would have been worse off, with a GDP decrease of 18.7 per cent over the same period (because the effect would be like a slump in world energy demand).[58] Moreover, any conversion to other sources of energy in other countries (apart from natural gas) would have been disastrous for their economies.

Perhaps not surprisingly, therefore, the Arab states began to take on much more visible roles in the climate change debate during the early 1990s. At the Second World Climate Conference, for example, they 'agreed to start negotiations on a climate change convention but objected to every mention of carbon dioxide'.[59] Moreover, they continued their defiance at the 1992 Earth Summit, where they both registered their disapproval of the Climate Change Convention and attempted to soften the final wording of Agenda 21.[60] In addition, they expressed concern about proposals for carbon taxes – arguing that they were punitive, did not take into consideration the welfare of producers, and, as was noted in Chapter 3, were based upon dubious science. If carbon taxes were to be implemented, some Arab representatives said that they would retaliate by taxing and limiting Western imports, reducing oil exports, and curbing planned increases in production capacity. (This call became even louder during 1993, in response to US President Clinton's proposal for a BTU tax.) So it continued into 1994. During the INC meeting in March, the Saudi Arabia representatives 'threw up roadblocks at almost every turn' during discussions about the possible inadequacies of the Convention's commitments.[61]

The Arab states were not, of course, the only energy exporters in the world. Any fossil fuel exporting country would have had good reasons to resist efforts to agree reductions in carbon dioxide emissions. For oil, look to the other OPEC member-states, particularly Nigeria and Venezuela. For coal, turn to countries like Australia and Columbia.[62] Natural gas, however, could present something of a different story. Major producers and exporters might have thought that they would have been able to package the commodity as the acceptable transition substance (the, if you like, HCFCs of the global warming debate). In any case, Russia, Indonesia, Algeria, Canada, the Netherlands and Norway were some of the world's major gas-exporting countries. What is clear is that fossil fuel exporters had a particular interest in the progress of the climate change negotiations.

At the beginning of 1994, a wide range of human activities was continuing to enhance the global greenhouse effect. Although there was some evidence that international commitments to reduce (or, at a minimum, stabilise) levels of carbon dioxide emissions might be agreed in time for the First Conference of the Parties (scheduled for Berlin in late March and early April 1995), they were by no means assured. As debate about potential regulation continued, a range of individuals and organisations attempted to assess the relative costs and benefits of alternative policy options. With such a diversity of actors and interests potentially affected by global warming, such work was set to occupy centre-stage in future efforts to realise international co-operation.

Notes

1   Another suggestion, with the aim of 'adjusting' global temperatures, involved the construction of huge parabolic mirrors in outer space, in order to reflect some of the sun's incoming radiation.

2   Of course, one set of greenhouse gases is already the subject of

extensive regulation – namely, CFCs.

3 Donella H. Meadows, Dennis L. Meadows, Jorgen Randers and William W. Behrens III, *The Limits to Growth* (New York, Universe Books, 1972).

4 William K. Reilly, 'A world in our hands', *Washington Post* (20 April 1990), p. B1.

5 The World Commission on Environment and Development, *Our Common Future* (Oxford, Oxford University Press, 1987).

6 Ibid., p. xii.

7 On 13 June 1990, the then West German Cabinet committed the country to a 25 per cent reduction in carbon dioxide emissions from 1987 levels by the year 2005. Moreover, on 7 November 1990, the Cabinet of the recently-reunified German Republic announced that its original target would remain for the former West Germany, but that 'in view of the high potentials for CO_2 reduction which is possible' in the former East Germany, 'higher reduction' targets would apply to this area. Moreover, during the INC negotiations, Germany was one of the states pushing for a protocol, to be adopted perhaps as early as the first Conference of the Parties (1995). This protocol would 'achieve a stabilisation of CO_2 emissions by the year 2000 based on the 1990 emission levels and in particular agree on ambitious CO_2 reduction commitments for the period after the year 2000. Moreover, it should adopt commitments to limit CH_4 and N_2O^6. (Statement by the German Delegation at the INC9', 7 February 1994.)

8 In its policy announced in February 1991, the US Government declared that as a result of currently planned actions, US greenhouse gas emissions in the year 2000 would be equal to or below 1987 levels; it did not, however, make a commitment to any kind of target (*America's Climate Change Strategy: an Action Agenda* (Washington, DC, US Government Printing Office, February 1991)). By the time of the 1992 UNCED conference, only one other OECD country (Turkey) had not made any commitment to stabilise or to reduce greenhouse gas emissions. Although five other countries (Greece, Ireland, Luxembourg, Portugal and Spain) had also not set individual targets, they had, nevertheless, agreed to the European Communities' target of the stabilisation of carbon dioxide emissions at the 1990 level by the year 2000. In the United States, there was some change under the Clinton Administration. This is examined below.

9 Federation of German Industries, 'Industry's Attitude', in H-J Karpe, D. Otten and S.C. Trinidade (eds), *Climate and Development: Climatic Change and Variability and the Resulting Social, Economic and Technological Implications* (London, Springer-Verlag, 1990), p. 298.

10 Federation of German Industries, *Inter-national Environmental Policy – Perspectives 2000* (Cologne, May 1992), p. 23.

11 One benefit of avoiding higher temperatures would be that German agriculture and forestry activities – relatively small contributors to national

GDP, admittedly – would escape disruption.

12   S. Glomsrod, T. Johnsen and H. Vennemo, *Stabilisation of Emissions of CO_2: a Computable General Equilibrium Assessment* (Oslo, Central Bureau of Statistics, Discussion Paper No. 48, 1990).

13   Given Germany's population density (the fourth highest among all OECD countries), and the consequent difficulties in externalising their societal costs of pollution, such 'local' environmental problems would have 'hit home' particularly hard.

14   David Pearce, 'The global commons', in David Pearce (ed.), *Blueprint 2: Greening the World Economy* (London, Earthscan, 1991), p. 21, Box 2.5.

15   'Growth can be green', *The Economist* (26 August 1989), p. 15. Writers from *The Economist* had, by the late 1980s, undergone their own 'green conversion', for this was a publication that had belittled the first environmental revolution during the late 1960s and early 1970s as 'fashionable nonsense'. See, for example, 'Changing Colour', *The Economist* (15 October 1988), pp. 15–16.

16   See, for example, Michael E. Porter, 'America's green strategy', *Scientific American*, 264:4 (April 1991), p. 96.

17   Federation of German Industries, *Inter-national Environmental Policy*, p. 58.

18   *BP Statistical Review of World Energy* (London, British Petroleum Company, 1992). Moreover, with over four-fifths of all European coal reserves, Germany's reserves to production ratio for coal was 231 years.

19   The original EC proposal was for a tax of US$3 to be applied to the equivalent of a barrel of oil in 1993; this would rise by US$1 annually until it reached US$10 in the year 2000 (*Proposal for a Council Directive Introducing a Tax on Carbon Dioxide Emissions and Energy* (Brussels, CEC, COM (92) 226 final, 1992)). The tax would not be a 'pure carbon-tax', for only one-half of it would be placed upon carbon emissions; the other half would be applied to the use of energy from any source other than renewables (including nuclear). The tax has a number of particular idiosyncrasies. First, the tax is not a 'true' carbon tax, but instead has the carbon/energy mix noted above. The rationale for this is that it means that the tax will not hit the coal industry (and coal users) as hard as it otherwise might have. Second, energy-intensive industries (those in which energy costs exceed 8 per cent of total production costs) are provided with some relief – in terms of either tax reductions or refunds. Finally, the directive insists that the application of the tax is conditional upon the introduction of a 'similar tax or of measures that have an equivalent financial impact' by other members of the OECD. Concerns about international competitiveness guaranteed this clause. Anyway, the discussion, as of April 1994, remained speculative, for no carbon-energy tax had yet been implemented by the EU.

20   Giuseppe Nicoletti and Joaquim Oliveira-Martins, *Global Effects of* the *European Carbon Tax* (Paris, OECD, Economics Department Working Paper No. 125, 1992), p. 16.

21 'Initiative of German business for world-wide precautionary action to protect the climate', in Federation of German Industries, *Inter-National Environmental Policy*, p. 65.

22 Author's calculations from World Resources Institute, *World Resources 1992–1993* (Oxford, Oxford University Press, 1992), pp. 316–17.

23 In 1991, the Dutch government set a target for the reduction of the emissions of greenhouse gases by 20 to 25 per cent of 1989/90 levels by the year 2000.

24 Quoted in Mary Fagan, 'Britain further isolated over CO_2 controls', *Independent* (London) (24 October 1990), p. 2. Emphasis added.

25 See, for example, Shinji Fukukawa, 'Japan's policy for sustainable development', *Columbia Journal of World Business*, 27 (Autumn and Winter 1992), pp. 96–105. Additionally, Japan's energy efficiency record at home also helps to explain the policy position.

26 See, for example, Gunnar Fermann, 'Japan's 1990 climate policy under pressure', *Security Dialogue* 24:3 (1993), pp. 287–300.

27 US Council of Economic Advisors, *Economic Report of the President* (Washington, DC, US Government Printing Office, February 1990), pp. 214 and 223.

28 IEA, *Energy Conservation in IEA Countries*, (Paris, OECD, 1987), p. 43.

29 Quoted in William Booth, 'Carbon dioxide curbs may not halt warming', *Washington Post* (10 March 1990), p. A8.

30 Peter Hoeller and Markku Wallin, *Energy Prices, Taxes and Carbon Dioxide Emissions* (Paris, OECD, Economics and Statistics Department Working Paper No. 106, 1991), pp. 26 and 11.

31 A number of studies challenge the validity of this hypothesis. See, for example, H. Jeffrey Leonard, *Pollution and the Struggle for the World Product* (Cambridge, Cambridge University Press, 1988).

32 Roger C. Dower and Mary Beth Zimmerman, *The Right Climate for Carbon Taxes: Creating Economic Incentives to Protect the Atmosphere* (Washington, DC, World Resources Institute, August 1992), p. 11.

33 The US has also invested heavily in developing clean-coal technologies.

34 Andrew Dean and Peter Hoeller, *The Costs of Reducing CO_2 Emissions: Evidence from Six Global Models* (Paris, OECD, Economics Department Working Paper No. 122, 1992), p. 28. Thomas Schelling argues that 2 per cent of GNP is 'a currently unmanageable amount politically, even though a 2 per cent loss of GNP through reduced productivity, phased in over a decade or two and maintained in perpetuity, would not be much noticed' (T.C. Schelling, 'Economic responses to global warming: prospects

for cooperative approaches', in Rudiger Dornbusch and James M. Poterba (eds), *Global Warming: Economic Policy Responses* (London, The MIT Press, 1991), p. 198.)

35   J. Whalley and R. Wigle, 'The international incidence of carbon taxes' (paper prepared to a conference on 'Economic policy responses to global warming', Torino, September 1990), cited in Peter Hoeller, Andrew Dean and Jon Nicolaisen (eds), *A Survey of Studies of the Costs of Reducing Greenhouse Gas Emissions* (Paris, OECD, Economics Department Working Paper No. 89, December 1990), p. 42.

36   The pump price of a litre of gasoline in 1989 was US$0.28 in the United States and US$0.65 in Germany (author's calculations from IEA, *Energy Efficiency and the Environment* (Paris, OECD, 1991), Figure III.20, p. 76).

37   'Earth Summit: U.S. business endorses international cooperation on climate change', *Press Release* (4 June 1992).

38   Frances Cairncross, *Costing the Earth* (London, Business Books, 1991), p. 132.

39   See, for example, IPCC, 'Emissions scenarios', *Report of the Expert Group on Emissions Scenarios (Responses Strategies Working Group Steering Committee, Task A) to IPCC* (New York, WMO and UNEP, 1990); and Joel B. Smith and Dennis Tirpak (eds), *The Potential Effects of Global Climate Change on the United States* (Washington, DC, EPA, 1989). Moreover, Cline argues that as the international community undertook negotiations towards a convention on climate change, there was considerable risk that 'the seeming concreteness of cost estimates for preventative action, set against the only fragmentary measurements of the benefits of limiting global warming, would bias the policy process toward inaction' (William R. Cline, *The Economics of Global Warming* (Washington, DC, Institute for International Economics, 1992), p. 82).

40   William D. Nordhaus, 'Economic approaches to greenhouse warming' in Dornbusch and Poterba, *Global Warming*, p. 44.

41   Ibid., p. 61. This has been called a 'no regrets policy' (C. Boyden Gray and David B. Rivkin Jr., 'A "no regrets" environmental policy', *Foreign Policy*, 83 (Summer 1991), pp. 47–65). Perhaps not surprisingly, the Americans consistently attempted to focus the climate change discussions on *all* greenhouse gases, not only carbon dioxide. Encapsulating this notion, they endorsed the idea of a so-called 'comprehensive approach'. In this way, they argued that by meeting their obligations in the Montreal Protocol, they were also helping to solve the global warming problem, because CFCs are also greenhouse gases. (Recall that Nordhaus's findings suggested that this strategy made the best economic sense for the US.) This stance, however, was given a setback when it was discovered that because the CFCs were stripping stratospheric ozone, which itself had played a more important greenhouse-gas role than previously thought, the net effect of CFC emissions may have

been largely neutral (J.T. Houghton, B.A. Callander and S.K. Varney (eds), *Climate Change 1992: the Supplementary Report to the IPCC Scientific Assessment* (Cambridge, Cambridge University Press, 1992)).

42 Michael Oppenheimer and Robert Boyle, *Dead Heat: the Race Against the Greenhouse Effect* (London, I.B. Tauris, 1990), p. 164.

43 Germany, for example, has replaced the United States as the principal manufacturer of photovoltaic cells (Norman Moss, *The Politics of Global Warming* (London, London Defence Studies No. 9, Brassey's, December 1991), p. 33.)

44 In addition, there was also a fear that any nationally based measure might be the 'thin edge of the wedge'. If, for example, there was eventually a global tax on carbon, which would then be redistributed by a global authority to poorer countries, then the US would have to contribute huge amounts. In one study, net transfers out of states of the EC over the period 1990–2030 amounted to 3,222.2 billion 1990 US dollars; while the same figure for North America was 9,059.4 billion 1990 US dollars, almost three times as much (John Whalley and Randall Wigle, 'The international incidence of carbon taxes', in Dornbusch and Poterba, *Global Warming*, Table 7.7, p. 252).

45 Cited in Michael T. Hatch, 'Domestic politics and international negotiations: the politics of global warming in the United States', *Journal of Environment and Development*, 2:2 (Summer 1993), p. 26.

46 National Academy of Sciences, *Policy Implications of Greenhouse Warming* (Washington, DC, NAS Press, 1991), p. 106.

47 Cline, *The Economics of Global Warming*, chapters 4 and 5.

48 Dower and Zimmerman, *The Right Climate*, pp. 18–19. For the debate about technological optimism and pessimism, see L.B. Lave, 'Comment on R.H. Williams', *The Energy Journal*, 11:4 (1990), pp. 61–4.

49 John Broome, *Counting the Cost of Global Warming* (Cambridge, White Horse Press, 1992).

50 See the debate between Cline and two World Bank employees in *Finance and Development* (March 1993), pp. 2–8.

51 Cline, *The Economics of Global Warming*.

52 Cited in Dower and Zimmerman, *The Right Climate*, p. 18.

53 In a 1993 study published by the World Economic Forum and IMD, a Swiss business school, the US came second in world competitiveness (up from fifth the previous year) (reported in *The Economist* (26 June 1993), p. 131).

54 See, for example, Rita Beamish, 'US President Clinton announces plans to reduce global warming', *The Associated Press* (19 October 1993).

55 Author's calculations from World Resources Institute, *World Resources 1992–1993*.

56 Quoted in John Pieraar and Colin Brown, 'Britain and EC head for row over "green taxes" ', *Independent* (London) (21 September 1990), p. 1.

Interestingly enough, during the early 1990s, the UK Government achieved this anyway!

57   *BP Statistical Review.*

58   Whalley and Wigle, 'The international incidence of carbon taxes', p. 250.

59   Cairncross, *Costing the Earth*, p. 140.

60   Seven major oil producing countries had not, as of March 1994, signed or ratified the Climate Change Convention (they were Brunei, Iraq, Kuwait, Qatar, Saudi Arabia, Syria and the UAE). Moreover, because they could not secure the elimination of references to things such as 'the need for more renewable energy resources', 'energy consumption as a problem' and 'emphasis on energy efficiency', many Arab states lodged their reservations in respect of Chapter 9 (entitled 'Protection of the atmosphere') of Agenda 21.

61   'Conference reports', *ECO Geneva* (18 February 1994).

62   However, Australia (and Canada, for that matter) were also major uranium exporters. If global warming gave nuclear power a new lease on life, then the utility matrix down-under would obviously change considerably.

7

Interests and global environmental politics

Interests play a pivotal role in politics. A general acceptance of this assertion led me to propose my second hypothesis – namely, that a situation in which all key actors, operating as self-interested utility maximisers, calculate the benefits of co-ordinating their policies to be greater than the costs is necessary for international co-operation. The experience on the issues of global atmospheric change, as outlined in Chapters 5 and 6, has, to some degree, confirmed this hypothesis. Let me consider each of the two issues in turn.

On the ozone layer depletion issue, the degree of correlation between the increasing net benefits (or, at a minimum, the decreasing net costs) of policies designed to reduce ozone layer depletion and international co-operation is high. Throughout the issue's history, the potential impact of any regulatory legislation upon the major states' domestic chemical industries was a key determinant of governments' actions. Much of the conflict between the members of the European Communities and the United States during the negotiations towards a Protocol can be best understood by examining how each perceived its own interests. After the middle of 1988, by which time substitute chemicals or alternative techniques had been developed for most CFC uses, the process of international co-operation accelerated. Once again, the simple establishment and continuing existence of a Panel for Technical Assessment and a Panel for Economic Assessment illuminates the importance attached to the economic costs of slowing and reversing ozone layer depletion.[1] Finally, the recurrence of similar arguments during the more-recent debates about controls over HCFCs and other chemicals lends further support to my second hypothesis. Thus, the ways in which the policies to reduce ozone layer depletion would impact the key states' perceived interests were held to be important.

On the climate change issue, the degree of correlation is moderate. By the early 1990s, some states' leaders (for example, in Germany) perceived a number of benefits associated with co-ordinated action. These were derived not only from the fact that their countries would avoid a warmer fate, but also from a number of secondary benefits including improvements in local environmental quality and potential gains in international trade. Such benefits were greater than the perceived costs.

This view, however, was not shared by leaders of all of the world's industrialised states. In particular (but by no means exclusively), some in the United States found the costs of co-ordinated action, primarily anticipated in terms of higher inflation and increased unemployment, to be excessive. The benefits, meanwhile, were modest in comparison. Given that leaders in countries like the United States were thwarting international co-operative measures, while those in countries like Germany were supporting them, it would appear that my second hypothesis holds. Additionally, it is given further strength by the importance placed upon 'economic considerations' and 'economic . . . effects' in the Climate Change Convention.[2]

However, observations like these are by no means unchallengeable. Arguments could be made to illustrate that it was not in, for example, Germany's interests to adopt some sort of co-ordinated policy to combat climate change. Similarly, a case could be made that demonstrated that it was in, for example, the United States' interest to push for international co-operation. Is it simply that post-hoc explanations of adopted policies have been constructed? Is it not the case that similar justifications for discarded policies still remain 'sensible'? Finally, is it really clear that those actors who endorsed co-ordinated policy responses were ready to fulfil their commitments? Might they not yet prove to be 'more talk than action'? These challenges might yet plunge the association between key states' interests and international co-operation into a murky mist.

Nevertheless, in spite of the fact that the correlation in each of the two issues is not exact, the results still suggest that it would unwise to overlook the role that interests play in the quest for international co-operation on issues of global atmospheric change. The ways in which actors perceive the costs and benefits of alternative courses of action are important. Indeed, without such information, it would be difficult to make sense of much of the politics of ozone layer depletion and climate change.

Still, *how* do interests and politics interact, particularly on global environmental issues? Within the existing literature (and as reflected in my second hypothesis), it is usually assumed that decision-makers – in order not only to make more effective decisions, but also to try to make sense of the world around them – often attempt to assess the costs and benefits of different policy alternatives. Labelled cost-benefit analysis (CBA), it is further postulated that states' leaders aggregate the preferences of the different actors within their borders. David Pearce expands:

> Arguably, the explanation [of the success of CBA] is very simple. Those who practised CBA had a real-world task to attend to. Someone had to decide on the priorities within any sub-budget of government expenditure. The niceties of academic interchange in the learned journals did little to aid those who had these tasks. Instead, it seemed that not only did CBA offer a technique for aiding the evaluative process, albeit subject to many caveats, it actually offered the *only* reasoned technique. Founded, as it is, in a very simple concept of rationality . . . CBA also had a fundamental attraction of reducing a complex problem to something less complex and more manageable.[3]

Moving from a theorist to a practitioner, the observations of a Canadian Member of Parliament also suggest that this approach has validity: 'When an environmental initiative reaches the political level, the first hurdle to be cleared is the financial one. Most significant initiatives require a substantial commitment of funds, often at a time when revenues are shrinking.'[4] Such notions are even entrenched in the guiding principles of policy. Matthias Mors, for example, notes that the European Communities are legally obliged to undertake this kind of analysis, for Article 130r of the Treaty specifies that 'in preparing its action relating to the environment, the Community shall take account of . . . the potential benefits and costs of action or lack of action'.[5]

Although such an assumption is nevertheless useful in the study of global environmental politics (for reasons that are explored below), sole reliance upon it would cause the analyst to overlook many elements important to the processes associated with international co-operation. A number of factors combine to make the interaction between interests and international co-operation highly complex. Let me turn to them now.

The operationalisation of some kind of cost–benefit analysis on environmental problems may be particularly challenging. Though calculation of the cost of action to curtail environmental damage may be straightforward enough – it will often be the total expense of adapting the processes that are causing the harm – the problems encountered when one tries to estimate the monetary value of the benefits are daunting. (Recall that the primary benefits result from the preservation of a stable, habitable, environment – that is, the value of the costs avoided.)

For one, the costs and benefits have different time horizons attached to them. Generally, the costs of stabilising the atmosphere have to be paid in the present, while the major benefits are not immediately available. Because the benefits will be obtained in the future, there is necessarily some sort of discount rate attached to them. 'Such problems are referred to as "paternalistic bias", or "intergenerational equity" problems.'[6] Although *any* policy analysis will involve costs and benefits spread over different time horizons, there are problems with time horizon that are peculiar to the issues of environmental change. As a 1977 report on the ozone layer notes:

> [A] problem arises because depletion of natural resources, or the use of an environment as a waste disposal sump, may bring about changes which within a given time-scale (sometimes in terms of several centuries, sometimes in terms of millenia) *are irreversible*. It is argued by some that a simple cost/benefit analysis does not take into account the costs of foreclosing of options to future generations that such a policy represents.[7]

A 1988 report on global warming expands:

> A major problem is the current practice of 'discounting' the future, since it is inappropriate to discount into present monetary values the risk of major transformations to the world of future generations. . . . Methods are needed that build on the best of risk-business analysis and intergenerational equity studies, in order to take into account the complex character of long-term, large-scale effects of climatic change.[8]

Uncertainty, irreversibility and uniqueness are three characteristics of this set of problems that suggest that a traditional CBA might not be able to take proper account of the benefits of actions to preserve the global environment.

Therefore, it should not be surprising to find that disagreements over a variety of issues associated with the operationalisation of CBAs persist, even within the economics community itself. Outstanding questions, for example, include: what factors should be included?; what techniques should be used to value things?; what discount rate should be employed?; and, how should uncertainty be incorporated? Debates about 'costing the environment' thus continue.

Nevertheless, let us suppose that the economists were able to agree a price for the proverbial elephant. The analysis of interests would still be problematic. In the search for a universal yardstick with which all consequences of a decision can be measured – that is, all costs and benefits quantified – money is often used. This, however, raises an important difficulty.

Recognise that not everything may be able to have a price determined for it. Granted, one might contend if a value can be found for an elephant, then a price should be able to be calculated for virtually anything. What about, however, things that may not be as tangible as an elephant – for example, security or justice? Although efforts can be made – no doubt surveys have been undertaken that ask people the amount of money that they would pay for these goods – such findings would be highly dubious. Will, therefore, money necessarily be the only quantity that actors try to maximise? If commodities like security and justice (and add to that others like leadership and reputation) cannot be accurately monetised, then must they be examined separately? If so, when will a actor place more value on one instead of another? How might they be aggregated? Universal answers to questions like these do not exist. Instead, they differ from actor to actor.

Helen Milner is one who picks up this point. In a review of studies on international co-operation, she concludes that one of the major faults with much of the literature is that most contributions are constructed at the systemic level. Consequently, they neglect (or assume) a theory of domestic politics. Arguing that this is a significant oversight, she maintains that '[c]onsideration of domestic politics seems essential for understanding international cooperation . . . domestic politics tells us how preferences are aggregated and national interest constructed'.[9] Therefore, in order to discover how interests are determined, the black box of the state should be opened up.

In a post-Cold War world – with 'butter' often thought to be more useful than 'guns' – it is usually assumed that interest is defined in terms of wealth; increased production and consumption are the goals towards which all states are working. Consequently, when examining interests in global environmental issues, many turn to business interests, assuming that they are broadly analogous with their respective states' interests. This, however, fails to consider the ways in which business interests influence government, something that is not necessarily constant across either space or time.

David Vogel, for example, reports that the 'most striking difference between the environmental policies of Great Britain and the United States has to do with the relationship between business and government'. He goes on to reveal that 'no other business community is so dissatisfied with its nation's system of environmental controls as the American business community. In Great Britain, by contrast, the relations between the two sectors have been relatively cooperative'.[10] The United Kingdom, Vogel argues, is like this because of the presence of a highly respected civil service, a business community that is prepared to defer to public authority, and a public that is not unduly suspicious of either the motives or the power of industry. In the United States, however, quite the opposite holds: civil servants hold a relatively low status, business is highly suspicious of government intervention, and the public tends to mistrust both institutions.[11] Consequently, business interests and state interests are not necessarily always one and the same.

For a variety of reasons, therefore, it appears that a rudimentary understanding of the relationship between interests and international co-operation might be incomplete. Experience from the two issues of global atmospheric change lends support to this conclusion. First of all, there is no agreement among economists as to the 'price of global atmospheric change'. In Chapters 5 and 6, examples abound in which different conclusions arise from studies of the same phenomenon – perhaps the Nordhaus/Cline debate is the most remarkable.[12] Second, there were numerous instances in which declared interests changed dramatically in the absence of any shift in the economic calculations. Instead, they were precipitated by other factors. These included heightened concerns about non-monetised commodities like the benefits accruing from leadership (for example, the British on the ozone layer issue) or desires to avoid the costs associated with being an environmental laggard (like the French on the same issue). Finally, an unpacking of the 'state' in the consideration of interests produces a number of fruitful findings. Experience on the ozone layer depletion issue confirms Vogel's observations about trans-Atlantic differences noted above. Maxwell and Weiner, for example, argue that '[r]ather than being at arm's length, as are U.S. government and industry, the British departments were unapologetic about the closeness of government–industry collaboration'.[13] On the climate change issue, however, it is not as clear. One of the main reasons for this is that the interests of industry do not, themselves, necessarily consolidate into a single position in any given country. Some industries – for example, coal – feel distinctly threatened by the possibility of international co-operation on global warming. Others – for example, renewable energy technologies – see it as an opportunity. Even within something as relatively restricted as 'the fossil fuels industry', views differ. Oil is certainly being challenged, but natural gas, at least in the short term, may find its global appeal heightened. Finally, nuclear power evokes polarised views, but for different reasons. Consequently, a better understanding of the ways in which different businesses within individual countries influence policy is crucial.

Although business output is important for a country, 'interests' can of course be made up of other elements as well. Vogel's comments noted above, for example, reveal that it would be wrong, certainly in the case of the United States, to think of states solely as conduits for business interests. Instead, a plurality of interests may be expressing themselves. Steve Rayner argues that this has been the case on issues of global atmospheric change: they 'already have demonstrated a dramatic broadening of the range of interest groups claiming legitimate roles as stakeholders in the decision-making process on both domestic US and international fronts'.[14] Moreover, he argues that individuals have made their voices heard:

> The optimal response is different for different stakeholders, and no number of appeals to higher collective rationality about the general welfare of society is likely to sweep away a concern for the welfare of individuals in a culture that derives so much of its strengths and vigour from its recognition of the sovereignty of each citizen.[15]

So when the interests of any particular state are analysed, attention should not necessarily be focused exclusively upon businesses. The interests of other actors – pressure groups, stakeholders, the 'general public', and even the state itself (a point to which I return in the Conclusions) – may be consequential.

Additionally, is it justifiable to identify selected states as the 'key actors' referred to in my second hypothesis? First of all, if you accept the importance of business interests for national interests (that is, 'What is good for General Motors is good for America'), do all industries ncessarily have an easily identifiable 'home' country? With the fading 'nationality' of many companies, the 'state' interest may not be the most consequential, but rather that of the transnational corporation itself may be paramount. At times, what is best for General Motors might also be best for the United Kingdom or Brazil, but only occasionally the United States. And if you believe that there are a plurality of interests present in world politics, then other transnational actors – for example, pressure groups, which are examined in Part V – may potentially be 'key actors'. Finally, the sheer profusion of states in the world today make the task of determining the 'key' ones (that is, if you accept the notion that states should be the object of the analysis) that much more challenging.[16] Caution should thus be exercised when selections are made.

In summary, then, there are a number of challenges to the notion that interests can be operationalised, let alone identified. Indeed, a variety of observations from the experiences on the ozone layer depletion and climate change issues suggest that states may not be simply 'self-interested utility maximisers'. Does this, therefore, totally discredit my second hypothesis? Not necessarily. First, the experience of global atmospheric change reveals that actors will often fight for what they understand to be their preferred outcome. Nevertheless, this 'preferred outcome' will not always be measured in terms of pounds, dollars or yen. Complex issues – such as global atmospheric change – can potentially affect the interests of every actor across time, as well as space. As a consequence, assessments of collective interests will prove difficult, even if not imprudent.

Second, the legitimation of the state as the key actor – and, thus, as the focus of the analysis – remains defensible. (This assertion is further explored in the Conclusions.) Indeed, in spite of the complexity of the issues of global atmospheric change, broadly-defined interests for different countries can be calculated. Scott Barrett, for example, maintains that on the climate change issue: 'In general, the US would prefer to negotiate on the basis of uniform per cent abatement (equivalently, uniform per cent abatement with trading or a uniform carbon tax); the EC on the basis of uniform CO_2 per capita; and Japan on the basis of uniform CO_2 per unit of GNP.'[17] Indeed, many states' policy positions can be explained in terms of these kinds of perceived interests. Nevertheless, one lesson discerned from the previous discussion is that it is important to unlock the black box of the state in order to examine the ways in which actors voice preferences and exercise power.

Third, the interests of business are significant to the interests of the state. Indeed, former UN Executive Director Mostafa Tolba maintains that: 'The difficulties in negotiating the Montreal Protocol had nothing to do with whether the environment was damaged or not. It was all about who was going to gain an edge over whom; whether Du Pont would have an advantage over the European companies or not.'[18] Moreover, the enthusiasm for 'joint implementation' shown by Norwegian and US industry (and subsequently their respective governments) during the climate change issue is another case in point. Consequently, the ways in which businesses operate in the international environmental debate will be influential. Let me briefly explore a couple of such possibilities here.

Consider developments in international environmental politics more generally. Note, in particular, the activities of the Business Council for Sustainable Development (BCSD). Founded and chaired by Swiss billionaire Stephan Schmidheiny during the run-up to the 1992 Earth Summit, the BCSD is a group of forty-eight top executives of multinational companies – including Dow, Du Pont, Mitsubishi and Shell. It members believe that: 'Progress towards sustainable development makes good business sense because it can create competitive advantages and new opportunities.'[19] The influence of the BCSD has been considerable, and groups like it – including the International Chamber of Commerce[20] – should continue to be important actors in the international environmental debate. Still, how will they impact efforts to achieve sustainable development? In answer, at least three scenarios are possible.

On the one hand, industry has important contributions to make. They possess significant financial, technical and management expertise, which could be utilised in the quest for global sustainable development. For the most part, it was the large multinationals that developed the alternative chemicals that allowed the phase-out of ozone-depleting substances to go ahead. Corporations have the resources to find solutions to the global environmental problems that the world faces today.

On the other hand, any progress towards the goal of sustainable development requires transformations in present patterns of consumption. Yes, industry did develop the 'solution' to the ozone layer depletion problem, but do not forget that it created the crisis in the first place! Because industry is in the business of making things that society consumes, it is part of the problem, not the solution. Putting, for example, unleaded petrol into your car may make you feel better, but you are still acting as a high-demand consumer and are consequently pushing the world down an unsustainable path. Any claims to the contrary by industry would be 'greenwash'.

Finally, some environmentally conscious businesses themselves are becoming disillusioned. They argue that they have responded positively to the demands of their stakeholders and have implemented strong environmental programmes. What they now see, however, are governments that are moving the goalposts: in other words, as the debate moves beyond 'reaching agreements' and towards 'enforcing compliance', governments are not keeping up their end of the bargain. They are not enforcing the laws on their books and therefore the 'free-riders' – other businesses that did not respond to the demands for stronger environmental standards – are reaping the benefits. Consequently, companies are becoming cautious, lest they be duped again.

In conclusion, it is important to recognise that, in efforts to realise international co-operation on global environmental issues, individual businesses and alliances within industries will have important roles to play. Broadly, states' representatives will continue to attempt to protect their national interest, which they often perceive mainly in broad economic terms, though other considerations are sometimes weighed. Nevertheless, the complexity of global environmental issues means that interests are not easily identifiable, and that they are by no means either universal or static.

Notes

1   Article 6 of the Montreal Protocol, 'Assessment and review of control measures'.

2   See, in particular, the Preamble, Article 4 and Article 7 of the Climate Change Convention.

3   D.W. Pearce, *Cost–Benefit Analysis*, Second Edition (Basingstoke, Macmillan, 1983), p. 21.

4   Charles Caccia, 'OECD nations and sustainable development', in David J.R. Angell, Justyn D. Colmer and Matthew L.N. Wilkinson (eds), *Sustaining Earth: Response to the Environmental Threats* (Basingstoke, Macmillan, 1990), p. 125.

5   Matthias Mors, *The Economics of Policies to Stabilize or Reduce Greenhouse Gas Emissions: the Case of CO_2* (Paris: Commission of the European Communities, Economic Papers, No. 87, October 1991), p. 13.

6   The Department of Economic and Social Affairs, 'Protection of the ozone layer – some economic and social implications of a possible ban on the use of fluorocarbons', in Asit K. Biswas (ed.), *The Ozone Layer* (Oxford, Pergamon Press, 1983), p. 146.

7   Ibid., p. 146. Emphasis added.

8   World Climate Programme (Impact Studies), *Developing Policies for Responding to Climatic Change*, (Geneva, WMO/TD, No. 225, April 1988), pp. 27–8.

9   Helen Milner, 'International theories of cooperation among nations: strengths and weaknesses', *World Politics*, 44:3 (April 1992), p. 493.

10   David Vogel, *National Styles of Regulation: Environmental Policy in Great Britain and the United States* (London, Cornell University Press, 1986), p. 21.

11   Ibid., p. 26.

12   For a more general review, see Samuel Fankhauser, *The Economic Costs of Global Warming Damage: a Survey* (University of Birmingham, Department of Economics, Working Paper No. 94–104, 1994).

13   James H. Maxwell and Sanford L. Weiner, 'Green consciousness or dollar diplomacy?: The British response to the threat of ozone depletion', *International Environmental Affairs*, 5:1 (Winter 1993), p. 30.

14   Steve Rayner, 'Prospects for CO_2 emissions reduction policy in the USA', *Global Environmental Change*, 3:1 (March 1993), p. 25.

15   Ibid., p. 26.

16   One potentially fruitful path for further study is that of the 'blocking state' – that is, 'states having such importance on a particular issue that they are able to prevent international agreement on it.' (Gareth Porter and Janet Welsh Brown, *Global Environmental Politics* (Oxford, Westview Press, 1991), p. 44.) By presenting such a proposition, Porter and Brown appear to be turning the HST argument on its head to posit that a powerful state cannot impose its own preferences, but can still block the imposition of its non-preferences – a kind of 'negative hegemony' perhaps?

17   Scott Barrett, *Negotiating a Framework Convention on Climate Change: Economic Considerations* (Paris, OECD, 1992), p. 35.

18   Quoted in Debora MacKenzie, 'Now it makes business sense to save the ozone layer', *New Scientist*, 120 (29 October 1988), p. 25.

19   Stephan Schmidheiny, *Changing Course: a Global Business Perspective on Development and the Environment* (London, The MIT Press, 1992).

20   See, for example, Jan-Olaf Willums and Ulrich Goluke, *From Ideas to Action: Business and Sustainable Development* (Oslo, ICC Publishing, 1992); and, more generally, the ICC's 'Business charter for sustainable development' and its newly formed 'World Industry Council for the Environment'.

IV
Equity

8
Equity and ozone layer depletion

Ozone layer depletion is a truly global issue. The destruction of stratospheric ozone would have consequences for all of the world's peoples. Truly global involvement is therefore crucial. However, during the initial discussions towards international co-operative arrangements on the ozone layer issue, relatively few countries were involved. More specifically, the developing world was not widely represented before 1986. At the 1985 Vienna Conference, for example, there were only twelve delegates from the South. Developing countries were not major players in the political process for reasons related to both cause and effect.

With regard to cause, countries of the Third World were responsible for very little ozone layer depletion. Only a handful of CFC producers were located in the developing world, and collectively their consumption of CFCs in 1986 was approximately 15 per cent of the global total (see Figure 8.1).[1] Southern countries did thus not appear to be part of the problem; there was no need for them to alter their behaviour significantly, and therefore they were not thought to be necessary participants in the co-operative process.

With regard to effect, many thought that ozone layer depletion would not impact developing countries. In hindsight, this might seem to be an inconceivable assertion, given the nature of the problem. However, recognition of 'global' environmental problems is relatively recent. During the 1970s, the world was just coming to grips with the notion of an 'international' environmental issue (versus merely a 'local' or, at most, a 'national' environmental issue). Truly 'global' environmental issues were not readily imaginable. Instead, many Southern decision-makers thought that the issue of ozone layer depletion was of little consequence to their citizens. The Bangladesh representative who spoke at the 1977 meeting of the United Nations Environment Programme's Governing Council, for example, seemed perplexed by the Council's preoccupation with the ozone layer issue:

> Bangladesh reminded the Governing Council of the real priorities as seen by a poor nation with repeated natural disasters such as floods and tidal waves. To us, said the Bangladesh representative, the controversy over harm caused to the ozone layer by spray products is simply not relevant. Increasing soil productivity, coping with natural disasters and meeting basic human needs are the areas in which the country must concentrate.[2]

The geographical reach of ozone layer depletion had, during the late 1970s, yet to be recognised fully.

Without a perceived concern in either cause or effect, most developing countries' leaders took little interest in the ongoing international negotiations. Consequently, any different interpretations of equity that may have existed between the North and South remained, for the most part, dormant. Although there was some recognition of the distinct circumstances – Article 4.2 of the 1985 Vienna Convention registers the necessity to take 'into account in particular the needs of the developing countries, in promoting, directly or through competent international bodies, the development and transfer of technology and knowledge' – there was little pressure to make such inexplicit statements more precise. North–South questions dominated neither the discussions working towards, nor the final text of, this framework convention. And until 1986, differences between North and South did not generate substantial political debate.

The onset of Southern concern

During the negotiations towards the 1987 Montreal Protocol, however, this changed. Attention was being drawn to the differences between North and South, and the particular problems that they raised for international efforts to preserve the ozone layer. Explanations of why this change occurred can again be related to the causes and effects of ozone layer depletion.

With regard to cause, consumption of ozone-depleting chemicals

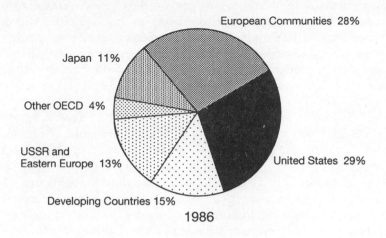

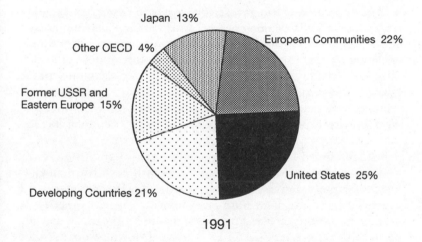

Figure 8.1 Global CFC consumption by region, 1986 and 1991

Note: All calculations weighted by ozone-depleting potential.

Sources: Author's calculations based upon the following sources: UNEP, 'The reporting of data by the Parties to the Montreal Protocol on Substances that Deplete the Ozone Layer' (UNEP/Ozl.Pro.5/5, 24 August 1993); A. McCulloch, P.M. Midgley and D.A. Fisher, 'Distribution of emissions of Chlorofluorocarbons (CFCs) 11, 12, 113, 114 and 115 among reporting and non-reporting countries in 1986', *Atmospheric Environment* (1994).

was increasing in the developing world. China's CFC consumption, for example, rose by 20 per cent annually during the 1980s.[3] Given, however, that initial quantities were so low, consumption levels remained, compared to Northern countries, relatively modest. What had a greater impact, however, was the potential for growth in the future. CFC production plants are typically small, they can be erected quickly and they can pay for themselves within a short time period as well. Consequently, any state – including a developing one – could become a manufacturer of CFCs quite rapidly. China, for one, was planning a massive increase in the production of refrigerators in the near future, and the logical chemical input for these units would be CFCs.[4] Thus, although the developing world's contribution to ozone layer depletion was recognised as relatively modest, future possibilities produced significant concern. Because developing countries were becoming part of the problem, some argued that they had to be part of the solution as well.

With regard to effect, the discovery of the ozone crater above Antarctica in 1985 demonstrated that ozone layer depletion was a global problem; no country could escape the impact of ozone layer depletion. It was the potential implications for food security that most concerned Southern states' representatives: a thinner ozone layer means increased ultraviolet radiation, which in turn, means reduced crop yields. Therefore, the consequences for countries that were heavily dependent upon agriculture were becoming increasingly clear.

Recognition of cause and effect, however, does not necessarily mean that consent to co-operative action will be forthcoming. In fact, for representatives of the developing world, eliminating the causes seemed to be much more costly than dealing with the effects – that is, the benefits accruing from the use of ozone-depleting chemicals were greater than the costs arising from the use of the same substances. The North's experience had, after all, shown that CFCs were an important element of industrialisation, their use contributing to higher standards of living. Calculations of costs and benefits, by themselves, seemed to discourage co-operative action.

The South's position was more diverse than this, however. Part of the ozone layer depletion which was occurring in the 1980s was caused by chemicals which had been released in the 1980s. This in itself suggested that the North was destroying a disproportionate amount of a global resource – in 1986, OECD countries were responsible for approximately 72 per cent of global CFC consumption. Once one added the fact that CFC consumption during the 1930s, 1940s, 1950s, 1960s and 1970s also caused depletion in the 1980s, the share of responsibility rose to over 90 per cent.[5] Because the North was primarily responsible for ozone layer depletion, representatives from the developing world argued that the North was also primarily responsible for addressing the problem. Unless there was some sort of preferential treatment, Southern countries would not become Parties to the Protocol. Given that the result would be an unrestricted growth in CFC consumption outside the Protocol, Northern decision-makers felt compelled to confront these concerns.

The first proposal to provide specifically for special treatment of developing countries came in April 1987 at a meeting in Geneva. At this time, the Canadian delegation suggested that developing countries be exempt from the provisions of any agreement for five years, or until their annual use of CFCs reached 0.1 kg per capita. Though not without its critics, this proposition proved to be a constructive starting point for discussions about provisions for developing countries.

During the ensuing five months, attention was paid to the particular problems of Southern states. Many hours of intense debate were thus generated as negotiators tried to agree a Protocol that would be as universal as possible. By the conclusion of the Montreal conference in September 1987, they had made two special provisions for Southern states. One followed the form of the original Canadian proposal: it permitted developing countries to delay their compliance with the control measures restricting CFC production and consumption for ten years, providing their annual level of consumption did not exceed 0.3 kg per capita. The other recognised the need to facilitate access to both technology and financial schemes that would enable developing countries to use alternative methods and substitute products more easily.

The Montreal Protocol attracted immediate support from some developing countries: representatives from eight of them signed the Protocol on the day that it was opened for signature.[6] With the 'prospect of preferential treatment in the continued use of the suspect chemicals, at least for the next twenty years, coupled with no trade discrimination and access to alternative technology and substitute safe chemicals',[7] most negotiators thought that the terms were attractive enough to encourage other developing countries to sign on to the document. Richard Benedick observes that: 'From the interest shown by developing-country delegates at Montreal, including even those who had not received authorisation to sign on the spot, it seemed likely that most would eventually ratify.'[8] Winfried Lang, head of the Austrian delegation, believes that the Southern countries had only one choice: 'Unless you join, you won't get those substances you need to meet your domestic needs, . . . [and because technology transfers are prohibited to non-Parties,] countries not signing the Protocol will be unable to produce their own.'[9] In the views of some in the North, the concerns of the South had been adequately addressed.

Post-Protocol protests

Others in the North, however, soon began to recognise that enough may not have been accomplished. A number of reasons were cited. First, future possible scarcities of CFCs might encourage low-producing countries to increase their production during the ten-year exemption period up to the 0.3 kg per capita limit. If China, for instance, were to take full advantage of its allowance, the country could, in good faith of the Montreal Protocol, produce approximately 350,000 tonnes of CFCs per year in 1999 (greater than pre-Protocol, US production). Even if Southern states signed on to the agreement, ozone layer depletion could well continue.

Second, Southern states' participation may not be a foregone conclusion. Although a number of sticks and carrots were included in the Protocol to encourage their involvement, the potential efficacy of each was subsequently challenged. The major carrots were promises of technology transfer and financial assistance from the North. They were, however, exceedingly vague. The sticks, meanwhile, were, as Lang mentions above, associated with trade restrictions. What they did not weigh, however, was the fact that some countries – for example, China and India – had potentially huge domestic markets. Restrictions on international trade in CFCs, therefore, might have little restraining effect.

Meanwhile, the predominant view among Southern analysts was also that the Protocol was unsatisfactory, but for different reasons. Many began to argue that the so-called 'concessions' in the Montreal Protocol did not address their special needs in a just manner. Kilaparti Ramakrishna reports that: 'Even among those countries that have signed on as parties to the agreements, a feeling that they were "caught napping" before and during the negotiations is gaining ground. If another opportunity were to present itself, many believe that they should react differently.'[10] A variety of arguments supported this view.

First, the terms of the Montreal Protocol served to increase Southern dependence on the North. More specifically, Article 2 allowed Northern states to exceed their production quotas by 10 to 15 per cent, so long as the excess went to the South. Additionally, Article 4.2 prohibited developing countries from exporting CFCs (even if they had the ability to do so), should they want to continue to benefit from the ten-year exemption period. The Montreal Protocol, therefore, seemed to be entrenching Southern dependence upon the North.

Moreover, the fact that the North seemed to have an undemocratic control over the emerging regime was also disconcerting. More specifically, Article 2.9 of the Protocol stipulated that any adjustments to the control measures would require a 'two-thirds majority vote of the Parties present and voting representing at least fifty per cent of the total consumption of the controlled substances of the Parties'. This effectively gave the United States and the EC veto powers. As Mukund Govind Rajan observes: 'To the developing states, however, it seemed absurd that when all states had an equal interest (theoretically) in preventing ozone depletion, a few states should have a veto over the decision of the rest of the states.'[11]

Consequently, the South's industrial production, their economies, their independence and their overall plans for development would be affected by the phasing out of CFCs. Thus, the costs were evident, but where was the compensation? As mentioned above, the carrots – the promises of technology transfer and financial assistance from the North to the South – were yet to materialise.

Upon the Montreal Protocol's entry into force (on 1 January 1989), it was evident that questions related to North–South issues had risen up the political agenda. The first major international ozone layer conference during 1989 was held in London in March. Sponsored by the United Kingdom Government and the United Nations Environment Programme, the primary purpose of this gathering was to encourage the developing states' representatives to sign and to ratify the Montreal Protocol.[12] The British organisers of the conference thought that this could be achieved quite easily: all that one needed to do was to show delegates from the developing world both that substitute chemicals existed and that it was in their own interests not to use ozone-depleting substances.

Immediately from the outset of the conference, however, it was clear that a strategy based on information and education would not be enough to convince some Southern countries to become part of the Protocol process. The Chinese and Indian delegation heads, in particular, declared that more would be necessary. Liu Ming Pu, the Chinese vice-chairman of the state commission for environmental protection, called for an 'International Ozone Layer Protection Fund'. Paid for by the Northern states, this fund would sponsor research into alternative methods and would also transfer technology, free of charge, to those Southern countries that agreed to limit their use of CFCs. Further, Ziul Rahman Ansari, the Indian minister of environment and forests, said that: 'Lest someone think of this [fund] as charity, I would like to remind them of the excellent principle of "polluter pays", adopted in the developed world.'[13] Thus, representatives from the two largest states in the developing world made it clear that they would not accede to the Montreal Protocol process until firmer commitments to provide them with financial and technical aid had been made.

The North's response was ambiguous. Although they acknowledged that they had a greater responsibility for the problem, they still maintained that there was no need for any new structures, particularly along the lines of those proposed by the Chinese delegation. Instead, they argued that existing institutions could deliver the goods. With these differences unresolved, delegates, in the final communique, could only agree that 'ways of helping developing countries should be a major feature of the protocol review and urgently examined in all appropriate international contexts . . . [and] . . . technical solutions are needed to help solve Third World human problems'.[14] Though nothing had been done in London to substantiate the commitments of the Montreal Protocol, all officials nevertheless realised that North–South issues were now of the utmost priority.[15]

Two months later, when the negotiations moved to Helsinki for the first official Meeting of the Parties to the Montreal Protocol, the negotiating chasm between North and South widened. On the one hand, officials from the US, the UK, Japan, West Germany, France and other countries remained opposed to the idea of an international fund, but instead continued to favour the use of existing mechanisms in order to address the particular needs of the developing world. They feared that a newly created institution would allow the South to wrest control of funds from the donor nations. The consequence, in their view, would be a bureaucratic nightmare: an inefficient and unaccountable body.

On the other hand, officials from China and other countries (including some from the North: Finland, the Netherlands, New Zealand and Norway) continued to press for a new fund. They argued that because such large amounts of cash were needed, a single central organisation should be in charge. At the same time, many in the South were suspicious of the International Monetary Fund, the World Bank and other established organisations; they thought that a new institution to look after their special needs might be more responsible.

Little movement from these two divergent positions took place, so once again no specifics could be agreed. Going through the same motions as they did two months earlier, all delegates duly recognised the special circumstances of the Southern countries in the final declaration. There was one additional development, however. Recognising the impasse in which they found themselves, the delegates established an Open-Ended Working Group, whose task it was to attempt to develop some more detailed proposals on the whole range of issues facing the Parties to the Montreal Protocol. This Working Group was to prove to be crucial in reconciling the differences between North and South.

Differences to resolve

The negotiations in preparation for the Second Meeting of the Parties in London in June 1990 thus proceeded in meetings of the Open-Ended Working Group during the second half of 1989 and the first half of 1990. With regard to the particular problems raised by differences between North and South, the negotiators had a number of issues to resolve.

The first was whether or not a fund should even exist. Although opposition to its creation among Northern states was waning, significant resistance was still emanating from some quarters – in particular, the United States. William Reilly (Administrator of the Environmental Protection Agency) and top State Department officials had become increasingly accepting of the idea of a fund, but John Sununu (White House Chief of Staff) and Richard Darman (Office of Management and Budget Director) remained fiercely opposed. Sununu and Darman harboured fears about the precedent that any ozone layer fund might set for subsequent negotiations on global warming. Together they were able to sustain the US Administration's position that established institutions, such as the World Bank, should be used to address the problem. Representatives from Southern states, however, continued to insist upon a new international fund.

Pressure from both inside and outside the United States was finally overwhelming, and the US Administration accepted the principle of a fund in mid June 1990. Inside the US, environmentalists and industry found common ground on this issue. In the case of the former, the rationalisation was that a fund was not only morally justified but that it would also help to slow ozone layer depletion; in the case of the latter, the rationalisation was in terms of dollars and cents. Du Pont officials pointed out to John Sununu that if the developing world did not have the money to buy the substitute products, then the chemical companies could be denied potentially lucrative markets. Pressure from outside the US, meanwhile, was coming from many sides. British Prime Minister Margaret Thatcher, in particular, encouraged US President George Bush to change his position. She maintained that continued US reticence could scuttle the entire international negotiations, which would undoubtedly put egg on the face of the US Administration. Nevertheless, in London, the United States' representatives still made it clear that they were not entering into anything that was open-ended and that the financial mechanism was 'without prejudice to any future arrangements that may be developed with respect to other environmental issues'.[16]

Given an agreement upon a fund, the next issue to resolve was about size: how much money would be necessary to help the states of the South meet their obligations as outlined in the terms of the Montreal Protocol? A variety of suggestions were initially put forward, ranging from US\$2 billion to US\$7 billion. Because the estimates being aired were so large and so varied, it was difficult to find a common starting point for negotiations. A turning point came, however, when it was decided to focus upon 'incremental costs', rather than 'full costs' – that is, the difference between the cost of processes that use ozone-benign substances and the cost of processes that use ozone-depleting substances. Moreover, a three-year starting period was also first considered. Given these more restrictive parameters, the estimates fell, and a UNEP suggestion of US$400 million annually became an initial point of reference.

This figure, however, was soon challenged, for many – the German and the Japanese delegates in particular – queried as to how it had been derived. All negotiators eventually agreed that more information was needed in order to estimate better the magnitude of the figures involved. To achieve this, studies of representative countries were contracted and undertaken. The results of these investigations were presented to the Working Group, where it was revealed that the required amount of money to cover costs would not be astronomical. In the end, a figure of US$160 million over an initial three year period was agreed. This amount would rise to US$240 million in the event that China and India became Parties to the Protocol.

A third point of discussion related to the question of upon whom the burden of financing the fund would fall – that is, who would contribute what share of the final amount needed. One suggestion that was put forward was that the contribution to the fund should be dependent upon 1986 levels of consumption, weighted by ozone-depleting potential.[17] In the end, however, it was decided, for reasons of both precedence and simplicity, that the traditional UN scale of assessment would be used.

Further, there was the question of what form each country's contribution should take. This debate had three major elements. First, could bilateral aid be counted as part of a country's contribution to the fund? The larger donor countries supported this idea, for their officials were eager to keep close controls on some of the aid. After some discussion, it was accepted that up to 20 per cent of a country's obligation could be met by bilateral assistance. Second, should all of the Fund's resources be in addition to existing aid transfers from North to South, or could some existing commitments be used to fulfil the donors' obligations? Supporting the latter, the Americans vocally fought against so-called 'additionality', arguing that funds should come from existing resources. After some heated debate, additionality was eventually accepted by all Parties. Third, should each country's contribution to the Fund be voluntary or obligatory? Benedick reports how this question was resolved:

On the issue of mandatory versus voluntary contributions [UNEP Executive Director Mostafa] Tolba attempted to bridge the gap between developing countries and major donors by promoting the concept of 'voluntary contributions on an assessed basis,' which conveyed a sense of implicit obligation.[18]

Thus, by the time that ministers gathered in London in June 1990, these three questions about the form of each country's contribution had been resolved to the satisfaction of all participants.

A fifth issue to be considered during this year-long process involved how this money – the new Fund – would be administered. Since the 1989 London gathering, this had continued to be one of the major points of contention. For over a year, leaders from the South had demanded a new organisation, while many representatives from the North had insisted that existing structures should be utilised. Although it appeared that the developing countries' officials would remain unwavering, they eventually:

accepted the concept of a tripartite division of responsibilities among the World Bank, UNDP [United Nations Development Programme] and UNEP. ... UNEP would pursue 'political promotion of the objectives of the Protocol,' as well as research, data collection, and clearinghouse functions. UNDP would take charge of the feasibility studies and other technical assistance activities. Other multilateral agencies, including regional development banks, could be invited by the executive committee to cooperate with the fund. But the World Bank, and specifically the president of the bank, was clearly designated as the administrator and manager of the central function of the fund: financing projects and programs to meet the incremental costs of article 5 parties [developing countries].[19]

Given the consistent adamancy of some Southern delegates on this issue, it may be somewhat surprising to find the World Bank playing such a significant role in the new institution. Recognise, however, that this arrangement was intended to cover the day-to-day administration of the Fund. Control of the Fund's executive council was another matter.

Being one of the most contentious issues, final agreement about the size and shape of the executive committee remained elusive during the Working Group's meetings. On the one hand, the US argued that because they would be the largest contributor to the fund, they should have the largest say on the council as a right. The

Southern states' representatives, on the other hand, responded that no one country should have a unique advantage – rather, there should be a democratic executive. By the beginning of the London conference in June 1990, the creation of a fourteen-member executive had been agreed, but just how the representatives should be chosen and how the voting should be weighted (if at all) remained unresolved.

After many hours of intense negotiations, a compromise was finally reached that allowed representatives to be chosen from defined regions – with, in total, seven from the North and seven from the South. Because the US was itself declared a 'region', a permanent seat was thus assured in a face-saving manner. Within the council, it was further agreed that a two-thirds majority, comprising separate simple majorities among North and South, would apply both to votes of the fourteen-member executive committee and to votes of the Parties as a whole concerning the financial mechanism.

Although the terms of the Montreal Protocol had noted that there would be a need to address both financial and technical issues, much more attention had been devoted to the former than the latter during the meetings of the Working Group. In the opinion of many representatives from the developing world, however, discussions about technical issues were just as important. As the Indian Environment Minister, Maneka Gandhi, argued in London: 'Money is irrelevant if we don't have access to the knowledge. Survival is about the spread of knowledge, not money.'[20]

It was accepted that the South would have to 'leap-frog' the ozone-depleting generation of chemicals and start to utilise the new ozone-benign chemicals that would replace them. What remained unclear was *how* they would obtain these substitutes. To that time, North–South transfers of technology consisted predominately of obsolete or prohibited products (DDT is the example that springs to mind). In fact, this had already been the case on the ozone layer issue: in London, Gandhi reported that Allied Chemical (an American multinational corporation) had sold CFC technology to India when CFCs were 'perceived as immoral' in the North.[21] While manufacturers' needs for replacement markets explain the transfer of old or discredited technology, their desires to protect their existing markets explain the withholding of new or state-of-the-art technology.

Without guarantees that their new products would not be subsequently given away to companies in developing countries, companies in the North would be hesitant to invest large amounts of money into research and development. Consequently, following the logic outlined in Chapter 5, many argued that the private sector had to be protected by patents so that the incentives to invest in research and development were maintained. Peter Lawrence expands:

> Where such intellectual property is held by a private company then a government in a developed State could not convey such intellectual property to a developing country without first either licensing, purchasing or compulsorily acquiring the particular copyright or patent involved from the owner. Without such consent, or adequate compensation in the case of compulsory acquisition, the intellectual property rights of the owner may be violated.[22]

Thus, a sixth significant point of contention concerned the question of guaranteed access to technology for Southern states. Throughout the Working Group's meetings, the representatives of Southern states made it clear that they wanted an assurance that, if they did not receive sufficient financial and technical assistance, then they would not be required to meet their obligations in the Montreal Protocol.

After late-night negotiating sessions in London, a compromise solution was finally agreed. Technology transfers could not be guaranteed, because technology is owned by companies, not governments. Still, it was accepted that if Southern states had problems gaining the technology to make CFC alternatives and thus found it difficult to meet their obligations under the agreement, then a meeting of the Parties to the Protocol would be convened in order to consider alternative paths of action. According to Benedick, resolution 'of the impasse was ingenious, realistic, and acceptable to all'.[23] Indeed, it seemed to satisfy the concerns of the Indian delegation, for Gandhi announced that she would recommend that her Government sign the amended Protocol.

By tackling these major issues – the fund's existence, size and other financial details, the structure of administration for the fund, and technology transfer – negotiators in London made significant progress towards answering fully the calls for equity as issued by Southern decision-makers. The success of their work can be measured by the fact that by the conclusion of the London conference in June 1990, fifty-nine nations had signed the Montreal Protocol and most of the other thirty-nine nations in attendance at the conference were expected to sign soon. Even China and India, the two most significant antagonists during the negotiations, indicated that they would soon join the process. In this way, it seemed that North–South disputes on ozone layer depletion had been largely resolved.

Continuing debate

All was not settled, however, for the mechanism that was established at the London conference was only an interim measure – states committed themselves to the Interim Multilateral (Ozone) Fund (IMOF) for an initial period of three years. When the Fund was to be made permanent – at the Fourth Meeting of the Parties in Copenhagen in November 1992 – divisions arose once again. I now turn to the major debates, arising from differences between North and South, which threatened to make things rotten in Denmark.

The IMOF was designed to exist only as long as the Protocol, as amended in London in June 1990, remained unratified by a sufficient number of Parties. Ratification of the Amendments was not as quickly forthcoming as had been initially expected, for the final of the necessary twenty instruments of ratification was not deposited until 12 May 1992. Therefore, the London Amendments did not come into effect until 10 August 1992 (ninety days later). Nevertheless, regardless of the date of ratification, the document stipulates that the Parties are subsequently obliged to establish a more permanent structure for international resource transfers. From a reading of the Protocol, one would not expect debate about this commitment to arise. However, during 1992, it did.

More specifically, an alternative proposition had been put forward at a meeting of the Protocol's Open-Ended Working Group in Geneva in July 1992. At that time, the British, supported by the Dutch, suggested that the responsibilities for funding on the ozone layer issue be transferred to the Global Environment Facility (GEF).[24] The GEF, which was established by the World Bank, the United Nations Environment Programme (UNEP) and the United Nations Development Programme (UNDP) in 1990, finances projects and training programmes that will help ameliorate the damaging global environmental impacts of any development project. (The GEF is examined in greater detail in Chapter 9.) The British–Dutch initiative was formally followed up by a proposal tabled by the French and the Italians.

Those who wanted the GEF to be the administering body for the resource transfers cited a variety of reasons to support their case. First, they claimed that the desire for efficiency dictates that there should be only one central body concerned with all of the different global environmental problems.[25] For this reason, some Northern states were pleased that the GEF had emerged from the 1992 Earth Summit in Rio de Janeiro with enhanced responsibilities: it was identified as the interim financial mechanism for the biological diversity and climate change conventions.

Second, they preferred the decision-making procedures that were used in the GEF – namely, that the World Bank (with its weighted voting structures) exercised considerable influence in the processes. The IMOF, by contrast, continued to be governed by an executive committee that was composed of an equal number of representatives from the developed and the developing worlds.

Third, representatives from these states complained that the IMOF had had a less than auspicious start. They maintained that it had taken an unacceptably long time to get projects up and running – anywhere from a year to eighteen months. Moreover, if the IMOF had had such difficulties in dealing with relatively small amounts of money, they worried about what would happen in the future as the Fund continued to expand. Therefore, both for reasons of support for the GEF and opposition to the IMOF, some Northern countries pressed for the funding responsibilities to be transferred.

This view, however, was adamantly and vigorously opposed by many other states. They maintained that the IMOF had had a promising start. In Copenhagen, the Chairman of the Executive Committee (Mexican Ambassador Juan Mateos) reported that '. . . a total of US$27,221,000 [had] been disbursed for investment projects in 12 countries, [which will lead to] the phaseout of 25,000 tonnes of [ozone-depleting substances]'.[26] Although they accepted that there had been some difficulties, they argued that those that could not be explained as simple 'teething problems' had arisen because some donor countries had been lax in fulfilling their financial obligations. While US$53 million had been pledged for 1991, only US$42 million had been received by 19 November 1992. Similarly, for 1992, US$73 million had been pledged, but only US$50 million received.[27] Therefore, rather than there being a fundamental problem with the structure of the IMOF, they argued that difficulties had arisen because of a lack of financial support for the fund. The decision-making machinery, they maintained, had worked well thus far: because all decisions of the Executive Committee had been made by consensus, no votes had yet to be held.

Many delegates from the developing world were just as adamant in their opposition to the GEF. Although nominally operated by three international organisations, many argued that, in reality, the World Bank dominated the Fund. Not only did they have problems with the decision-making procedures that the Bank used (in particular, its use of weighted voting and general lack of transparency) but also given the World Bank's dubious environmental record, many in the South questioned the Bank's genuine commitment to sustainable development.

In response to the argument that the GEF had been given additional responsibilities in Rio, they also pointed to the fact that Agenda 21 endorsed the GEF as only one part of the financial picture.[28] Finally, they were ready to challenge any inflation of the GEF's experience – they noted that it was not an established mechanism, for it was only just coming out of its 'pilot stage'. It was absurd, therefore, to suggest that it was a 'fully developed' example.

On a more general level, representatives from the developing world argued that since the establishment of the financial mechanism, they had played a full and constructive role in the development of the ozone layer regime. They thought that it was generally accepted that the IMOF was a necessary condition for their ongoing support. Therefore, they found it not only surprising but also disturbing to discover some Northern countries reneging on their part of this understanding.

Debate about the Fund was closely linked to negotiations about control measures on ozone-depleting substances (in particular, methyl bromide – the debate about which is analysed below), and in the end, it was agreed that the IMOF would be made permanent.[29] It was further accepted that the level of funding for the period 1994–96 would be between US$340 million and US$500 million, with the amount for 1994 to be at least as much as 1993 (that is, US$113 million).[30] A review mechanism, although not explicitly mentioning the GEF, was also approved.

The question of the Fund was not the only issue that divided North and South in Copenhagen. Technology transfer remained an unresolved problem. Although it was still accepted that countries of the developing world must bypass ozone-depleting substances, it remained to be determined how the transfer of the next generation of technologies would be facilitated. The parallel debate about the issue within the GATT rounds revealed the breadth and importance of this issue. Little, meanwhile, was achieved to advance the discussions in Copenhagen.

Another significant debate revolved around the question of whether control mechanisms should be brought in on methyl bromide. In 1990, anthropogenic uses of methyl bromide included the fumigation of soils (82 per cent of all consumption), quarantine and commodity fumigation (13 per cent) and structural fumigation (5 per cent). About 67,000 tonnes of the substance were produced commercially, 42 per cent of that in North America, 29 per cent in Europe and 22 per cent in Asia.[31]

Industrialised states, led by the United States, called for a substantial cutback in the use of this chemical. They were persuaded by the scientific reports, which highlighted its ozone-depleting potential, and moreover believed that a 25 per cent reduction could be achieved simply by more efficient use of the chemical. In addition, the experience of the Netherlands suggested that even more dramatic cutbacks were possible. That country had responded to public concerns about the impact of methyl bromide upon the local environment by phasing it out completely during the 1980s.

On the other hand, however, developing countries, led by Israel, were adamant in their opposition to any regulation.[32] Not only did they maintain that the science was still plagued by too many uncertainties[33] but they also had two major fears related to economic issues. First, if cutbacks in the production of methyl bromide did occur, then the subsequent decrease in supply and increase in price would affect the availability of the product in the developing world. (In this respect, it is important to note that the use of methyl bromide was increasing in the developing world.) Second, Northern countries might not only impose restrictions upon methyl bromide as a bulk chemical, but they might also regulate those products that use the substance in their production process (as is the case for CFCs). In this way, non-tariff barriers upon the developing world's agricultural products might be erected (for both fumigation procedures and quarantine requirements mean that many of these products are 'produced' with methyl bromide).

As noted above, the debate about methyl bromide was closely

linked to the debate about the international funding mechanism. In the end, a compromise was reached, for it was agreed that developed states would freeze their methyl bromide production at 1991 levels by 1995. However, further action would await the completion of a fuller report by the Protocol's Assessment Panels. Thus, though addressed in Copenhagen, the debate was nevertheless still poised to arise again in the future.

A number of North–South issues have been successfully resolved during the political negotiations on the ozone layer issue. A number of carrots and sticks – with the most significant of these being the establishment of a Fund – have helped to extend participation in the Montreal Protocol process. For developing countries, the advantages of becoming a Party are many. They include: financial and technical assistance through the Multilateral Fund; and transfer of latest technology and access to world markets (through technical and financial assistance, Parties are in a better position to acquire technologies for producing and using substitutes as well as for reducing use and emission of controlled substances). Similarly, there are a number of disadvantages of not becoming a Party. These include: the inability to import controlled substances from Parties (thus making it difficult to service existing equipment); closed access to world markets, because Parties are banned from importing products containing controlled substances; and difficulties in obtaining new technologies.[34] Such measures have had an impact. When Burma (Myanmar), for example, announced its accession to the Montreal Protocol process in 1994, its officials revealed that one of the major motivating factors for its signature was the desire to avoid trade restrictions.[35]

Nevertheless, the issue of developing world participation may not yet be fully resolved. First of all, it is accepted that the use of ozone-depleting substances is increasing, rather than decreasing, in Third World countries.[36] Although this might be expected, because of the ten-year 'period of grace' accorded such countries in the Montreal Protocol, it is still a cause of concern among many scientists and policy-makers, for the objectives of the Protocol are not being fulfilled.

Additionally, the Multilateral Fund continues to be a subject of much debate. Questions about governance, like those raised in Copenhagen (particularly with respect to the rate of disbursement of the Fund's resources), persist. Moreover, there are also potential problems associated with its size. To date, the Fund has been relatively small. Nevertheless, there have been problems in securing the modest quantities that have been pledged by donor countries. Some wonder what will happen both now that the Fund has more than doubled in size and in the future when it is expected that even more money will be needed. Two forces in particular could drive this future demand: continuing increases in the number of Parties to the Protocol (with all of them being developing countries) and a growing number of substances being regulated. A consultant's report prepared in 1992 estimated that about US$2 billion would be needed for the period 1997–2010,[37] and a more recent study estimates that the cost of eliminating ozone-depleting substances in China alone by the year 2010 will be US$1.4 billion.[38] In addition, a UNEP report has recognised that 'the incremental costs which the Fund has to meet will be much higher if the developing countries are not assisted to adopt alternative technologies/substances sooner through higher allocations now'.[39] Moreover, the requisite size of the Fund would grow significantly if some developing countries' representatives decided that they wanted financing for the full costs of CFC replacements, rather than just the incremental costs:

> If, for example, a developing country wishes to build a refrigerator plant to take the place of an existing facility that makes CFC-based refrigerators, it must pay what a new CFC facility would have cost; the fund makes up the difference. But the developing nation must still invest a large amount of capital in the new plant – and swallow the costs of shutting down the old one.[40]

If donor countries do not pay now, then they may be asked for even more in the future. With the financial mechanism set to be reviewed at the Seventh Meeting of the Parties in 1995, the question of resource transfers should continue to be a crucial issue during the coming years.

Notes

1   Their share of production was even less, approximately 4 per cent. See Figure 5.1.

2   Quoted in Allan L. Springer, *The International Law of Pollution: Protecting the Global Environment in a World of Sovereign States* (London, Quorum Books, 1983), pp. 23–4. With hindsight, it is clear that the concerns raised by the Bangladesh representative are all exacerbated by stratospheric

ozone depletion, by 'spray products'.

3   Richard Elliot Benedick, *Ozone Diplomacy: New Directions in Safeguarding the Planet* (London, Harvard University Press, 1991), p. 150.

4   See, for example, Robert D. Perlack, Milton Russell and Zhongmin Shen, 'Reducing greenhouse gas emissions in China: institutional, legal and cultural constraints and opportunities', *Global Environmental Change*, 3:1 (March 1993), p. 84.

5   Author's calculation from figures in Grant Thornton, *Chlorofluorocarbons (CFCs) 11 and 12: Annual Production for the Years 1931–1975 and Annual Production and Sales for the Years 1976–1992* (Alternative Fluorocarbons Environmental Acceptability Study, 1993).

6   The Protocol was opened for signature on 16 September 1987. The Southern countries that signed the document on that day were Egypt, Ghana, Kenya, Mexico, Panama, Senegal, Togo and Venezuela.

7   Peter Usher, 'Climate change and the developing world', *Southern Illinois University Law Journal*, 14 (1990), p. 262.

8   Benedick, *Ozone Diplomacy*, p. 99.

9   Quoted in Annette M. Capretta, 'The future's so bright, I gotta wear shades: future impacts of the Montreal Protocol on Substances that Deplete the Ozone Layer', *Virginia Journal of International Law*, 29 (1989), p. 232, n. 138.

10   Kilaparti Ramakrishna, 'North–South issues, the common heritage of mankind and global environmental change', in Ian H. Rowlands and Malory Greene (eds), *Global Environmental Change and International Relations* (Basingstoke, Macmillan, 1992), pp. 152–3.

11   Mukund Govind Rajan, 'Bargaining with the environment: a new weapon for the South?', *South Asia Research*, 12:2 (November 1992), p. 138.

12   At this time, only eight Southern states (Egypt, Kenya, Malta, Mexico, Nigeria, Singapore, Uganda and Venezuela) had ratified the Montreal Protocol.

13   Quoted in Richard North, 'Appeal for fund to help Third World cut CFCs', *Independent* (London) (7 March 1989).

14   Reprinted in Pearce Wright, 'Banning CFCs is only remedy', *The Times* (London) (8 March 1989), p. 6.

15   Despite the rather vague conclusion of the final communique, organisers could claim success in the fact that, by the end of the conference, fourteen developing countries said that they would ratify the Montreal Protocol.

16   Quoted in Benedick, *Ozone Diplomacy*, p. 184. Many, however, maintain that although the Americans were insistent that the issue not be viewed as any kind of precedent, it was generally agreed that a precedent had indeed been set.

17   In 1989, one delegation had suggested a minimum contribution of

US$1,000 plus a premium on each kilogramme of CFCs produced equal to one cent (UNEP/OzL.Pro.1/5, p. 8). See, also, UNEP/OzL.Pro.Bur.1/2, p. 4.

18 Benedick, *Ozone Diplomacy*, p. 161.

19 Ibid., pp. 161 and 186. See, also, UNEP/OzL.Pro.2/3, Annex IV, p. 50, Paragraphs B2 and B3.

20 Quoted in Paul Brown, 'India insists on recipe for green fridges', *Guardian* (London) (29 June 1990), p. 4.

21 Comments of Maneka Gandhi, press conference, London, 28 June 1990.

22 Peter Lawrence, 'Technology transfer funds and the law – recent amendments to the Montreal Protocol on Substances that Deplete the Ozone Layer', *Journal of Environmental Law*, 4:1 (1992), p. 20.

23 Benedick, *Ozone Diplomacy*, p. 196.

24 The ozone layer issue was already within the GEF's remit to a limited extent – namely, it was responsible for assistance to those countries that were not 'Article 5' Parties (for example, states of Eastern Europe).

25 The GEF's four original areas of concern were climate change, biological diversity, international waterways and ozone layer depletion.

26 UNEP/OzL.Pro.4/8. Moreover, the Executive Committee had approved a further sixty projects that would lead to another 31,600 tonnes being eliminated.

27 Informal document entitled 'Status of contributions by Parties towards the trust fund for the Interim Multilateral Fund for the implementation of the Montreal Protocol for 1991, 1992 and 1993' (19 November 1992).

28 See Chapter 33, 'Financial resources and mechanisms', of Agenda 21.

29 While the developing world 'conceded' new controls on methyl bromide, the developed world 'conceded' the establishment of a permanent ozone fund.

30 In fact, at the Fifth Meeting of the Parties in Bangkok, in November 1993, Parties approved a budget of US$510 million for the 1994–96 period.

31 See, generally, UNEP, *Methyl Bromide: Its Atmospheric Science, Technology, and Economics* (Nairobi, UNEP, Synthesis Report of the Methyl Bromide Interim Assessment Panels, June 1992).

32 Although Israel was the most vocal in opposition to the ban, the alternative amendment – which simply proposed that states be obliged to report their use of the chemical – was proposed by Chile (UNEP/OzL.Pro.4/2, p. 18).

33 A group called the 'Methyl Bromide Global Coalition' claimed that 85 per cent of methyl bromide released into the atmosphere emanates from natural sources.

34 'The Montreal Protocol and its implications', *OzonAction*, 4 (September 1992), p. 4.

35 'Burma avoids trade restrictions on CFCs by signing ozone protection agreements', *BBC Monitoring Service, Summary of World Broadcasts* (12 January 1994).

36 At the Fifth Meeting of the Parties, it was reported that only nine developing countries had cut their emissions of ozone-depleting substances. Consumption in others, meanwhile, was 'growing fast'. In China, for example, it increased by almost 70 per cent between 1986 and 1990. (UNEP/OzL.Pro.5/5, 24 August 1993.)

37 Anil Markandya (Metroeconomica), *The Montreal Protocol, Funding the Incremental Costs for Article 5 Countries: a Review and Update* (London, June 1992), p. 6.

38 'World Bank grant targets China's ozone depletors', *Reuter News* (1 December 1993).

39 UNEP/OzL.Pro.5/2, p. 5.

40 Robert Pool, 'A global experiment in technology transfer', *Nature*, 351 (2 May 1991), p. 6.

9

Equity and climate change

Just like ozone layer depletion, climate change is a truly global issue. A shift in temperature and precipitation patterns would have consequences for all of the planet's inhabitants. Therefore, global involvement is once again crucial. However, North–South issues were not important elements of the climate change negotiations before the late 1980s. To substantiate further this assertion, look no further than the conference declaration agreed at one of the first major international gatherings to examine the question – the First World Climate Conference in Geneva in 1979. In this document, an agenda for research into various issues surrounding climatic change was agreed, one element of which was the socioeconomic impacts of climatic variability. The closest reference to the North–South question, however, was a stated desire to improve the understanding of the 'characteristics of human societies at different stages of development and in different environments that make them especially vulnerable or resilient in the face of climate variability and change'.[1] Nevertheless, there were no explicit recommendations for political actions to address any special needs that the Southern states might have.

During the middle part of the 1980s, the concept of transnational assistance for developing countries in light of projected global climate change began to be mooted at international gatherings. At the Villach-Bellagio conferences in 1987, for example, it was recognised that '[i]nternational assistance would be needed to pay for anticipatory adaptation in many developing countries, so additional bilateral and multilateral funding would be required'.[2] We should recall, however, that the vast majority of participants at these meetings were scientists.

Why were North–South issues a relatively small element of the climate change agenda during the period before 1987? The answer is quite simple. Recall that the discussions did not attract significant participation outside of the scientific community before the 1987 Villach–Bellagio conferences. Thus, North–South issues were not being discussed, because virtually no political issue of any kind was being discussed.

The rise of North–South issues

The degree of politicisation on the climate change issue, however, increased dramatically during 1987 and 1988. Moreover, North–South issues appeared upon the broader global warming agenda almost immediately. To explain this rapid emergence, I can take a page from the ozone layer analysis to consider, initially, both cause and effect.

With regard to cause, the developing world was contributing to global warming to a significant extent, and their leaders' policy plans suggested that their share would increase in the future. In 1990, for example, Southern states were responsible for just over 30 per cent of all energy-related carbon dioxide emissions in the world (see Figure 9.1). Moreover, the Chinese government had plans to expand its coal consumption five-fold between 1990 and 2020. Realisation of this policy proposal would add nearly 50 per cent to the 1990 level of *global* carbon emissions.[3] Moreover, carbon dioxide from fossil fuel combustion is not the only contributor to global warming. Countries of the Third World also produce significant quantities of methane and carbon dioxide from land use, both of which contribute to global warming as well. Depending upon the mode of measurement employed, inclusion of such substances could increase their contribution to over 40 per cent.[4]

With regard to effect, the global nature of environmental problems was, by the mid-1980s, becoming increasingly evident. It was also becoming clear that no developing country could exempt itself from the repercussions of a warmer world – sea-level rises and climatic shifts would be particularly consequential. Because North–South questions had already been raised in the political negotiations on other environmental issues, they arose rapidly during the discussions on global warming. Not only has Chapter 8 revealed that they

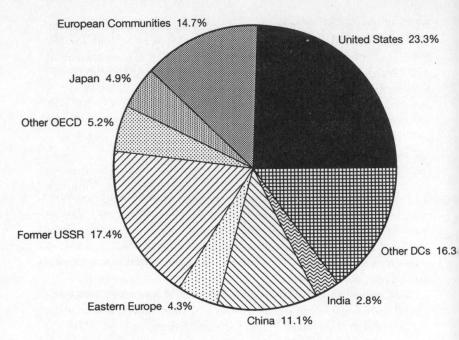

Figure 9.1 Global energy-related carbon dioxide emissions by region, 1990

Source: IEA, *Climate Change Policy Initiatives* (Paris, OECD, 1992), pp. 28–31.

were being given greater visibility during the ozone layer negotiations, but by 1987, the emerging 'environment and development' debate had pushed them still further up the international environmental agenda.[5] Therefore, North–South issues were already on the minds of decision-makers when they embarked upon the global warming negotiations. For these three reasons, this element of the climate change issue became a prominent concern during the late 1980s.

A 'climate fund', to deal explicitly with global warming, was first proposed to policy-makers at the Toronto Conference on the Changing Atmosphere in June 1988. In the final conference statement, delegates agreed to establish a 'World Atmosphere Fund. Financed in part by a levy on fossil fuel consumption in industrialised countries, it would mobilise a substantial part of the resources needed for implementation of the *Action Plan for the Protection of the Atmosphere*.[6] Further, the conference statement also recognised that the North had an obligation to bear the main responsibility to ensure that the problem was addressed, but not at the expense of development opportunities in the South. Although this declaration was not legally binding, it nevertheless set the terms of reference for the ensuing debate by putting forth the idea of a climate fund to assist the developing world.

After the UN General Assembly approved its first resolution on climate change – thus entrenching the global scope of the political discussions[7] – a conference of legal experts was convened in Ottawa, Canada in February 1989 to discuss the possible legal responses to global warming. One of the principles identified in Ottawa endorsed:

> [the] possibility of establishing a World Climate Trust Fund for use in initiating and supporting all necessary activities to reduce emissions of greenhouse gases and to mitigate effects of climate change. The beneficiaries of that Fund should be developing countries. The Trust Fund should be funded from three possible sources: contributions by countries (voluntary or assessed), 'user fees' for activities causing climate change, and fines for violations of the convention.[8]

Although this declaration further reinforced the visibility of North–South issues, it remained that such proposals focused upon the validity of various principles, rather than upon detailed and specific recommendations.

A month later, in March 1989, the governments of Norway, France and the Netherlands hosted an international conference in The Hague. One commentator notes that this conference was 'the first public attempt to think through the effects on North–South relations of greenhouse warming, and its proposal for a new world environment authority with teeth, sets the agenda for an international debate on the international politics of the environment that seems certain to grow louder and louder'.[9] The final declaration attempted to highlight the importance of the issue, for 'calls for help from industrialized nations to help developing countries in pollution abatement' were made.[10] Once again, however, the importance of this conference should not be overstated. It did not have broad-based support (the US and the Soviet Union were not invited, and the

British did not attend), and its haughty declarations again lacked specifics.

Earlier in this chapter, the political linkage between the two issues of global atmospheric change was flagged. Mostafa Tolba, Executive Director of UNEP, was one of the individuals who identified this linkage in order to try to achieve agreements on the global warming issue by directing officials towards the wake left by the ozone layer negotiators. At the 1989 Helsinki Meeting of the Parties to the Montreal Protocol, for example, Tolba called for the creation of a climate fund, which would be similar to the ozone layer fund being called for at the same time. In response, the Northern states' decision-makers were non-committal on the issue (recall that they had delegated the ozone layer issue to a working group), and British Environment Secretary Nicholas Ridley not only mocked the idea as simplistic but he also highlighted its perceived infeasibility and argued that a climate fund 'implies a degree of sovereignty over sovereign nations which can never really be there'.[11] Although the establishment of a link between global warming and ozone layer depletion brought attention to the former, divergence between the North and South was just as great on the former as Chapter 8 has already shown it was on the latter.

In general, therefore, the discussion surrounding North–South issues during 1988 and the beginning of 1989 was long on vague statements of intent, but short on specific proposals. As 1989 progressed, however, this changed to some degree, for a variety of concrete proposals were made. In April of that year, for example, the Norwegian government 'called for the establishment of a UN fund to support measures aimed at alleviating global climate changes, and pledged the equivalent of [UK]£60 million [0.1 per cent of its GNP] for the project'.[12] Their officials reiterated the fact, however, that any Norwegian policy action was conditional upon the concurrent involvement of other developed countries. Jim MacNeill identifies two other unilateral proposals from Northern states:

> The 1989 budget of the Netherlands included provision for an annual contribution of 250 million guilders to a global climate fund, and the government is currently assessing the various options for financing and managing such a fund. . . . At the September 1989 meetings of the World Bank and the International Monetary Fund in Washington, DC, the French finance minister announced that France would contribute a similar amount, about US $140 million.[13]

Specific proposals, however, remained the exception rather than the rule. More indicative of the feeling of most Northern decision-makers is the Declaration that emerged from the Group of Seven's (G7) Paris Summit in July 1989. Although many commentators have noted that this was the G7's first 'green' meeting, a closer look at the fine print suggests that it may not be all that it appeared. Although the seven nations' leaders did recognise that some sort of assistance from the North to the South was needed – they specifically noted 'economic incentives may include the use of aid mechanisms and specific transfer of technology [and] in special cases, ODA debt forgiveness and debt for nature swaps can play a useful role in environmental protection'[14] – they still stopped short of any mention of a climate fund. Rather, they believed that the issue should be addressed by traditional routes and channels, most notably bilateral aid.

While many Northern leaders were being vague, prominent decision-makers in the South were being much more exact. Indian Prime Minister Rajiv Gandhi, for example, put forward a plan at the Non-Aligned Movement's meeting in Belgrade in September 1989. He proposed a 'Planet Protection Fund': this fund, under UN control, would promote the development of environmentally friendly technologies, which would in turn be given, free of charge, to states. He proposed that all UN members should contribute one thousandth of their GDP to the fund. If realised, this would generate approximately US$18 billion per year.[15]

Because of Gandhi's party's subsequent defeat in the Indian parliamentary elections, he was not able to press his case at the Commonwealth Heads of Governments gathering at Kuala Lumpur during the following month. Nevertheless, the declaration agreed there did acknowledge that the North was responsible for a great deal of global pollution and should therefore bear most of the burden of cleaning it up.[16] MacNeill maintains that this 'was the first intergovernmental meeting, to my knowledge, at which world leaders talked about this question [a climate fund] using numbers that bear some relationship to the needs'.[17] Though such talk was evident during the meeting, British officials were able to ensure that the final declaration did not refer to specific sums. Instead, the Commonwealth Heads of Government agreed to:

> strengthen and support the development of international funding mechanisms and appropriate decision-making procedures to respond

to environmental protection needs which will include assisting developing countries to obtain access to and transfer of needed environmental technologies and which should take account of proposals for an international environment fund/Planet Protection Fund.[18]

British Prime Minister Margaret Thatcher maintained that the United Kingdom was ready to contribute its share; however, she remained adamantly opposed to the creation of any new bureaucracy.

Further calls for an international climate fund were made at a ministerial conference in Noordwijk, the Netherlands, in November 1989. A consultant's report prepared for the conference estimated the costs of achieving significant reductions in carbon dioxide emissions at approximately US$50 billion per year. The report also recognised, however, the difficulties in estimating the specific price of assistance required for the developing world. The authors could place a figure upon the cost of forest management (which, at full potential, they calculated at US$10–15 billion per annum), but encountered problems when projecting costs in other areas, particularly the funding of fossil fuel conservation and methane emission reductions. Although decision-makers discussed the specific details of a fund to a greater degree, a number of Northern representatives remained resistant to any substantive action (including movement on the question of resource transfers from North to South).

Much of this resistance was led by the US, their opposition becoming more firmly entrenched at the beginning of 1990. In fact, some signs of movement towards additionality – signalled by Secretary of State James Baker in February 1990 – had disappeared by the time of the Bergen conference only three months later. In Norway, US negotiators disclosed that they 'feared being drawn into an "open-ended commitment" for virtually infinite sums of aid money to cope with global warming if they conceded the principle that environmental overseas aid should be in a separate category from other aid programmes'.[19]

Although American action precluded ambitious proposals from being endorsed in the final declaration, the Bergen conference is nevertheless noteworthy for a consideration of North–South issues for two particular reasons. First, one commentator argues that it was the first time that the North's leaders accepted the fact that massive amounts of money would need to be transferred from the North to the South;[20] and second, the declaration acknowledged that the South might have to have higher emission targets than the North, in order to allow for economic growth. However, Tom Burke (then of the Green Alliance) argues that there was not really any significant change: The conference, he said, '. . . will send a signal to the developing world that we don't care and that we will not take any measures that cause pain'.[21]

Leaders of the G7 countries considered the question further at the Houston Summit in July 1990. David Runnalls reports that the politicians appeared to have come close to approving a suggestion from German Chancellor Helmut Kohl to create a global fund of US$5 billion at this meeting. In the end, however, the proposal was blocked by the hosts.[22]

North and South met again in August 1990, at a meeting of the Intergovernmental Panel on Climate Change (IPCC) in Sundsvall, Sweden. At this conference, the Southern states' representatives continued to press their demands for assistance, and, at the end of the conference, all of the IPCC members could agree that there was a need to use existing multilateral agencies (for example, the World Bank and UNDP) and bilateral agencies (for example, the US Agency for International Development) in order to assist developing countries. When, however, a number of delegations strongly supported the need for new institutions, such as a climate fund, opposition on the part of the leaders of particular Northern states (most significantly, the United States) prevented this call from being unanimous.

Later that same year, the Second World Climate Conference was held in Geneva in November. Transfers were again on the agenda, and the final declaration recognised that the net greenhouse gas emissions of developing countries 'must grow from their, as yet, relatively low energy consumption to accommodate their development needs'.[23] Further, it recommended that the South be given 'adequate and additional financial resources . . . [and that the] best available environmentally-sound technologies [should be] transferred expeditiously on a fair and most favourable basis'.[24] The Americans, the Soviets and the Saudis, however, prevented the delegates from doing more than giving 'consideration' to the need for funding facilities.

Differences between North and South existed on a variety of issues – in particular, the specifics related to sums of money, and whether any new organisation should be created to manage transfers for climate change. Another difference was much more fundamental – the two groups of countries had different ideas about *where* the issue should be discussed. The North wanted the United Nations Environment Programme to continue to play an important role, as it had for the ozone layer issue. The South, on the other hand, wanted the responsibilities for climate change to be transferred to the United Nations General Assembly. They not only felt that they would be better able to keep on top of the issue if it were handled by their best professional diplomats in New York rather than Nairobi, but many also had differences of opinion with UNEP Executive Director Mostafa Tolba. Tolba's particular style – as is discussed in Chapter 12 of this book – had alienated some countries' representatives. Moreover, they were recognising that the climate change issue was so important – and so interlinked with other social, economic and political issues – that it should be considered by the 'broader' United Nations. With the December 1990 UN General Assembly resolution on 'the protection of global climate for present and future generations of mankind', the Southern states had achieved their aim.[25]

The history of North–South discussions on global warming to this point suggests that the question was unfolding much as it had during the ozone layer negotiations: demands for a fund, articulated by Southern states' leaders, being met with resistance or indifference by officials from the North. Continuing the parallel, one might expect discussions on the global warming issue to have been heading towards the creation of some sort of massive, new, issue-specific 'climate fund'. Indeed, given the South's diplomatic victory noted above, the chances of a such an outcome would seem even greater. Although up until the late 1980s, such a progression seemed not only possible, but even probable, the emergence of another mechanism did not allow such a fund to develop unhindered.

The Global Environment Facility and the Climate Change Convention

By the early 1990s, a significant amount of international attention had been diverted to the Global Environment Facility (GEF). The GEF was first officially proposed by French and German representatives during the September 1989 meeting of the World Bank's Development Committee. Given the questionable interest accorded the environment by multilateral banking institutions during the 1980s, it might come as a surprise to some to find the World Bank at the forefront of this new initiative. David Reed, however, notes that by 'the late 1980s, multilateral lending institutions had changed from being cautious, if not resistant, to seeking a more central role in the search for new sources and forms of international environmental funding'.[26] World Bank participation was being seen as crucial to the successful resolution of global environmental problems. 'Crucial', that is, by some in the North.

The GEF was established by the World Bank, UNEP and UNDP. As reported in Chapter 8, the Facility financed projects and training programmes that would avert the ill effects upon global change of any development project. The original definition of 'global change' meant that the GEF was concerned with four specific areas: reducing the destruction of the ozone layer, countering global warming, halting the loss of biological diversity and preventing the pollution of the international waterways. Valued at US$1.4 billion over a three-year period, the Fund was not meant to address *all* problems, but simply to fund *some* projects during the initial demonstration phase (1991–93).

Each of the three operating organisations took responsibility for projects that would normally fall within its mandate. Therefore UNDP co-ordinated and managed project preparation and technical assistance work, UNEP provided scientific and technological guidance in identifying and selecting projects, and the World Bank administered the GEF Trust Fund and was responsible for appraising and supervising investment projects. The Fund's administrators met twice a year, and to be eligible to send representatives to take part in these meetings, a country must have contributed US$5.5 million to the Fund. During the first year of operation, more than twenty countries contributed to the Fund and thereby took a seat at the negotiating table.

Although the GEF was the most significant body to deal with North–South issues on global warming during the early 1990s, it was by no means the only one suggested, for a number of other possible funding mechanisms were also being proposed. Intergovernmental organisations, such as the OECD's Group on Development Assistance and the Environment, were studying different alternatives. In addition, MacNeill and colleagues identify other proposals:

A tax of 0.5 percent on the value of international trade has been suggested, which would yield about [US]$7 billion annually. Egypt has proposed a levy of 1 percent on international passenger and freight transport, which would provide approximately [US]$250 million per year, with a growth of 10 to 15 percent per annum. Other proposals would place a small levy on the commercial value of ocean fish catches, toxic incineration at sea, and river-borne wastes.[27]

Furthermore, non-governmental organisations were also contributing to the discussions. In 1989, for example, the World Resources Institute in Washington, DC published a report which, one commentator argues, 'broadened the parameters of public debate on innovative financial mechanisms'.[28] In addition, other international environmental organisations were further expanding 'the menu of mechanisms for financing environmental programs through innovative approaches, including debt-for-nature swaps'.[29] Most of these different proposals, however, were just that – proposals. During the early 1990s, the GEF was the only existing multilateral mechanism for North–South transfers on global warming.

Against this background – that is the establishment and initial activities of the GEF – intergovernmental negotiations towards a climate change convention commenced in February 1991. Although North–South issues remained visible, they did not dominate the negotiations. Two reasons explain this. First, there was significant West–West conflict – particularly between the United States and some members of the EC, as has been outlined in Chapter 6. And, second, the 'South' was by no means a united entity, for different countries of the South had different priorities. The particular interests of the Arab countries (and some other oil producing countries) has already been explored, also in Chapter 6. Additionally, given the potential impacts of climatic change, the issue was a question of survival for many small-island states. Approaching the negotiations with unique interests, many of them collaborated together under the auspices of the Alliance of Small Island States. At the fourth negotiating session of the INC (1991), this divergence of views nearly caused the Group of 77 to '[fly] apart over the issue of commitments'.[30]

In spite of these differences, almost all Southern countries could subscribe to one fundamental position: they opposed any restrictions on their future use of fossil fuels until they had reached a higher level of development (this being implied by a higher average per capita emission levels). Indeed, before they would consider any kind of control upon their activities, they demanded a firm commitment to the stabilisation of emissions in Northern countries. Because this could not be agreed, any calls for obligations to be imposed upon Southern states in the Convention were successfully resisted.

With respect to helping the Southern countries meet the challenges of climate change, however, there were some obligations placed upon the Northern countries. Informing these were a number of fundamental principles governing North–South relations on the issue. They are: the 'common but differentiated responsibilities' of the two sets of countries (preamble, Article 3.1); the assertion that 'developed country Parties should take the lead in combating climate change and the adverse effects thereof' (Article 3.1); and the recognition that 'the share of global emissions originating in developing countries will grow to meet their social and development needs' (preamble). Moving from general statements of principle to specific commitments of action, three in the Convention are particularly noteworthy. First, Northern countries agreed to 'provide new and additional financial resources to meet the agreed full costs' of communication (to the Conference of the Parties) of developing countries' national inventories (of greenhouse gas sources and sinks) and their national programmes on climate change (Article 4.3). Second, Northern countries also consented to meet the 'agreed full incremental costs' of the developing world's commitments (Article 4.3). These commitments ranged from preparation of national inventories of sources and sinks (Article 4.1(a)) to 'education, training and public awareness related to climate change' (Article 4.1(j)). Finally, Northern states pledged to 'take all practicable steps to promote, facilitate and finance' technology transfer (Article 4.5). The Parties also agreed to establish a mechanism for looking after all of these transfers (Article 11). Since such a mechanism would have to be implemented by the Conference of the Parties (which was not scheduled to be convened until after the Convention had entered into force), it was accepted that the Global Environment Facility would be entrusted with the operation of the financial mechanism in the interim (Article 21).

Given the vagueness of some of these agreements, along with the inclusion of the GEF as a key participant (at least initially) in the operationalisation of the convention, it should come as little surprise to discover that the Climate Change Convention was not the final word on North–South issues and global warming. After 1992, the outstanding questions on this set of issues generally fell into four different areas: transfer size, burden-sharing, governance and technology transfer. I now consider each of these in turn.

Southern discomfort

First, the size of the necessary North–South transfer was the subject of much debate. Figures ranged widely. Academics put forward a variety of estimates: Michael Grubb quotes a figure of US$100 billion annually,[31] Geoffrey Bertram suggests about US$50 billion annually,[32] and Peter Hayes arrives at a figure of about US$30 billion annually.[33] Northern NGOs also advanced estimates: the Worldwatch Institute in the United States proposed a US$28 billion fund to pay for 'massive investments in energy efficiency and reforestation in developing countries',[34] and Greenpeace advocated 'a [US]$30 billion fund to be made available to Third World signatories of a climate convention as well as to support the development of renewable energies'.[35] Meanwhile, Southern NGOs also arrived at estimates. A 1990 report published by the Centre for Science and Environment in India argues that, under the scheme that they developed, the 'top 15 polluting nations would have to pay individual developing countries a total of [US]$20 billion dollars annually'.[36] A further analysis, under a different scenario, yields a figure of US$90 billion annually.[37] Moreover, at the ninth session of the INC in February 1994, representatives from Southern NGOs suggested that, because 25 per cent of the world's people (that is, those living in the North) had emitted 75 per cent of the world's carbon, the 'developing countries [had] provided environmental space to the industrialised countries at no cost for decades. Annually, this subsidy is estimated to be around US$75 billion.'[38]

Of course, the amount of money estimated depends upon the assumptions that are made, the most critical of which relate to the aim of any transfers. As noted above, the most potentially most expensive commitment in the Convention (Article 4.3) obliges Northern states to cover the 'full incremental costs' of the developing world's commitments. It, however, fails to define this phrase. Katrina Brown and colleagues identify two alternative interpretations: '[First, the] funding of incremental costs should occur where the benefits to the global environment would not accrue to domestic economies even if the domestic economies invested in environmental protection. [And second, the] funding of incremental costs should occur where there are net environmental benefits no matter whether these accrued to domestic economies or globally.'[39] What definition is agreed will obviously impact significantly the amount required. Although accepted that its application should be flexible, pragmatic and applied on a case-by-case basis, two years after the Convention had been agreed, a working definition remained elusive.[40] What is clear, however, is that no matter what definition is chosen, the amounts required appear to be at least one, and perhaps two or even three, orders of magnitude larger than the amount of money disbursed for global warming projects from the GEF.[41]

Consequently, a number of representatives from the developing world argued that other organisations (in addition to the GEF) should be brought on board to help to implement the Climate Change Convention. In response, however, others wondered what other organisations would qualify as 'financial mechanisms': while TNCs and the multilateral development banks might have the required resources, (particularly the TNCs) they were not in the business of disbursing grants, or even concessional loans; moreover, they did not have transparent systems of governance, and therefore would not satisfy the conditions listed under Article 11 of the Climate Change Convention. The formal participation of such entities, therefore, might well have been a non-starter.

This did not, however, preclude the involvement of such entities in the global effort to address the climate change challenge. While they might not be officially recognised as the 'financial mechanism', they might still be effectively 'leveraged'. At the ninth session of the INC, for example, a US representative stated:

> we recognize that the funds available under the financial mechanism will be limited, and will form only a fraction of the total resources summoned to combat the threat of climate change and simultaneously promote sustainable development. For this reason, we think it vital that the financial mechanism serve to leverage other funds as fully as possible, and that priority be given to projects that do so.[42]

Nevertheless, while discussions continued about how the resources would be obtained, it remained that the differences between 'demand' and 'supply' had yet to be reconciled.

Although there was agreement that the North had a particular responsibility for addressing the global warming problem, it remained to be determined how the costs would be divided among the developed countries. Three parameters that could define responsibility from a polluter pays perspective include: which greenhouse gases are counted; which sources are included; and what time frame is used for estimating them. Susan Subak notes how the choice made would have significant practical impact upon each country's relative responsibility:

> A New Zealander who lives in a country with twenty methane emitting sheep for every person may prefer to keep the gases limited to carbon dioxide only. A Swiss citizen mostly emits carbon dioxide by burning fossil fuels, and may be unhappy if only this gas is controlled. And someone from a recently industrialized country such as Singapore might feel justified in pushing for the inclusion of historical emissions in global greenhouse negotiations.[43]

The most obvious candidates for regulation were: carbon dioxide from energy use; carbon dioxide from land use; methane from energy production and land use; and, other greenhouse gases. Although proposals for protocols at the beginning of 1994 focused upon the first of these, all were significant elements in the debate.[44]

The question of time-frame was potentially even more controversial. Because of the significant lifetimes of greenhouse gases, the substances that are causing enhanced global warming today have been expelled over the previous 200 years. Therefore, some studies suggest that historical rates of emissions should be used in order to estimate each countries' relative contribution to the enhanced greenhouse effect that the world is experiencing today. The major findings from one of these investigations are that:

> First, North Americans bear the largest historical responsibility for the present carbon problem. Second, some regions currently emitting high amounts of carbon per capita, notably the USSR, Eastern Europe and Asia have contributed relatively little historically to the problem. Third, historic rebalancing of carbon emissions would require only modest annual per capita cuts in emissions by most industrialised regions, but major cuts by North America. Fourth, expected high rates of population growth in developing regions would quickly overwhelm any emissions credits inherited from past generations, leaving them with CO_2 allocations no greater than in most developed regions.[45]

A pattern of burden based upon past emissions, rather than present emissions, would change figures significantly. For example, Western Europe was responsible for 16 per cent of the carbon dioxide added in 1990, but 26 per cent of the carbon dioxide rise since 1800. Similarly, Asia was responsible for 19 per cent of the rise in 1990, but only 9 per cent of the rise since 1800.[46] Although some argued that this idea was a political non-starter,[47] it was, nevertheless, an important negotiating tool for leaders of Southern states.

Another suggestion was that countries should be allowed to release a quantity of greenhouse gases into the atmosphere that was proportional to their population.[48] In this way, those states that were above their quota would have to compensate those that were below their quota. Once again, decision-makers in the North were resistant to this sort of approach (for it is in opposition to the principle of 'grandfathering', which they prefer), while those in the South felt that it was the most equitable manner in which the issue could be addressed. The way in which burden-sharing should be calculated continued to be the focus of much controversy.

A third issue key point of debate between the North and the South related to governance. As noted above, Article 11 of the Climate Convention establishes a mechanism for the management of financial transfers. Also noted above, it was agreed that the Global Environment Facility would be the interim entity entrusted with the operation of the financial mechanism. An addendum to that commitment, however, states that the GEF should be restructured so that it has 'an equitable and balanced representation of all Parties within a transparent system of governance' and its membership 'made universal' (Articles 11 and 21). These qualifiers were included at the insistence of many representatives from developing countries, for they felt that the Facility had some serious deficiencies.

More specifically, although the GEF was supposedly being run by three international organisations, it was, in fact, dominated by the World Bank's officials: the World Bank managed the core fund, distributed most of the resources, and provided the bulk of the secretariat services (indeed, the GEF itself was created by a resolution (91–5) of the World Bank's Executive Directors (14 May 1991)). As a consequence, the GEF had adopted many of the Bank's worst characteristics and habits. It was unaccountable: dominated by donors, membership was conditional upon a fee of US$5.5 million. And it was untransparent: acquisition of documentation was difficult and NGO participation was severely restricted. Many of these criticisms were identified in a report entitled 'The Independent Evaluation Report of the GEF', which assessed the Facility's pilot phase. Commissioned by the Bank, it was published towards the end of 1993.

At the end of negotiations for the Facility's replenishment (held in Geneva in March 1994), some of the GEF's problems had been addressed. By rejecting sole use of the 'one dollar, one vote' system of the international financial institutions, recipient countries were given some say in the decisions of the Facility. More specifically, the Facility will have a Governing Council, which will have two voting methods, both of which will need a minimum of 60 per cent of the votes to pass a resolution. The first is based on money: the four largest donors (France, Germany, Japan and the United States) will, by virtue of holding 63 per cent of the votes between then, predominate. The second is based on membership of the council: of the 32 members, 16 are from the developing world, 14 from the donor countries, and 2 from the 'economies in transition'.

With respect to efforts to achieve 'a transparent system of governance', meanwhile, it was agreed that the GEF would 'provide for full disclosure of all non-confidential information'.[49] It remained, of course, to discover how the definition of 'confidential' will be operationalised. It was not spelt out at that time.

Regardless of the extent to which the GEF had met the conditions outlined in the Climate Change Convention, the Facility's relationship to the Convention's Conference of the Parties still remained unclear. One reading of Article 11 of the Climate Convention suggested that the GEF had to accept some form of supervision of its activities by the Conference of the Parties. (The Conference would provide guidance to the GEF and decide on its policies, programme priorities and eligibility criteria with respect to its climate change activities.) One of the reasons, however, for Northern support of the GEF was that its control was not in the hands of a Southern majority of states. Would they, therefore, really accept this interpretation of Article 11?

It is also important to recognise Southern concerns about the GEF's scope. Many argued that the highest priorities for the developing world were poverty alleviation and the resolution of local environmental problems. The global environmental problems identified by the GEF, meanwhile, represented the priorities of the industrialised world.[50] Indeed, many of the GEF's grants simply helped to 'green' larger loans.[51] Moreover, the sheer structure of the Facility, some claimed, embodied a view that sustainable development was a problem for the South, rather than a global challenge that required changes in socioeconomic policies throughout the world.[52]

The position among Northern decision-makers, meanwhile, was that all support should be given to the GEF as it was then structured, because Northern decision-makers wanted one fund, administered by an established international organisation, to address a broad range of issues. Their worst-case scenario was a series of issue-specific funds – the ozone layer fund, they hoped, was the exception rather than the rule. The South's demands for new, all-inclusive funds and organisations were seen as efforts by Southern politicians to place a multitude of issues under the broad environment umbrella, and thus demand a host of concessions.

The fourth major issue arising from North–South differences concerned the transfer of technology. Early in the debate, Grubb argued that:

> Technology transfer is a more fundamental issue than many realise. The dire predictions of future global carbon emissions cannot be avoided if the developing countries industrialise along the same broad path as the developed have done. They will need to 'leapfrog' directly to more advanced and efficient technologies than would occur naturally in the course of development.[53]

Just as on the ozone layer, however, it remained unclear how developing countries would be able to obtain the relevant technologies. During the Uruguay Round of the GATT negotiations, representatives from the Northern states – in particular, the United States – made it clear that they were eager to ensure that patents, copyrights or other trademarks were awarded to the owner or the investor in order to protect intellectual property. Their representatives continued to argue that such rights had to be conferred in order to provide incentives for research, development and innovation. Northern leaders also expressed their desires for *all* countries to adopt intellectual property laws, like those in the North, so that there could be one standard, which would be administered in the GATT (or subsequently, the WTO).[54]

Developing countries' officials, for their part, were not content with this prospect. They feared that tighter protection for intellectual-property rights would strengthen the power of Northern transnational corporations,[55] with the result being less technology transfer and higher prices of essential patented goods. Moreover, they were not convinced by the Northern representatives' arguments that stronger protection of intellectual property rights would boost foreign investment and technology transfer by reducing TNCs' fears of theft. Instead, Southern decision-makers remained sceptical that it would not just be the outdated and harmful technology that would be transferred to their countries. The stalemate therefore continued.[56]

Consequently, a range of questions related to 'equity' on climate change issues remained controversial during the first few months of 1994. Indeed, they occupied considerable efforts during the negotiations of the INC – the second of the two working groups was devoted to discussions of such issues. With the financial mechanism set to be debated by the Conference of the Parties at its first session (in early 1995), North–South issues were set to continue to be important elements of the broader intergovernmental deliberations.

Notes

1 'Declaration of the world climate conference', reprinted in *Environmental Policy and Law*, 6 (1980), p. 103.

2 World Climate Programme (Impact Studies), *Developing Policies for Responding to Climatic Change* (Geneva, WMO/TD, No. 225, April 1988), p. 31.

3 James K. Sebenius, 'Designing negotiations toward a new regime: the case of global warming', *International Security*, 15:4 (Spring 1991), p. 129.

4 Author's calculation from World Resources Institute, *World Resources 1990–91* (Oxford, Oxford University Press, 1989), p. 15. The measurement of responsibility for the enhanced greenhouse effect is by no means uncontroversial. This particular report engendered a large amount of controversy. I return to the broader debate below.

5 See, for example: the address of Maumoon Abdul Gayoom, President of the Maldives, to the United Nations General Assembly on 19 October 1987 (UN Doc A/42/PV.41).

6 'The changing atmosphere: implications for global security' (Toronto, Canada, 27–30 June 1988), *Conference Statement* (Ottawa, Environment Canada, 1988), p. 6.

7 UN General Assembly Resolution, 'Protection of global climate for present and future generations of mankind' (A/RES/43/53, 6 December 1988).

8 'Protection of the atmosphere: international meeting of legal and policy experts', *Meeting Statement* (Ottawa, Canada, 20–22 February 1989), p. 11.

9 Quoted in 'The Hague environment summit', *Environmental Policy and Law*, 19:2 (April 1989), p. 45.

10 Ibid.

11 Quoted in Tim Radford, 'Ridley pledges CFC aid for Third World', *Guardian* (London) (4 May 1989).

12 Tony Samstag, 'Climate call', *Independent* (London) (29 April 1989).

13 Jim MacNeill, 'The greening of international relations', *International Journal*, 45:1 (Winter 1989–90), p. 32.

14 Reprinted in 'Economic declaration: section on the environment', *Environmental Policy and Law*, 19:5 (1989), p. 183.

15 'Gandhi urges an environment fund', *International Herald Tribune* (6 September 1989).

16 Reprinted in 'The Langkawi declaration on environment', *Commonwealth Law Bulletin*, 15:4 (October 1989), p. 1546.

17 MacNeill, 'The greening of international relations', p. 32.

18 Reprinted in 'The Langkawi declaration on environment', p. 1546.

19 Michael McCarthy, 'Global warming to cost "trillions" ', *The Times* (London) (16 May 1990), p. 22.

20 'Facing up to global damage', *Independent* (London) (17 May 1990), p. 26.

21 Quoted in Richard North, 'Fight against pollution "will cause anguish" ', *Independent* (London) (17 May 1990), p. 8.

22 David Runnalls, *United Nations Conference on Environment and Development: Institutional and Financial Options for Sustainable Development* (Ottawa, United Nations Association in Canada, Briefing Paper No. 30, July 1991), p. 4.

23 *Ministerial Declaration of the Second World Climate Conference* (Geneva, SWCC, 1990), point 15, p. 5.

24 Ibid., point 15, p. 5.

25 UNGA Resolution, 'Protection of global climate for present and future generations of mankind' (A/RES/45/212, 21 December 1990).

26 David Reed, *The Global Environmental Facility: Sharing Responsibility for the Biosphere* (Washington, DC, Multilateral Development Bank Program, WWF-International, 1991), p. 4.

27 Jim MacNeill, Pieter Winsemius and Taizo Yakushiji, *Beyond Interdependence: the Meshing of the World's Economy and the Earth's Ecology* (Oxford, Oxford University Press, 1991), p. 101.

28 Reed, *The Global Environmental Facility*, p. 4. The WRI report was entitled *Natural Endowments: Financing Resource Conservation for Development*.

29   Reed, *The Global Environmental Facility*, p. 4.

30   Sten Nilsson and David Pitt, *Protecting the Atmosphere: the Climate Convention and its Context* (London, Earthscan, 1994), p. 56.

31   Michael Grubb, *Energy Policies and the Greenhouse Effect. Volume One: Policy Appraisal* (London, Royal Institute of International Affairs, 1990), pp. 287–8.

32   Geoffrey Bertram, 'Tradeable emission permits and the control of greenhouse gases', *Journal of Development Studies*, 28:3 (April 1992), pp. 441–4.

33   Peter Hayes, 'North–South transfer', in Peter Hayes and Kirk Smith (eds), *The Global Greenhouse Regime: Who Pays?* (London, Earthscan, 1993), p. 153.

34   Christopher Flavin, *Slowing Global Warming: a Worldwide Strategy* (Washington, DC, Worldwatch Paper No. 91, 1989), pp. 70–1.

35   'Prevent climate holocaust – Greenpeace', *Geneva ECO NGO Newsletter*, 3 (21 June 1991), cited in Patrick McCully, 'The case against climate aid', *The Ecologist*, 21:6 (November/December 1991), p. 244.

36   'Environmental colonialism to the fore', *Ecoforum*, 15:1 (February 1991), p. 13.

37   Anil Agarwal and Sunita Narain, *Global Warming in an Unequal World* (New Delhi, Centre for Science and Technology, 1990).

38   Educardo Sanhueza, quoted in 'JI: Southern statement', *ECO Geneva* (11 February 1994).

39   Katrina Brown, W. Neil Adger and R. Kerry Turner, 'Global environmental change and mechanisms for North–South resource transfers', *Journal of International Development*, 5:6 (November–December 1993), p. 584.

40   Determination of the elements of Articles 4.1 and 4.4 that would be eligible for funding through the financial mechanism were also still to be agreed.

41   In March 1994, the GEF was replenished at just over US$2 billion for three years. If about 40 per cent of the Facility's funds continue to go to global warming projects (as was the case through the first five tranches of the pilot phase), about US$267 million a year will be distributed.

42   'Program priorities' (Statement of the United States Delegation, INC9, Geneva, 10 February 1994).

43   Susan Subak, 'Assessing emissions: five approaches compared', in Hayes and Smith, *The Global Greenhouse Regime*, p. 51.

44   Following upon my comments in note 4 above, some representatives from the developing world argued that you should make a distinction between 'survival' and 'luxury' emissions of greenhouse gases (Agarwal and Narain, *Global Warming*). The former – which would include emissions from land use – should not be 'counted' the same as the latter – which would include emissions from automobiles.

45   A study by Yasumasa Fujii at the International Institute for Applied System Analysis, Laxenburg, Austria, reported in 'CO_2: a balancing of accounts', *Options* (December 1990), p. 13.

46   Ibid., p. 12.

47   See, for example, Michael Grubb, *The Greenhouse Effect: Negotiating Targets* (London, Royal Institute of International Affairs, 1989), p. 24, n. 47.

48   See, for example, Michael Grubb, *The Greenhouse Effect* and Agarwal and Narain, *Global Warming*.

49   Quoted in a report by Mark Halle (Director of Central Policy, IUCN–The World Conservation Union), 'IUCN report from GEF meeting' (18 March 1994).

50   In addition, the GEF defined incremental costs narrowly around global benefits, meaning that the impact upon the local environment was of secondary importance.

51   An estimate from the World Bank found that, in 1992, 85 per cent of the money (although only two-thirds of the numbers) of World Bank GEF projects were estimated to be associated with larger loans (quoted in Pratap Chatterjee, 'Green fund at the World Bank: victory or menace?', *Inter Press Service* (16 March 1994)).

52   See, for example, Oliver Tickell and Nicholas Hildyard, 'Green dollars, green menace', *The Ecologist*, 22:3 (May/June 1992), pp. 82–3. This fear has been exacerbated among some by the growing popularisation of 'joint implementation' – that is, the notion whereby one state (usually in the North) fulfils its obligations by paying for changes in another state (usually in the South).

53   Grubb, *The Greenhouse Effect*, p. 24.

54   See, for example, Martin Khor Kok Peng, 'The Uruguay Round and the Third World', *The Ecologist*, 20:6 (November/December 1990), pp. 208–13; and 'Thought control: GATT and intellectual property', *The Economist*, 7 July 1990, p. 80. Officials of Northern corporations were also 'cautious about selling their latest and best technology to countries such as India and China, both of which have reputations for not being completely respectful of intellectual property rights' (Robert Pool, 'A global experiment in technology transfer', *Nature*, 351 (2 May 1991), p. 6).

55   They observed that 99 per cent of all patents were held by citizens or companies in the North to support their position.

56   See, for example, Touche Ross Management Consultants for the UK Department of Trade and Industry and Overseas Development Administration, *Global Climate Change: the Role of Technology Transfer* (London, Touche Ross, February 1991). A working group on technology transfer was established in 1993, within the ongoing programme of the Commission on Sustainable Development.

10

Equity and global environmental politics

Equity is significant in politics. A general belief in this assertion inspired my third hypothesis, which was that adequate resolution of North–South issues – that is, developing countries' concerns about 'equity' – is necessary for international co-operation. The experience on the issues of global atmospheric change, as outlined in Chapters 8 and 9, has delivered somewhat inconclusive results with respect to this hypothesis. Let me consider each of the two issues in turn.

On the ozone layer issue, the degree of correlation between the satisfaction of demands for equity and international co-operation is high. The North–South equity issue did not occupy a prominent position upon the broader ozone layer agenda until after agreement was reached on the Montreal Protocol in 1987. Leaders from the developing world maintained that the so-called concessionary terms for their countries that were included in the Protocol were unsatisfactory. Consequently, in working group meetings through the second half of 1989 and the first half of 1990, representatives from the North and the South negotiated changes to the terms of the Montreal Protocol – these were finalised in London in June 1990. The new arrangements were subsequently consolidated at the Fourth Meeting of the Parties in Copenhagen two years later. Although the established framework continues to be the subject of some debate, unprecedented proposals have been initiated. In this way, it appears that much progress had been made towards meeting Southern demands for equity on the ozone layer issue.

On the climate change issue, the degree of correlation is unclear. The question of global equity in terms of North–South concerns emerged soon after the global warming issue took on political dimensions of any significance. Since 1988, furthermore, North–South matters have been the focus of much attention in the international negotiations. The relationship between calls for a resolution of North–South concerns and co-operation, however, is indistinct.

From one perspective, it appears that a generally accepted mechanism for dealing with equity issues on the climate change issue is in place – namely, the Global Environment Facility (GEF). During its renegotiation in March 1994, the GEF was restructured to make it more democratic. Indeed, a Governing Council with equal representation from North and South was established – echoes of the Multilateral Ozone Fund's Executive Council. More generally, a number of further changes, which were designed to increase the Facility's transparency, were also promised. Some degree of 'equity' might, therefore, have been realised.

There is, however, a different perspective. Exclusive attention directed towards the share of seats on the Governing Council misses the point. Real power continues to rest with the GEF secretariat's Chief Executive Officer – an individual who just so happens to be an employee of the World Bank (namely, the World Bank Vice-President for Environmental Affairs, Mohamed El-Ashry). Granted, there is a co-chair, elected by the Council's members, but this individual's primary responsibilities will be for administrative matters. Because money-decisions still rest with the World Bank, critics believe that the GEF will continue to be donor-driven. Thus, the conditions for 'equity', as laid out in the Climate Change Convention, have yet to be fulfilled.

There is, furthermore, a final view. Recall that the GEF was only intended to be an 'interim' measure. Consequently, it is still early days; the heart of the debate about North–South issues lies ahead. (The true direction of the discussion might not be revealed until the first Conference of the Parties in early 1995.) Thus, the hypothesis about equity has yet to be put to the test.

In spite of the inconclusive nature of the second application of this hypothesis, the experience on the ozone layer depletion and climate change issues suggest that it would unwise to overlook the role that North–South issues play in the process of international co-operation on issues of global atmospheric changes. The ways in which actors defined and attempted to operationalise 'equity' were significant, and their recognition helps to increase understanding of the politics of ozone layer depletion and climate change.

Nevertheless, following the pattern adopted in previous chapters, one can still question whether the relatively simple hypothesis put forward allows for the capture of all key elements in global environmental politics. Indeed, a deeper examination reveals that reliance upon it might cause a number of important factors to be neglected.

Most fundamentally, can notions of 'equity' be easily operationalised? Within international society, it seems to be accepted by all that developing countries are in a 'special situation' (Principle 6 of the Rio Declaration). Because countries of the North have caused most of the damage to the global environment, these countries have a responsibility for taking the lead in addressing this set of problems. As a consequence, it is generally agreed that 'states have common but differentiated responsibilities' (Principle 7 of the Rio Declaration). But how might these statements of principles be spelt out in policy terms? In other words, what would 'equity' actually look like?[1]

Another problem arising from our hypothesis is that it encourages us to look at two entities, called 'North' and 'South'. Just as Chapter 7 revealed that there are problems associated with looking at individual states as 'unitary entities', the difficulties proliferate once we look at groupings of states as single actors. For one, a number of industrialised states – particularly Scandinavian countries and the Netherlands, to a lesser extent France and Canada – have traditionally displayed greater concern for 'equity' on North–South issues than some others. In addition, the bloc that is commonly referred to as the 'South' is by no means a solitary unit. Study of the climate change issue has already revealed how different countries have adopted markedly different policies on the issue – perhaps the positions of the OPEC states and the AOSIS members were the most polarised.

Another lesson from Chapter 7 is that uniformity of views within any particular Southern country should not necessarily be assumed either. Granted, the search for a single position might yield success in some instances: China, for example, a county that has no non-governmental organisations, and a centralised government, and a command economy, could be one such candidate. But substantial differences exist in other instances – for example, India. Sheila Jasanoff reveals that while most Indians endorse the notion of 'sustainable development', different parts of the population interpret the concept in different ways.[2] Thus, the debate within India has remarkable similarities with the broader North–South debate.

My third hypothesis also presumes a capacity for the state, or indeed, for any entity, which may not be present in many parts of the developing world. For a number of reasons, many Southern countries have found it difficult to take part effectively in global atmospheric change discussions. At the outset, simple participation in the international negotiations has proved trying for a number of them. The IPCC's Special Committee on Participation of Developing Countries identified five areas of particular concern which might inhibit Third World involvement in its deliberations: 'insufficient information, insufficient communication, limited human resources, institutional difficulties and limited financial resources'.[3] In order to pre-empt these problems, a fund was established to assist developing country participation. Lack of money, however, meant that it was only mildly successful: in 1994, many countries were being represented by only one individual. This has both immediate and far-reaching implications. During the actual negotiations, it proved to be very difficult for these representatives (and, consequently, these 'states') to be fully informed of all deliberations. Additionally, because an increasing amount of 'soft' law is eventually 'hardening' up, absence from these seemingly specific negotiations might yet have broader ramifications for these countries.

After an international agreement has been reached, there are a number of additional difficulties involved in operationalising its terms. Initially, there is the trial of ratification. In many countries, this has to be effected by an environment department which lacks bureaucratic clout, technical knowledge and financial resources. Its officials may find it impossible to overcome obstacles within their respective states.

Still, getting the desired legislation on the books may seem positively effortless compared to the challenge of enforcing it. In the absence of the appropriate human, financial and technological resources, this would invariably prove difficult. There are in many countries, however, bodies that will serve – either consciously or not – to impede the process of implementation. Within the nation's borders, there will be any of a number of powerful actors (some within government) that are benefiting from the present (unsustainable) forms of development. Externally, not only will there be the demands of economic adjustment policies, but all actions will also be susceptible to international economic forces (particularly transnational corporations). Generally, then, the state may not be able to 'deliver the goods'. Given, moreover, that in many developing countries there are few effective NGOs (or other semblances of 'civil society') to support, or even to perform, the required tasks, a general lack of capacity will make any change difficult to achieve.[4]

Any focus upon this third hypothesis, moreover, suggests the need for *global*, rather than simply *international*, co-operation. Some argue that, because of the profligate waste of resources and damage to the environment caused by Northern countries, attention should be focused, at least initially, upon these countries: all energy should be directed towards efforts to achieve co-operation among OECD countries. Consequently, scarce resources should not be used to try to resolve North–South issues. If this advice were acted upon, equity would still play a role; only in a different way.

Among Northern states, there have been instances when one state's leaders have felt that uniform standards should not be applied across all states, because such a policy would overlook the actions that that state had taken in the past. In these situations, the demand for equity also derived from a consideration of historical factors. (Recognise, for example, the US demand that their 1970s 'can ban' be taken into consideration in the formulation of international CFC regulations during the 1980s[5] and a similar call for consideration of historical action by the Japanese on the global warming issue.[6]) More recently, in the international negotiations, representatives from Eastern Europe have argued that their 'economies in transition' warrant special consideration.[7] In this way, endorsement of my third hypothesis may encourage limited resources to be misused.

However, perhaps the most damning challenge upon the third hypothesis involves its relation to my second hypothesis – more specifically, is 'equity' simply a short-form for 'interests across both North and South'? Supporting this challenge, consider the particular characteristics of the two cases of global atmospheric change. Greater ozone layer depletion occurs near the planet's poles than at its equator, and any increase in exposure to ultraviolet radiation has a more severe impact upon fair-skinned individuals than dark-skinned individuals. Consequently, the issue was perceived to be a unique threat to the inhabitants of the northerly latitudes (in particular, North America and Europe), and public opinion was thus stimulated.[8] Moreover, Chapter 8 has already shown that the costs of dealing with ozone layer depletion were relatively small and contained. Therefore, any Southern 'successes' on this issue may have owed as much to a fortuitous coincidence of circumstances – that is, a certain distribution of interests – than to broader shifts in Northern attitudes towards global equity. The climate change issue, by contrast, does not have this particular characteristic.

But is it really simply a case of perceived self-interest? When North–South relations are examined, should references to 'equity' be thought of as a veneer masking selfish motivations? Will, therefore, any definition of 'equity' depend upon the values, the interests and so on of the actor doing the defining? There will, obviously, be some truth to this. Nevertheless, an analysis based solely upon the simple calculations of interests would be hard pressed to explain many of the actions that have happened on issues of global atmospheric change to date. Concern for equity thus remains significant.

Let me, as well, come back to some of the other challenges laid out above. First, the placing of North–South issues on the back-burner – justified by the dominance of the North in these issues – would be a mistake. The present path of development in the South is unsustainable.[9] Continued travel along it will cause substantial environmental degradation and human misery. All actors, therefore, must think about how sustainability in the developing world could be achieved. This should be done as soon as possible – not only is this warranted for moral concerns for the earth and, its inhabitants but cost considerations also encourage it. History provides a wealth of examples that reveal that it is cheaper to take the sustainable path the first time then to change paths (that is, to 'retrofit') at a later date. Consequently, a focus upon North–South issues is vital for both normative and analytical reasons, though the ways in which 'equity' can be part of the debate between other actors should still be recognised.

In summary, then, although there are limits to the utility of my third hypothesis, there remains sufficient justification for its inclusion. Indeed, Chapters 8 and 9 showed that, first, the correlation between North–South equity and international co-operation is high on the ozone layer depletion issue, and, second, discussions about equity are significant parts of the broader climate change negotiations. Let me now consider more closely the dynamics associated with North–South issues on global environmental politics.

Much of the recent North–South discussions on environment and development have been dominated by a small number of elements – namely, the transfer of finances and technology by multilateral agencies. This is best supported by the observation that the GEF has captured so much of the debate: although questions continue to be asked about the appropriateness of the GEF, it seems to be widely accepted that the Facility will play a major role, at least in the short and medium term.

By being framed in such a way, many elements of the broader debate have become increasingly marginalised. While attention has focused upon the 'how much is being given in ODA?' question, other channels for assisting the developing world appear to have been forgotten. Some of these other channels were identified in Chapter 33 of Agenda 21 and labelled 'innovative financing' possibilities. They include: various forms of debt relief, apart from official or Paris Club debt, including greater use of debt swaps; the use of economic and fiscal incentives and mechanisms; the feasibility of tradeable permits; new schemes for fund-raising and voluntary contributions through private channels, including non-governmental organisations; the reallocation of resources presently committed to military purposes.[10] Still other prospects include: removing subsidies; international emissions charges (for example, taxes on air travel); reforming tax systems by 'greening them'; development of private sector financing mechanisms; and environmental mutual funds to support sustainable development.[11] Non-governmental organisations, additionally, have tried to widen the agenda by asking for attention to be directed to, for example, structural adjustment programmes, debt relief and terms of trade. In this way, they have attempted to challenge the conventional wisdom that sustainable development must be 'bought'. On the contrary, they maintain, many actions to promote sustainable development simply involve the reformation of existing injustices in the international economic system.[12]

Though most of these are being discussed, few anticipate that they will be acted upon in the near future. Instead, there seems to be an endorsement, even by most developing countries' representatives, of the liberal economic order. Behind closed doors, all negotiators – North and South – now speak the same language. Even in public, although some speeches are still made up of rhetoric straight from the pages of the New International Economic Order, a more general shift in pitch is nevertheless evident. Supporting this, Jasanoff notes that the Beijing Declaration, a major statement of policy objectives by developing countries, still 'highlighted equity but softened the NIEO "ideological template" with language drawn from the Brundtland Commission report, which was rightly judged to be more acceptable to the North'.[13] Additionally, the endorsement given to a 'supportive international economic environment' (that is, a liberal global economic order) in Chapter 2 of Agenda 21 and Principle 12 of the Rio Declaration lends further weight.

Attempting to explain this apparent convergence of views, a number of reasons are offered. Many of them relate to the apparent failure of other (non-liberal) models – in particular, the collapse of the command economies in Eastern Europe. Because liberal economics has become the 'only game in town', one rejects it only at one's peril. Many decision-makers in the South thus feel that if greater integration with international markets is not pursued, then further marginalisation will be forthcoming. In order to maintain good relations with Northern countries – something they see as crucial – the game is played.

In conclusion, it appears that North–South issues will continue to be a major axis around which the global environmental debate revolves. These issues are characterised by both conflict and concurrence. On the one hand, a number of points of contention persist between those in the developed countries and those in the developing countries. Conceptually, the most fundamental involves the meaning of the term, 'sustainable development'.[14] Though universally supported, different ideas about its operationalisation will preclude the near-term conclusion of any new 'global bargain'. On the other hand, common ground has also been reached in a number of areas. All actors agree now that 'the environment' cannot be considered in isolation from other issues, most significantly 'development'. Practically, there is some agreement that both donor and recipient countries should have a voice in the governance of any resource transfers. Finally, both have an interest in preserving the controlling role that the state now holds.[15] As discussions continue, within both the frameworks of the two sets of agreements on issues of global atmospheric change, and the broader work of the Commission on Sustainable Development, equity will continue to be a major factor in efforts to achieve and to extend international co-operation.

Notes

1 See, for example, a report in which ten international equity principles are identified and subsequently transformed into operational rules for allocating carbon allotments on the climate change issue (Adam Rose, 'Equity considerations of tradeable carbon emission entitlements', in UNCTAD, *Combatting Global Warming: Study on a Global System of Tradeable Carbon Emission Entitlements* (Geneva, UNCTAD, 1992), pp. 55–83).

2 Broadly, there is one group who 'put the blame on individual moral behaviour – the reckless consumption of the rich – and [another group] who prefer a collective, almost ecological explanation for non-sustainability, focusing on the pressure of population and the physical limits of the biosphere' (Sheila Jasanoff, 'India at the crossroads in global environmental policy', *Global Environmental Change*, 3:1 (March 1993), p. 51).

3 Quoted in Gerald Foley, *Who Is Taking the Heat?* (London, Panos Institute, 1991), p. 80.

4 On this point more generally, see Robert H. Jackson, *Quasi-states: Sovereignty, International Relations and the Third World* (Cambridge, Cambridge University Press, 1990).

5 See Chapter 5.

6 Michael Grubb, 'The greenhouse effect: negotiating targets', *International Affairs*, 66:1 (January 1990), p. 75.

7 So too has South Africa.

8 See the section in Chapter 11 entitled 'Issue tangibility', where I explore this idea further.

9 It is in the North as well!

10 Agenda 21, Chapter 33.18.

11 These are taken from both other parts of Agenda 21 and the initial discussions of the CSD's 'Working group on financial flows and mechanisms'.

12 Additionally, not all financial transfers are necessarily good and desirable. Sending money to developing countries may contribute to unsustainable development. An examination of the impact that resource transfers have upon recipient societies needs to be undertaken in order to identify the most effective means of providing new and additional money to developing countries. See, more generally, Ian H. Rowlands, 'Paying for sustainable development: progress and prospects', *The Oxford International Review*, 5:1 (Winter 1993), pp. 28–31.

13 Jasanoff, 'India at the crossroads', p. 37.

14 Consider, for example, the difference in emphases in two of the Rio Declaration's principles. Principle 3 asserts that '[t]he right to development must be fulfilled so as to equitably meet developmental and environmental needs of present and future generations', whereas Principle 4 maintains that 'in order to achieve sustainable development, environmental protection

shall constitute an integral part of the development process and cannot be considered in isolation from it.' See, more generally, Ian H. Rowlands, 'Achieving sustainable development: getting a good thing', *Third World Quarterly*, 14:2 (1993), pp. 387–95.

15   See, not least of all, Principle 21 of the Stockholm Declaration, which was further consolidated by Principle 2 of the Rio Declaration. I return to this point in the Conclusions.

V
Catalysts

11

Catalysts and ozone layer depletion

Political entrepreneurs

During the international political negotiations on the ozone layer, United Nations Environment Programme (UNEP) Executive Director Mostafa Tolba was undoubtedly the most visible and dominant individual. Mere evidence of visibility and dominance, however, do not necessarily qualify one as a 'political entrepreneur'. Indeed, whatever Tolba's accomplishments, they could have conceivably been derived from his position as the head of a major UN organisation, and not from his own, personal qualities. This was not, however, the case. On the ozone layer issue, Mostafa Tolba was a decisive political entrepreneur.

Oran Young, for one, reports that 'Tolba played a key link in translating the rapidly evolving scientific picture regarding ozone depletion into terms that were relevant to processes of institutional bargaining at the international level'.[1] Richard Benedick, additionally, singles out Tolba for his unique efforts, particularly highlighting his role as a broker:

> UNEP's Mostafa Tolba provided overall personal leadership, initiating critical consultations with key governments, private interest groups, and international organizations. During the negotiations, he moved from group to group, arguing for flexibility, applying pressure, often floating his own proposals as a stimulus to the participants.[2]

Others echo these sentiments. Tolba often used his creativity to steer negotiators around potential obstacles. Moreover, his inspiration and obvious desire to find ways to preserve the ozone layer, attributes that were more abstract, were also central to the success of the process. Thus, particular organisational and management skills built upon a background of deep, personal commitment helped Mostafa Tolba function as an effective political entrepreneur during efforts to achieve international co-operation on the ozone layer.

A number of representatives from individual states were also important entrepreneurs. Richard Benedick, in particular, played a vital role. During the negotiations leading up to the 1987 Montreal Protocol, Benedick (who was US Deputy Assistant Secretary of State for environment, health and natural resource issues) was the lead negotiator for the United States. Although Young identifies him as a 'structural leader', because of his ability to use American power to 'urge' the EC representatives to accede to an international agreement,[3] his performance may well have been more multifarious than Young acknowledges. Indeed, during the negotiations, there were a number of instances when Benedick drew upon his personal skills, rather than the power derived from the position that he occupied. Many of these are documented (often in anecdotal form) in his own book on the ozone layer negotiations.[4]

In addition to Benedick, other representatives of the United States government also served as important catalysts in the drive for an international agreement. Perhaps not surprisingly, Benedick himself highlights this, but so too does Peter Haas: the former reports that US officials 'undertook extensive diplomatic and scientific initiatives to promote an ozone protection plan to other countries, many of which were initially hostile or indifferent to the idea',[5] while the latter recounts how 'able US diplomacy' was crucial in selling policy positions to other countries.[6] Although many of the actions of the American diplomats were undoubtedly, like their leader, 'structurally based', others were, nevertheless, 'entrepreneurially based'.[7]

On the other side of the Atlantic Ocean, meanwhile, Laurens Brinkhorst, the European Communities' chief negotiator during this period, also played an important role. Although the EC members were more hesitant about concluding an agreement than the Americans, his ability to forge a common EC view on the issue was a significant accomplishment.[8]

Former British Prime Minister Margaret Thatcher is another individual whose efforts catalysed efforts to realise international co-operation on the ozone layer issue. Prior to her well-known speech to the United Kingdom Royal Society in September 1988,[9] Thatcher was not thought to harbour much concern for the environment. In

1985, for example, she labelled environmentalists as 'the enemy within',[10] and during the 1982 Falklands/Malvinas War, she remarked: 'when you've spent half your political life dealing with humdrum issues like the environment . . . it's exciting to have a real crisis on your hands'.[11] Nevertheless, from the end of 1988 until the end of her tenure as British Prime Minister in November 1990, Thatcher adopted a noticeably different stance. She hosted two important conferences on the ozone layer depletion issue in March 1989 and June 1990,[12] at which significant progress towards the goal of international co-operation was made. The higher profile accorded these gatherings, because of Thatcher's personal interest and involvement, was integral to their success.

Additionally, some Scandinavians and Canadians also acted as important political entrepreneurs on the ozone layer issue, particularly during the period of negotiations before September 1987. In addition to educating other countries' representatives about the importance of the environment, the Canadians and the Scandinavians did much to 'build bridges' between the opposing US and EC delegations. While the Canadians generally had had a close relationship with the Americans since the nineteenth century, the warmth of this friendship increased significantly in 1984 with the election of a pro-US, conservative government to Ottawa. On the other side of the Atlantic Ocean, meanwhile, the Scandinavians not only had had strong political, economic and geographical bonds with the states of the European Communities but also the fact that Denmark was a member of both the unofficial 'Nordic' grouping and the official EC organisation provided a more direct link between Scandinavia and Western Europe. Although this dual membership might sometimes give rise to crises of identity for the members of the Danish government, it was often used by the Nordics as a conduit to feed both research and policy ideas into the discussions of the European Communities. These respective links meant that the conflicting Americans and Europeans had intermediaries through which they could negotiate and communicate.

Furthermore, the Canadians put forth their own proposals in order to try to break the trans-Atlantic stalemate during the mid-1980s. A number of participants recognise that the Canadian compromise proposed during the Leesburg (VA) meeting in 1986[13] not only helped to resolve a negotiating impasse but also helped to create a better (small-'a') atmosphere – the 'Leesburg Spirit' – in which the negotiations were subsequently conducted.[14] By drawing attention to important concepts, by building bridges and by inventing new policy options, particular individuals' creativity and ingenuity often helped the participants in the ozone layer discussions to clear negotiating hurdles, or simply to keep on track.[15]

Delegations from the developing world also yielded political entrepreneurs. Consider, for example, one who emerged at the Fourth Meeting of the Parties – namely, Indian Environment and Forests Minister, Kamal Nath. As the number of Parties to the Montreal Protocol grew during the late 1980s and, particularly, the early 1990s, the ways in which the negotiations were structured and chaired became increasingly important. This was perhaps never better evident than at the meeting in Copenhagen in 1992. Nath not only chaired the conference's plenary sessions but together with the UNEP Executive Director and the Dutch Environment Minister, he also chaired the informal consultations that took place among smaller (ad hoc) groups of states. His particular skills in these positions were revealed most vividly during the last scheduled day of the conference.

The meeting's final plenary began approximately an hour and a half late, because last-minute details were still being worked out behind closed doors. Once the proposed document (which contained the various 'deals' that had been agreed) was brought to all of the delegates, Nath made it clear that if it were not accepted in its entirety, then the whole package would have to be reopened for negotiation. While cautiously optimistic of its acceptance, UNEP Secretariat officials nevertheless thought that an afternoon session would be needed, so that work on it could continue. Nath, however, had other plans. Proceeding at a brisk pace, he allowed little to stand in the way of the proposal's acceptance. In the end, therefore, the Indian Minister's piece of brinkmanship proved to be very astute, and the champagne was poured with lunch.

The list of individuals who acted as political entrepreneurs during the ozone layer negotiations does not end there. A complete catalogue needs to include a number of others, many of whom come from within the ranks of national delegations. Steve Lee-Bapty (from the United Kingdom), for example, displayed considerable skill while serving as the chair of numerous meetings. Juan Mateos (from Mexico), additionally, commanded significant respect from a number of delegations, particularly within the developing world. He served as chair of numerous meetings, the most important of which was the Executive Committee of the Interim Multilateral Ozone Fund. Officials from international organisations also served to aid the process of co-operation. UNEP officials, in particular, were important. Working within the Global Environmental Monitoring Service (GEMS), Peter Usher and others helped to maintain momentum, especially when a number of states' representatives were not particularly enthusiastic about the negotiations. Moreover, the Ozone Secretariat in Nairobi, after 1991 adeptly headed by K. Madhava Sarma, did much to facilitate the formal process. In these ways, therefore, political entrepreneurs emerged from a range of quarters on the ozone layer issue.

Non-governmental organisations

The involvement of non-governmental organisations (NGOs) on the ozone layer issue can be traced back to the original SST debate in the United States during the late 1960s and early 1970s. Douglas Ross highlights, in particular, the involvement of the Citizens League Against the Sonic Boom, the Friends of the Earth and the Environmental Defense Fund.[16]

With the greater popularisation of the issue after the publication of the CFC hypothesis in 1974, the most active NGOs continued to be found in North America. Their initial efforts concentrated upon 'spray cans', arguing that CFCs should be banned as aerosol propellants. A number of campaigns, largely orchestrated by environmental organisations, effectively mobilised public opinion and thus helped to prompt US legislation. After this success (in 1977), it was left to the Natural Resources Defense Council to continue to highlight the issue after it fell from political agendas during the early 1980s. Indeed, the study in Chapter 5 has shown how the 1984 lawsuit brought against the Environmental Protection Agency, forcing them to agree to formulate further CFC regulations, was instrumental in extending US policy action.[17]

After the discovery of the ozone crater above Antarctica, the ozone layer depletion issue became internationalised to a greater extent; so too did the work of the NGOs. Consider, for example, the following: in Canada, a public awareness campaign about the damage being done to the ozone layer had been started well in advance of similar campaigns in the states of the European Communities. Therefore, once West European NGOs started to campaign actively on the ozone layer issue during the late 1980s, they were briefed and given information by their Canadian counterparts. The international network of Friends of the Earth affiliates proved particularly conducive: the Canadian branch provided the British group with information that enabled the latter to campaign on the issue so successfully. Under the charismatic leadership of Jonathan Porritt, Friends of the Earth UK targeted CFCs in spray cans, launching a public education programme and threatening a consumer boycott. This was particularly effective. As a result, 'three major British manufacturers of aerosol cans (Unilever, Beecham, and Gillette) switched propellants after learning from surveys that one-third of the British consumers were not buying those with CFCs'.[18] The construction of such transnational channels of communication between north American and European NGOs, Michael Oppenheimer argues, allowed 'technical information on ozone depletion and the potential availability of CFC substitutes [to be exchanged]'.[19] On the other side of the Atlantic, meanwhile, US NGOs continued their work: most significantly, targeting McDonald's fast-food packaging in a 'Styro-Wars' campaign.[20] The NGOs' work at the grass-roots, therefore, was influential.

Non-governmental organisations also played a significant role at the 'elite-level' – that is, in the technical debate and the formal negotiations.[21] Benedick, for one, recognises that environmental groups provided ideas, opinions and actions that 'often proved critical to the successful outcome' of the negotiations.[22] Meanwhile, Oppenheimer argues that, during the Montreal Protocol discussions, the NGOs' 'unique viewpoint probably swayed negotiators on not a few points'.[23] The groups that were particularly active in these regards were the Natural Resources Defense Council (US), the World Resources Institute (US), Friends of the Earth (which was based in the United Kingdom, although it operated around the world) and Greenpeace International (based in Amsterdam, but with affiliates worldwide).

Nevertheless, many maintain that NGOs' contributions should not be overstated. Peter Haas, for example, argues that:

> In general, public sentiment and the activities of nongovernmental organizations such as Friends of the Earth had little impact on the adoption of CFC controls. Instead, they tended to merely reinforce government regulations that had already been introduced.[24]

Perhaps if there had never been an ozone crater, they maintain, might the NGOs have had a more important role to play?

Issue tangibility

The ozone layer issue is a highly tangible one. Many perceive a fundamental cause–effect link on the ozone layer depletion issue: an individual act (the use of certain aerosol sprays) directly increases the chances of harm to the individual (in the form of skin cancer).[25] This feeling was reinforced by media reporting on the issue, particularly after 1985. Stunning, dynamic and colourful pictures on the television evening news were able to demonstrate, both quickly and dramatically, how a hole in the sky was allowing destructive forces to hit the earth's surface.[26] Similarly, the effects of such penetration – increased incidence of skin cancer – could also be displayed in an equally dramatic and alarming manner. Because the media were able to present three straightforward images – a spray can, a map of Antarctica with a large crater over it and a person suffering from skin cancer – to demonstrate cause and effect, they helped sensitise the public on the issue.[27] Benedick argues that in the United States, in particular, the 'interest of the media in the ozone issue and the collaboration with television and press by diplomats, environmental groups, and legislators had a major influence on governmental decisions and on the international negotiations'.[28]

A number of scholars argue that mobilised public opinion was influential in the ozone layer depletion issue. While examining its impact in Europe, Markus Jachtenfuchs, for example, asserts that: 'It was the pressure of their respective national public opinion which has finally pushed the negotiators to forward-looking behaviour.'[29] John Gribbin reinforces this general argument by specifically citing the importance of environmental issues for the West German electorate.[30] Oppenheimer and Boyle, in fact, suggest that pressure from the German public acted as the original catalyst in a process that culminated in the Europeans' change of policy during the late 1980s.[31] A report from the Canadian House of Commons, meanwhile, effectively demonstrates that the impact of public opinion on the ozone layer issue was by no means restricted to only one side of the Atlantic Ocean:

> Public pressure has been an effective force in accelerating the removal of CFCs from some products. The two most notable examples are the

recent removal of CFCs from most aerosol products, and the substitution of an HCFC and pentane for CFCs in some cups and
packaging materials made from rigid foam. The public can do even
more, for example, by choosing non-pressurized dispensers, or products packaged in non-petroleum-based material, or products with
substantially reduced packaging. . . . Just as consumers have been a
driving force for industrial responsibility in the use of CFCs in the
past, they can be a potent lobby for future initiatives to ban ozone-
depleting substances and to control use of their substitutes. Public
involvement is essential. That involvement in turn depends on a well
informed public.[32]

Furthermore, Richard Benedick notes the influence of public opinion
in the United States:

[E]ducating and mobilizing public opinion can be a powerful force to
generate pressure for action on often hesitant politicians. . . . [On the
ozone layer depletion issue, a]roused consumers brought about the
collapse of the CFC aerosol market.[33]

Oppenheimer, in addition, echoes these sentiments, for he argues
that the pressures exerted upon both government and industry
accelerated efforts to realise international co-operation by shifting
US officials' perception of the issue.[34] The ozone layer was perceived,
by many, to be an issue of significance, one that could have consequence for their personal well-being.

A conducive international environment

When political negotiations towards an ozone layer agreement
began in 1982, they did so under the shadow of the Second Cold
War. Although Cold War politics did not control the activities of the
Co-ordinating Committee on the Ozone Layer (CCOL) during the
early 1980s, they did nevertheless play some role.[35] Consider, for
instance, the apparently trivial matter of participants' lists – those
documents that record the attendance of delegates at the CCOL's
meetings. Once they were produced, the Soviet Union's representatives would lodge a formal protest because the participation of
the West German Environment Ministry would be recorded on this
document. Their opposition was not to West German attendance;
rather, they objected to the fact that the West German ministry was
located in West Berlin, a fact that contravened the terms of the

Quadripartite Agreement on Berlin.[36] Efforts to preserve the ozone layer would thus be distracted, because the four powers' representatives would have to be brought together and the obligatory protocol would have to be enacted. UNEP officials realised that this was always likely to happen, so they would not release the participants' list until the last possible moment. Nevertheless, Cold War politics would still disrupt the proceedings, which were primarily directed at preserving the ozone layer.

The Cold War, however, dissipated during the middle of the 1980s, and this had some important ramifications for the ozone layer negotiations. The policy of *glasnost*, for example, contributed to the Soviet Union's decision to release its CFC production figures for the first time in 1986. Greater openness, on both sides of the Iron Curtain, allowed more interactions to be tolerated. Therefore, ministerial contacts, a minimum quantity of which would be necessary for any progress to be realised, could be more easily undertaken. Moreover, scientific links, again important catalysts to progress, could also be more easily forged. In fact, atmospheric scientists from the United States and the Soviet Union began collaborative work in 1987. Richard Benedick argues that this type of interaction 'contributed to a gradual weakening of Soviet opposition to international controls on ozone-depleting compounds'.[37] Renewed East–West calm, therefore, was a spur to the international negotiations to preserve the ozone layer.

Notes

1 Oran R. Young, 'Political leadership and regime formation: on the development of institutions in international society', *International Organization*, 45:3 (Summer 1991), p. 294.

2 Richard Elliot Benedick, *Ozone Diplomacy: New Directions in Safeguarding the Planet* (London, Harvard University Press, 1991), p. 208.

3 Young notes that Benedick was able to make 'good use of threats to restrict access to the American market as a means of gaining acceptance of the principle of across-the-board cuts in the production and consumption of CFCs' (Young, 'Political leadership and regime formation', p. 290).

4 Benedick, *Ozone Diplomacy*.

5 Ibid., pp. 205–6.

6 Peter M. Haas, 'Obtaining international environmental protection through epistemic consensus', in Ian H. Rowlands and Malory Greene (eds), *Global Environmental Change and International Relations* (Basingstoke,

Macmillan, 1992), p. 50.

7 The work of both Robert Watson (originally from the United Kingdom, but subsequently employed by NASA) and Eileen Claussen (from the United States) also deserves recognition. MacKenzie argues that Watson's efforts, in particular, were crucial:

> It could be argued that, if Bob Watson had been hit by a bus in 1980, we would not now have a treaty to save the ozone layer. . . . Watson did not discover the hole in the ozone layer, calculate how CFCs reach the stratosphere, or write the models that predict the damage. What he did do, however, was to bring the scientists who did that work together to reach a consensus on what was happening. He then helped to translate what they said into a language that politicians could not obfuscate or ignore. The result was the ozone treaty.

(Debora MacKenzie, 'How to use science and influence people', *New Scientist*, 122 (29 April 1989), p. 69.)

8 Brinkhorst's identification as a political entrepreneur redresses an imbalance that is evident in Benedick's book (Benedick, *Ozone Diplomacy*). In that work, Benedick suggests that Brinkhorst impeded efforts to realise international co-operation. This view, however, is not shared by others who were involved in the negotiations. See, more generally, the review of Benedick's book by a member of the British government's negotiating team: Fiona McConnell, 'Book reviews', *International Environmental Affairs*, 3:4 (Autumn 1991), pp. 318–20.

9 See, for example, Martin Jacques, 'Why Thatcher turned green', *The Sunday Times* (London) (2 October 1988).

10 Cited in Larry Tye, 'All environmental talk, no action', *Citizen* (Ottawa) (22 July 1989).

11 Quoted in Jonathan Porritt, 'Can the Conservatives go green?', *Earth Matters*, 2 (no date given), pp. 2–3.

12 They were, respectively, the 'Saving the ozone layer conference' and the 'Second Meeting of the Parties to the Montreal Protocol'. Both were held in London.

13 See G.V. Buxton *et al.*, 'A Canadian contribution to the consideration of strategies for protecting the ozone layer', presented at the UNEP Workshop on Economic Issues Related to Control of CFCs, Leesburg, VA, 8–12 September 1986.

14 Geoffrey Lean, *Action on Ozone* (Nairobi, UNEP, 1989), pp. 7–8.

15 Some, however, argue that many of the representatives from these states have subsequently reduced their entrepreneurial activities. In 1992, for example, delegates from non-governmental organisations complained that the usually 'progressive' states were no longer pushing the larger states to take more stringent measures to protect the ozone layer.

16 Douglas Ross, 'The Concorde compromise: the politics of decision-making', *Bulletin of the Atomic Scientists*, 34:3 (March 1978), p. 49.

17   See, for example, Paul J. Allen, 'Overview', *Environment*, 32:10 (December 1990), p. 3.

18   Gareth Porter and Janet Welsh Brown, *Global Environmental Politics* (Oxford, Westview Press, 1991), p. 50.

19   Michael Oppenheimer, 'Responding to climate change: the crucial role of the NGOs', in H-J Karpe, D. Otten and S.C. Trinidade (eds), *Climate and Development: Climatic Change and Variability and the Resulting Social, Economic and Technological Implications* (London, Springer-Verlag, 1990), p. 345.

20   Elizabeth Cook, 'Global environmental advocacy: citizen activism in protecting the ozone layer', *Ambio*, 19:6–7 (October 1990), p. 335.

21   This was particularly the case after the discovery of the ozone crater in 1985. As for before that discovery, Sand reports that 'no conservation NGOs attended the Vienna Conference [in March 1985]', and that while 'industry spokesmen were also official members of several national delegations (for example, those of Japan and West Germany), not one of the more than one hundred national and EEC delegates and observers came from the environmental NGO community' (Peter H. Sand, 'Protecting the ozone layer: the Vienna Convention is adopted', *Environment*, 27:5 (June 1985), p. 42).

22   Richard Elliot Benedick, 'Protecting the ozone layer: new directions in diplomacy', in Jessica Tuchman Mathews (ed.), *Preserving the Global Environment: the Challenge of Shared Leadership* (London, W.W. Norton & Company, 1991), p. 146.

23   Oppenheimer, 'Responding to climate change', p. 345.

24   Peter M. Haas, 'Banning chlorofluorocarbons: epistemic community efforts to protect stratospheric ozone', *International Organization*, 46:1 (Winter 1992), p. 218.

25   Although conceived in this way, there is no link between the recently recorded increase in rates of skin cancer and the recorded depletion in the ozone layer. There is a greater incidence of skin cancer, not least because of changing habits among the populace. This led one researcher to label it 'the "yuppie disease" because it was to be observed more among affluent indoor workers who holiday in the sun' (Professor Mark Elwood, University of Nottingham, quoted in Tim Radford, 'Ozone loss spells end of sunbathing', *Guardian* (London) (30 November 1988)). Regardless, ozone layer depletion incited a fear among individuals of a tangible and personal harm. Indeed, the fact that President Reagan had two skin cancers removed (in 1985 and 1987) may have had an accelerating influence upon the process of international co-operation!

26   The unexpected discovery of the ozone crater in 1985 was, in this instance, crucial. Further, the similarity with the US Strategic Defense Initiative (the 'Star Wars' programme) – that is, instead of a nuclear weapon penetrating a 'peace shield', the aggressive weapon is ultraviolet radiation

penetrating an 'ozone shield' – may have helped members of the general public in the United States envisage the issue more easily.

27   Indeed, Hollywood even got into the act. In 1977, a film entitled *Day of the Animals* was produced. A writer for *The Financial Times* describes it as follows: 'An imbalance in the Earth's ozone layer causes animals living at high altitudes to become vicious – and a mountain trek turns into a nightmare for a group of hikers.' (*The Financial Times* (London), no date given.)

28   Benedick, *Ozone Diplomacy*, p. 205.

29   Markus Jachtenfuchs, 'The European Community and the protection of the ozone layer', *Journal of Common Market Studies*, 28:3 (March 1990), p. 275.

30   He says that: 'The reason [for action on ozone layer depletion] is simply public pressure, in a country [West Germany] where environmental politics matter . . .'. (John Gribbin, *The Hole in the Sky* (London, Corgi, 1988), p. 146).

31   They also note the importance of 'pressure brought by German greens' (Michael Oppenheimer and Robert Boyle, *Dead Heat: the Race Against the Greenhouse Effect* (London, I.B. Tauris & Co., 1990), pp. 48 and 193).

32   The Standing Committee on Environment, House of Commons, Canada, *Deadly Releases CFCs* (Ottawa, Canadian Government Publishing Center, June 1990), p. 45.

33   Benedick, 'Protecting the ozone layer', p. 145.

34   Oppenheimer, 'Responding to climate change', p. 343.

35   See, generally, Tapani Vaahtoranta, 'The control of atmospheric pollution: is there an East–West conflict?', in Jyrki Kakonen (ed.), *Perspectives on Environmental Conflict and International Politics* (London, Pinter, 1992), pp. 44–54.

36   This agreement was signed by the Soviet Union, the United States, Great Britain and France on 3 September 1971.

37   Benedick, *Ozone Diplomacy*, p. 101.

12

Catalysts and climate change

Political entrepreneurs

In order to discover if any political entrepreneurs were able to influence the politics of climate change, it makes sense to begin the search among the entrepreneurs from the ozone layer negotiations. Given the analogous nature of the two issues, the same individuals could have acted in similar entrepreneurial fashions on both issues of global atmospheric change.

I begin by examining the role of former UNEP Executive Director Mostafa Tolba, for there is wide agreement that his actions during the negotiations leading to international co-operation on ozone layer protection were pivotal. His methods for achieving such ends have, however, been questioned by some. Mark Imber reports that: 'Numerous individuals attest to the strong personal style of Mostapha Tolba's term of office, to his extraordinary work-rate, his reluctance to delegate authority (in particular in the matter of appointments) and to his single-mindedness in the promotion of the work and role of UNEP.'[1] While Benedick refers to his manner of 'applying pressure', others have been less diplomatic. No one doubted Tolba's extraordinary abilities, but his style led some to resent his level of influence. Because many individuals – particularly representatives of Latin American states – felt that they had been cajoled and manipulated by Tolba during the ozone layer negotiations, they wanted to ensure that it did not happen again. By 1990, consequently, they had become automatically suspicious of any proposal that he put forward. Additionally, they thought that Tolba (and UNEP more generally) was too concerned with the North's 'global environmental agenda' – that is, issues like ozone layer depletion, climate change and biological diversity. Therefore, a loss of confidence in the individual and the organisation prompted a number of developing countries to want to wrest control of the climate change issue from UNEP. With the creation of the INC by a UNGA Resolution in late 1990, this had been achieved.[2] The UNEP Executive-Director, accordingly, lost his ability to 'tweak the process', as he had done during the ozone layer negotiations. A significant political entrepreneur who had catalysed the international co-operative process on the ozone layer was, thus, barred from playing the same role during the climate change negotiations.

In lieu of solely UNEP, a number of institutions became involved in the political negotiations on climate change. It seems logical, therefore, to direct attention to the bureaucratic summits of these organisations in order to discover if a surrogate political entrepreneur arose on the climate change issue. The most significant institutions were the Intergovernmental Panel on Climate Change (IPCC) and the Intergovernmental Negotiating Committee for a Framework Convention on Climate Change (INC) Secretariat. The former was headed by Bert Bolin, a Swedish scientist who had been involved in climate change issues for over a decade, and the latter by Michael Zammit Cutajar, a Maltese national who had worked in the United Nations system for twenty years. In addition, similar claims of responsibility were being made by other international organisations, including UNEP.[3] Although no one doubted the capabilities of any of the individuals who headed these various bodies, the sheer fact that the climate change responsibilities were the concern of a larger number of international organisations lessened the ease with which any single individual might be able to play a strong, entrepreneurial role.

Political entrepreneurs during the ozone layer negotiations, however, also emerged from among the ranks of national governments. Once again, using this experience as a guide, I turn to the United States. Before looking at specifics, however, note that the question of whether American entrepreneurial efforts are needed in this area is addressed by Benedick:

> As the largest emitter of both ozone-destroying chemicals and greenhouse gases, the United States has enormous potential to influence the policy considerations of other governments in favor of environmental protection. In fact, because of the geographic size and population of the United States, its economic and scientific strength, and its inter-

national interests and influences, progress in addressing global environmental problems can probably not be achieved without American leadership.[4]

Although his Amerocentric analysis should not be accepted passively, it seems reasonable to suggest that enthusiastic American participation would, *ceteris paribus*, quicken the realisation of international co-operation.[5] The chief negotiator for the United States during the duration of the Bush Administration was William Reilly, Administrator of the Environmental Protection Agency. Like some others in the international negotiations, he was generally recognised to be a highly competent individual. His ability to act as an effective entrepreneur, however, was hindered during this period by the US Administration's position on the issue. Although it was generally believed that Reilly supported a more active policy posture on climate change, the reluctance of other individuals in the US White House to endorse any policy commitments effectively served to suppress Reilly's entrepreneurial talents.[6] Once again, where there had been an effective political entrepreneur catalysing the drive towards international co-operation on the ozone layer issue, none existed on the global warming issue through its early political days.

The issue, nevertheless, was not totally devoid of such catalysts. The route that the negotiations followed, however, revealed that some of the most significant political entrepreneurs on this issue were European. The organisation of a number of key conferences during the late 1980s helped to focus attention on the issue; many of these took place in Europe. Two of the most important were held in 1989: one of the first conferences to consider the issue of global atmospheric pollution was convened by the Dutch, French and Norwegian governments in The Hague in March; and the Dutch, under the enthusiastic leadership of Ed Nijpels (Minister of Housing, Physical Planning and Environment), organised the Ministerial Conference on Atmospheric Pollution in Noordwijk, the Netherlands in November. The French, furthermore, by pushing for the creation of some sort of global environmental fund, advanced a new idea that helped negotiators overcome some initial bargaining impediments. Jean Ripert from France, who chaired the INC meetings in pursuit of a Climate Change Convention, also deserves mention.[7] Finally, former UK Environment Secretary Michael Howard is widely credited with brokering the compromise wording of the Climate Change Convention that realised US participation. By convening conferences, proposing policy options and mediating disagreements, therefore, these governments' representatives helped both to create fora for discussions and to accelerate the process of negotiation. By their actions, both the leaders and the 'nameless' bureaucrats acted as political entrepreneurs.

Non-governmental organisations

There was an incredible rise in the number and size of non-governmental organisations (NGOs) during the 1980s. In the United Kingdom, for example, membership of the Friends of the Earth increased almost seven-fold to 200,000 between 1985 and 1990, while in the United States, membership of Greenpeace more than quadrupled to two million during the same period.[8] With this growth in size came an expansion of resources, many of which were successfully used to heighten the level of sophistication. The scope of the NGO conference that was held in parallel to the 1992 United Nations Conference on Environment and Development (called the 'Global Forum') is evidence of the size, while the construction of a variety of electronic communication networks is testimony to the sophistication.

The result was that NGOs were being given access to the formal, intergovernmental negotiations to a greater extent. The Bergen conference in May 1990 is particularly noteworthy. At this meeting, Paul Brown reports that for 'the first time industry, trade unions, environmental groups, women and youth groups took part in the conference and were consulted by ministers in an attempt to bring democracy to the Bergen Process'.[9] Although this meeting was not necessarily meant to set a precedent, it almost certainly did. Indeed, any NGO that could demonstrate its competence in and relevance to the debate received formal accreditation during the UNCED process. Although their rights did not equal those of states, NGOs were entitled to make oral and written statements to formal meetings, and, at the discretion of the Chairman, to attend 'informal' inter-governmental negotiating sessions as well. Additionally, a number of NGO representatives were members of states' delegations.

Thus, by the late 1980s and the early 1990s, the days when all environmental pressure groups were made up of 'fruit juice drinkers and sandal wearers'[10] appeared to have been long-gone.[11] Instead,

NGOs were staffed by individuals who were well equipped – both intellectually and materially – to participate in the various debates. Lynton Caldwell contends that: 'Resources of money and appropriately skilled personnel have increased the ability of [NGOs] to influence the policy agendas of governments and to follow through to obtain action.'[12] Consequently, as the politically formative years of the climate change issue arose, NGOs were much better placed to play a role in the political process.

And NGOs were active on the issue. Michael Oppenheimer reports that there was 'an incipient international [NGO] network on the atmosphere in place which served as a mechanism for dissemination of information on climate warming'.[13] This was formalised in March 1989, when, at a meeting held in Germany, a number of NGOs from the North decided to establish a 'Climate Action Network'. Membership of the network has since grown to include NGOs in the South as well. The members of this network all shared a common concern for the greenhouse effect and agreed to co-operate in the development and implementation of short- and long-term strategies.

A combination of increased capacity and greater access allowed NGOs to take highly visible roles during the negotiations towards the Climate Change Convention. Numerous groups – most significantly, CAPE (Consortium for Action to Protect the Earth), an alliance of six of the most established US NGOs – contributed to the policy debate, critiquing drafts emerging from the negotiations and proposing alternatives.[14] Pulvenis expands:

> The NGOs not only provided delegations with copious documentation, they also published daily a bulletin reporting on the work carried out in the various working groups. This was specially important – and particularly for small delegations – due to the absence of summary records. In addition, a number of seminars, forums and meetings were also organized by NGOs in order to provide an opportunity for a more flexible exchange of points of view.[15]

Additionally, NGOs were invited to express their views during official meetings, and their participation in the ongoing process is now recognized under Article 7.6 of the Framework Convention on Climate Change.

However, this increased level of participation by NGOs during the formal negotiations was not viewed favourably by all government representatives. While the input of some NGOs' representatives during the meetings was helpful to negotiators, others (from several major developing countries, and to a lesser extent, some industrialised countries) viewed them as undesirable interlopers. Indeed, at least one country's delegation regretted their choice of NGO representatives to sit on their delegation:

> David McRobert, Pollution Probe's [a Canadian NGO] global warming programme coordinator, who attended some of the policy-making sessions [at the Second World Climate Conference in Geneva in 1990], caught Canadian bureaucrats red-handed trying to convince delegates from other countries to take a lenient line on the international response to global warming. At a drafting session for the ministers' statement, which all countries would sign, McRobert listened in disbelief as two Canadian delegates encouraged other countries to gut the wording of the final statement and eliminate all references to the Toronto target. McRobert, who released the details of the Canadian deception to the media, was later chastised by Kirk Dawson, a senior civil servant with Environment Canada.[16]

There was deep disappointment on the part of some Canadian government officials at this time.

Additionally, 'stunts' by NGOs like Greenpeace at different conferences irritated many officials from national delegations. Indeed, such actions caused some of them to exercise extreme caution during dialogues with NGO representatives. One effect was to restrict the access of NGOs' representatives to some states' officials. Moreover, notwithstanding the greater access of NGO representatives to the negotiation process, the meetings' chairs (state representatives) were still able to convene small 'informal-informals', 'contact groups' and 'friends' gatherings, which thus allowed her or him to negotiate among personally selected representatives (predominantly from national governments). This happened during the run-up to the deadline of the Climate Change Convention negotiations in May 1992. With the deadline fast approaching, much of the hard negotiating took place among representatives from thirty (or so) key states. Consequently, when the chips were down, the NGOs' representatives were not in the room.

Issue tangibility

Is climate change a tangible issue? There is some evidence to suggest that it is tangible enough to generate concern. Riley Dunlap, for one, cites a 1989 report which found that 75 per cent of Americans felt that the problem posed by the greenhouse effect was 'very serious' or 'somewhat serious'.[17] There was, nevertheless, still great confusion regarding global warming.

A number of studies, supported by experimental and survey work, found that although people were concerned about climatic change, the complex scientific realities were making it difficult for them to comprehend the phenomenon fully. Baruch Fischoff, from Carnegie-Mellon University, elaborates by reporting that: 'Climate change is tricky. . . . People have a limited understanding of the scientific processes contributing to it. They may know a fair amount, but the pieces don't fit together.'[18] Another investigation, by the Public Agenda Foundation, found 'tremendous confusion [about the causes of global warming among lay people]. People may think they know. But once you get beneath the surface, their understanding is very fragmentary, very unclear.'[19]

This is understandable. Global warming, as far as disasters go, is much more diffuse than most others. Sheldon Ungar argues that global warming 'is not founded on everyday experience, has not immediate effects, and is not readily observable'.[20] Indeed, it is difficult for any individual to make the link between a personal act that enhanced global warming – for example, driving a car – with the consequences of a warmer world – for example, rising sea levels. One survey, for example, found that only 21 per cent of respondents felt that they could 'do a lot about' the greenhouse effect.[21] Even if the link could be made, the perceived impact of the identified 'harm' upon the individual was not readily apparent. Although the consequences might eventually be personal, the image of a sea that was three or four inches higher did not give rise to any significant level of personal concern among most people. Thus, it is not surprising to find that Holdgate notes that most people 'in the developed countries have yet to recognise their own personal involvement in global systems of interdependence'.[22]

In the developing world, moreover, the perceived cause–effect link among the population was even more diffuse. At an international meeting in Nairobi, Maneka Gandhi (Indian Environment Minister at the time) allegedly told UNEP Executive Director Mostafa Tolba of the difficulties she had in making the global warming issue 'real' for the people of her country. One of the difficulties, she explained, was that most of the 800 million citizens of India could not actually picture a sea, let alone a sea-level rise![23] Survey work in the developing world supports this assertion. One study found that environmental concerns are 'highly coloured by [peoples'] personal experience. No room here for abstract concerns about the global environment.' More specifically, it also found that 'global warming is not a priority'.[24]

The climate does, at time, have impact in this way, but usually only when it manifests itself in changes in the weather. Two examples from the history of the climate change debate support this assertion. One report from 1978 notes: 'Two severe winters and a period of prolonged drought in California have, like the proverbial hangman's noose, had a wonderful concentrating effect on the collective minds of US political administrators.'[25] Secondly, exactly ten years later, Chapter 3 has already shown how the hot North American summer focused attention upon an international conference in Toronto and Congressional hearings in Washington, DC.[26] However, subsequent cold winters, particularly in North America, eradicated memories of hot summers from the minds of many.

Global warming's complexity did not allow issue tangibility to force the pace of international co-operation. This meant that traditional mobilisers of public opinion were not able to act as effectively in the absence of a perceived cause–effect link: for the media, global warming could not easily be adapted to a 'sound bite'; for NGOs, meanwhile, their members were not able to organise campaigns on the issue as easily as on other issues. The conclusion for Frances Cairncross, therefore, is that the global warming issue was in this way 'disadvantaged', *vis-à-vis* the ozone layer depletion issue: 'One reason for the successful negotiation of the Montreal agreement was the evidence that ozone depletion was dangerous to health. Global warming does not yet enjoy this perverse advantage.'[27]

A conducive international environment

Just as global warming was becoming a major international political issue, revolutions were sweeping through Eastern Europe. Still, some caveats from before the collapse of the Soviet empire are worth noting as we explore the processes associated with international co-operation on climate change.

One of the most remarkable acts of international co-operation, which (in a small way) helped to advance the political process, took place during the early 1980s. In 1980, an ice core, more than 2 kilometres long and thus covering more than an entire glacial cycle (160,000 years), was recovered from a drillhole at Vostok in the Antarctic. From the *Soviet* station where it was drilled, the core was taken by a specially equipped *American* transport to a laboratory in *France*, where it was analysed during the following three years. This co-operative, tripartite effort took place at the height of the Second Cold War. Though only a single episode, it nevertheless suggests that scientific co-operation need not be dependent upon broader political relations.[28]

By the mid-1980s, the gradual opening in the former Soviet Bloc countries most probably was having an impact upon the early international negotiations in ways similar to those which have been described on the ozone layer case in Chapter 11 – that is, increased information exchanges and personal interactions. As time passed, however, the changes within these countries may have also had a retarding impact upon the prospects for international co-operation.

The disintegration of the Soviet Union and some of the former sovereign states in Eastern Europe had five important ramifications. First, their internal difficulties – economic crises and political instability – meant that the attention of their leaders was primarily focused upon domestic issues. As a consequence, international negotiations did not receive high priority, and many of these countries were indeed 'paralysed' during much of the climate change negotiations.[29] Second, there was, at times, uncertainty as to where the locus of sovereignty rested; it was unclear as to which level of government had the authority or the power to discuss international environmental issues, to negotiate international treaties and to implement contractual obligations (for example, between Russia and the CIS). Third, findings brought to light by Mancur Olson suggest that the sheer fact that there are a greater number of states in international society could make it more difficult to achieve co-operation.[30] It is not yet clear if European 'unification' will be able to slow this trend. Fourthly, a number of West European states had their attention diverted. The most important example in this instance is, of course, Germany, for its reunification efforts diverted substantial energy and resources. More generally, though, the lifting of the Iron Curtain revealed a series of ecological disasters in Eastern Europe. In particular, many West Europeans were eyeing, fearfully, the old Soviet-style nuclear reactors, at work throughout Eastern Europe. Finally, the extent to which changes in Eastern Europe gave rise to conflict among the peoples of the former Yugoslavia meant further diversion of concern for countries of not only the Western Alliance but also the entire world. Consequently, institutional disintegration in Eastern Europe and the former Soviet Union might have had arresting effects upon the rate of international co-operation on climate change.

Notes

1   Mark Imber, 'Too many cooks?: the post-Rio reform of the United Nations', *International Affairs*, 69:1 (January 1993), p. 62.

2   UNGA Resolution, 'Protection of global climate for present and future generations of mankind' (A/RES/45/212, 21 December 1990).

3   Many analysts recognise that the international environmental agenda was becoming increasingly crowded during the late 1980s and early 1990s. Glen Plant reviews the numerous organisations involved in the climate change issue in particular. (Glen Plant, 'Institutional and legal responses to global climate change', in Ian H. Rowlands and Malory Greene (eds), *Global Environmental Change and International Relations* (Basingstoke, Macmillan, 1992), pp. 122–44.)

4   Richard Elliot Benedick, *Ozone Diplomacy: New Directions in Safeguarding the Planet* (London, Harvard University Press, 1991), p. 206.

5   Benedick's comments point not only to entrepreneurial leadership, but also to the need for the United States' leaders both to find it in their national interest to help to build a global warming regime and to exercise structural leadership. See Chapter 6 for a further discussion of the US position.

6   See, for example, Michael Weisskopf, 'U.S. to fight aid to halt global warming', *International Herald Tribune* (10 May 1990), p. 7.

7   Ripert took a number of initiatives: he altered the organisation of the work of the INC, he prepared a number of working documents, and he convened a number of *ad hoc* negotiation groups. On the basis of such activities, Pulvenis concludes that '[c]learly it is only as a result of this forceful drive led by Chairman Ripert that the INC was able to adopt the Convention in time for the Earth Summit' (Jean-Francois Pulvenis, 'The Framework Convention on Climate Change', in Luigi Campiglio *et al.* (eds), *The Environment After Rio: International Law and Economics* (London, Graham & Trotman, 1994), p. 91).

8   Frances Cairncross, *Costing the Earth* (London, Business Books, 1991), pp. 12–13, Tables 1 and 2.

9   Paul Brown, 'Global slow-step trips up', *Guardian* (London) (18 May 1990), p. 27.

10 George Orwell, quoted in Editorial, the *Independent* (London) (26 May 1990), p. 18.

11 Richard North observes that, by the end of the 1980s, American environmentalists had abandoned their sandals for suits ('Markets and law push US towards voluntary change', *Independent* (London) (27 September 1989), p. 26), while two others support this observation with more substantive evidence (Helen M. Ingram and Dean E. Mann, 'Interest groups and environmental policy', in James P. Lester (ed.), *Environmental Politics and Policy: Theories and Evidence* (London, Duke University Press, 1989), pp. 152–3).

12 Lynton K. Caldwell, 'Beyond environmental diplomacy: the changing institutional structure of international cooperation', in John E. Carroll (ed.), *International Environmental Diplomacy: the Management and Resolution of Transfrontier Environmental Problems* (Cambridge, Cambridge University Press, 1988), p. 19.

13 Michael Oppenheimer, 'Responding to climate change: the crucial role of the NGO's', in H-J Karpe, D. Otten and S.C. Trinidade (eds), *Climate and Development: Climatic Change and Variability and the Resulting Social, Economic and Technological Implications* (London, Springer-Verlag, 1990), p. 345.

14 See, for example, Angela Harkavy, 'The Earth Summit: a progress report on preparatory negotiations for the UNCED: the final effort', (Washington, DC, CAPE '92, 1992); Jessica T. Mathews *et al.*, *Greenhouse Warming: Negotiating a Global Regime* (Washington, DC, World Resources Institute, 1991); and William A. Nitze, *The Greenhouse Effect: Formulating a Convention* (London, Royal Institute of International Affairs, 1990).

15 Pulvenis, 'The Framework Convention on Climate Change', p. 84.

16 Andrea Imada, 'Canada's cool response to global warming', *Probe Post* (Spring 1991), p. 27.

17 Cambridge Reports and Cambridge Reports/Research International, cited in Riley E. Dunlap, 'Public opinion in the 1980s: clear consensus, ambiguous commitment', *Environment* 33:8 (October 1991), p. 36, Fig. 8.

18 Susan E. Davis, 'Greenhouse effect: the human response', *The Washington Post* (Health Section) (17 April 1990), pp. 9–10.

19 Ibid.

20 Sheldon Ungar, 'The rise and (relative) fall of global warming as a social problem', *Sociological Quarterly*, 33:4 (1992), p. 489.

21 Cited in Dunlap, 'Public opinion in the 1980s', p. 34.

22 Martin Holdgate, 'Changes in perception', in David J.R. Angell, Justyn D. Colmer and Matthew L.N. Wilkinson (eds), *Sustaining Earth: Response to the Environmental Threats* (Basingstoke, Macmillan, 1990), p. 89.

23 Author's interview with official of a national embassy, Nairobi,

Kenya, July 1991.

24   Maria Elena Hurtado, 'Lukewarm response to controls', *PS (Panoscope)*, 24 (May 1991), pp. 8 and 14.

25   David Dickson, 'A bad year for weather, a good one for climate', *Nature*, 273 (11 May 1978), p. 388.

26   Ungar argues that: 'What rendered 1988 so extraordinary was *concatenating* physical impacts *felt* by the person in the street.' Emphasis in original. (Ungar, 'The rise and (relative) decline', p. 490.)

27   Cairncross, *Costing the Earth*, p. 128.

28   Cheryl Simon Silver with Ruth S. DeFries, *One Earth One Future: Our Changing Global Environment* (Washington, DC, National Academy Press, 1990), pp. 24–5.

29   Sten Nilsson and David Pitt, *Protecting the Atmosphere: the Climate Change Convention and Its Context* (London, Earthscan, 1994), pp. 59–60.

30   Mancur Olson, *The Logic of Collective Action: Public Goods and the Theory of Groups* (Cambridge, Harvard University Press, 1965).

13

Catalysts and global environmental politics

A belief that certain elements had received insufficient attention in the literature encouraged the inclusion of my fourth hypothesis, which was that the prospects for international co-operation will increase when any of four catalysts – namely, political entrepreneurs, non-governmental organisations, issue tangibility and a conducive international environment – are present. The experience on the two issues of global atmospheric change has delivered mixed results with regard to this hypothesis. Let me briefly consider each of the four elements in turn.

The first concerns political entrepreneurs. The results seem to vindicate the decision to consider explicitly the role that individuals play in the processes associated with international co-operation. Nevertheless, there were differences between the two issues of global atmospheric change: a small number of political entrepreneurs were particularly dominant on the ozone layer depletion issue, while a larger number of individuals each had less overall impact on the climate change issue. This can be explained by the fact that the latter became a highly political issue relatively 'earlier' than the former. Consequently, individuals were less able to exercise their own free will during the negotiations, but instead were watched over more closely by their political superiors. Thus, spontaneity, ingenuity and creativity may have been suppressed and replaced by standard-operating procedures. Additionally, the increased politicisation of the climate change process *vis-à-vis* the ozone layer negotiations ensured that the same forces that propel bureaucratic politics made it difficult for a single entrepreneur to arise from among the international organisations involved.[1] Consequently, though a number of political entrepreneurs did play some role during efforts to achieve international co-operation on the climate change issue, the considerable breadth of the issue hindered the ability of any single individual to attain a significant level of entrepreneurial effectiveness.

What the investigation did not explicitly pursue, however, was the extent to which individuals can also have a *retarding* effect. On the climate change issue, one individual probably did more to thwart the effort to achieve an international co-operative agreement than any other did to advance it – namely, John Sununu. While White House Chief of Staff under US President George Bush, Sununu harboured a deep scepticism about the issue, and believed that 'the science of climate prediction [was] not developed well enough to take actions that might cause economic pain'.[2] Therefore, political entrepreneurs – or 'leadership', as Young and Osherenko have more recently called it[3] – is important, but do not assume that the leader out front should necessarily be followed.

The second catalyst is non-governmental organisations. Assessments of their influence appear to be mixed. On the one hand, it is accepted that they made some positive contributions to the process of global atmospheric change: both at the grass-roots level (mobilising public opinion to expand support for pro-active government policies) and the elite-level (proposing policy alternatives within the negotiations). Their classification as a 'catalyst', on the other hand, still appears appropriate, for there is little evidence to suggest that their involvement was essential to the achievement of international co-operation on ozone layer depletion; moreover, their influence on the climate change issue was severely restricted at times.[4]

With regard to their future role in global environmental politics, there are arguments that support apparently contrasting conclusions. On the one hand, NGOs could well play a more important role, primarily for three reasons. First, much that is needed to be done in order to achieve sustainable development involves substantial change in practices at the lowest level – that is, the everyday activities of individuals. Many NGOs have valuable experience both in education and in small-scale projects, and will therefore continue to be called upon for guidance.[5] Indeed, on issues of global atmospheric change, Greenpeace has advanced its own ozone-benign refrigerator, and, more generally, NGOs have advocated a variety of technologies to reduce carbon dioxide emissions.

Second, by bringing together groups with overlapping interests (indeed, their constituencies cut across states, issues and even time), NGOs are able to explore cross-sectoral issues in ways in which governments, for reasons of protocol, political preservation or information-overload, are not able to. 'Synergy' is the current buzz-word used to capture some of these ideas. In terms slightly more passé, ideas about functionalism – that is, the proposition that 'form follows function' – suggest that NGOs may have vital path-breaking to do as efforts are made to understand further how international co-operation on global environmental issues might be achieved.

Third, now that agreements for a range of environmental issues are in place, NGOs have important roles to play in ensuring that commitments are honoured. While monitoring governments' and industries' efforts, they can promote compliance by translating popular sentiment into political pressure. Factors like these, therefore, point to greater NGO activity on global environmental issues in the future.

Alternatively, however, a number of other arguments support the notion that the influence of NGOs might decline. Most of them emerge from differences among the NGOs – for example, in goals, in capabilities and in style. These, in themselves, are not bad things – indeed, it is argued above that this would prove particularly beneficial in the exploration of cross-sectoral issues. The problem, however, stems from the fact that this diversity is often accompanied by a widening chasm in communication. Perhaps the most significant gap in this respect is between Northern NGOs and Southern NGOs.

Such differences are not surprising, for the two sets of groups have had substantially divergent experiences. For a start, the former have traditionally been concerned with the 'environment', while the latter have been more interested in 'development'. In addition, NGOs from the Southern countries have not typically been engaged by the 'global issues'; their Northern counterparts, meanwhile, have significant experience with this set of questions. Citizens of Southern countries are also acutely aware of the enormous power that some of the Northern NGOs exert. By influencing the actions of governments and large international organisations (for example, the World Bank), Northern states' NGOs have been able to influence outcomes in the South, sometimes with less-than-favourable consequences for citizens of developing states. Consequently, there is a feeling that the large international NGOs groups from the North (many of whom

have dominated international meetings on issues of global atmospheric change[6]) may not necessarily represent broader public
opinion.

Finally, with environmental issues now being taken up (at least to
some degree) by government and industry, NGOs have had to
change roles – from 'stone-throwers' and 'watchdogs' to something
else. That 'something else', however, has yet to be defined to universal approval. On the one hand, some argue that participation in
decision-making processes is now crucial. Others, however, argue
that too close an involvement would compromise their ability to
criticise. Consequently, while some work from the inside, others
work on the outside – perhaps arguing that this is more effectual
anyway. I return to this idea in the Conclusions.

The third proposed catalyst is issue tangibility. A rudimentary
exploration of the nature of the two issues of global atmospheric
change – in particular, the extent to which each is definite and clearly
intelligible – suggests that there may be some value to the
identification of this factor as a catalyst. Indeed, it was shown that,
on the issue on which international co-operation has been realised
(that is, ozone layer depletion), there was a high degree of issue
tangibility, while on the issue without co-operation (that is, climate
change), there was not. Two arguments, however, challenge this
apparent correlation.

First, it might well be that all environmental issues are doomed to
travel through Antony Downs's 'issue-attention cycle'.[7] If this is
indeed the case, then the particular nature of any individual environmental problem will not be decisive. Instead, because all environmental issues will inevitably have a period of high public attention
('[a]larmed discovery and euphoric enthusiasm', in Downs's
words[8]), other factors will determine whether international co-
operation is realised during this 'window of opportunity'. In this
view, all environmental issues are considered the same.[9]

Second, this catalyst may be so closely related to my second
hypothesis that it does not merit special investigation elsewhere. In
other words, issue tangibility relates so intimately to perceived
interests that a thorough exploration of 'interests' would uncover the
ways in which any particular environmental issue impacts individuals' calculations of costs and benefits – that is, it would reveal the
extent to which an issue is perceptible. No repetition, therefore, is
needed. Nevertheless, the focus upon individual human beings does

remind the analyst that interests cannot necessarily be easily aggregated – some unpacking of the 'self-interested utility maximiser', as was argued in Chapter 7, is desirable.

Finally, a conducive international environment is proposed as the fourth catalyst. Analysis in Chapters 11 and 12 has focused upon the ways in which developments in relations between 'East' and 'West' affected the prospects for international co-operation. During the mid-1980s, the general thawing of East–West relations did accelerate the process on the ozone layer issue. However, the continuing disintegration of the old Soviet empire, in turn, may have hindered continued progress on the climate change issue. If, therefore, 'conducive international environment' is taken to mean a reduction of East–West tensions, then some correlation is evident.

In a more general sense, it appears that factors not directly related to the issue-area under examination appear to have an impact upon developments relating to it. Consequently, more systematic study of the role of a 'conducive international environment' in global environmental politics is desirable. Nevertheless, the question being begged is obviously, 'what is a "conducive international environment" '? While the Cold War raged, the state of relations between East and West seemed to be a highly logical (and hence defensible) candidate. With, however, the disintegration of the East–West axis, such a definition of the phrase is no longer sensible. Consequently, one should look elsewhere.

But, where? The world is, of course, a huge place; the landscape for any particular issue will consist of numerous elements. Those that might appear to be consequential could well be captured by other elements of the framework. Indeed, the motivation for the inclusion of this catalyst is that hitherto unanticipated factors will exercise influence. Some guidance is therefore needed. At this point, however, it is not clear where that search should proceed.

In summary, it was anticipated that these four catalysts affected the process of international co-operation to such an extent, and in such a unique manner, that each warranted an explicit investigation. This decision appears to have been vindicated with respect to political entrepreneurs and non-governmental organisations, for their importance as catalysts was confirmed. The influence of issue tangibility, meanwhile, may best be incorporated into other elements, while the importance of a conducive international environment has yet to be determined.

Notes

1   Graham T. Allison, *Essence of Decision: Explaining the Cuban Missile Crisis* (Boston, Little, Brown, & Company, 1971).

2   Tim Beardsley, 'Profile: political engineer', *Scientific American* (April 1991), p. 17. Hatch argues that recognition of Sununu's dismissal in late 1991 helps to explain subsequent US movement on the climate change issue. With Sununu gone, discussions within the Administration opened up to a wider range of views. (Michael T. Hatch, 'Domestic politics and international negotiations: the politics of global warming in the United States', *Journal of Environment and Development*, 2:2 (Summer 1993), pp. 27–8).

3   Oran R. Young and Gail Osherenko, 'International regime formation: findings, research priorities, and applications', in Oran R. Young and Gail Osherenko (eds), *Polar Politics: Creating International Environmental Regimes* (London, Cornell University Press, 1993), pp. 254–5 and 259.

4   Additionally, as is the case for political entrepreneurs, scholars should also be alert to the ways in which NGOs might retard efforts to realise international co-operation.

5   'By 1989, NGOs from the North were distributing an estimated [US]$6.4 billion to developing countries – about 12 per cent of all public and private development aid' (Robert Livernash, 'The growing influence of NGOs in the developing world', *Environment*, 34:5 (June 1992), p. 15).

6   At the ninth meeting of the INC in Geneva in 1994, for example, less than one-quarter of the NGO attendees were from the developing world (author's calculations from 'NGO attendees at INC-9', *ECO Geneva* (7 February 1994)).

7   Anthony Downs, 'Up and down with ecology – the "issue-attention cycle" ', *The Public Interest*, 28 (Summer 1972), pp. 38–50.

8   Ibid., p. 39.

9   Citing a number of Cambridge Reports used by Riley Dunlap ('Public opinion in the 1980s: clear consensus, ambiguous commitment', *Environment*, 33:8 (October 1991), pp.10–15 and 32–37), Ungar '. . . finds that the greenhouse effect was regarded as a "very serious" problem by 12% of respondents in 1982, 24% in 1986, and 41% in 1989'. He goes on to argue that global warming has since lost its standing as a 'celebrity' social problem (Sheldon Ungar, 'The rise and (relative) decline of global warming as a social problem', *Sociological Quarterly*, 33:4 (1992), pp. 492–3 and 483). Additionally, in 1987, 37 per cent of respondents identified the greenhouse effect as a 'clear threat' to personal health and safety; by 1989, the figure had risen to 66 per cent. (Riley E. Dunlap and Rik Scarce, 'Trends: environmental problems and protection', *Public Opinion Quarterly*, 55:4 (Winter 1991), p. 663).

Conclusions

The examination in this book of the politics of global atmospheric change gives rise to a number of findings that have implications for the study and practice of international relations. In these Conclusions, I identify and develop these implications. By doing so, I hope to contribute to the broader discussion within the field concerning both the theories with which the academic discipline of international relations conducts its investigations and the possible evolution of world politics more broadly. Thus, although these Conclusions form the final part of this book, one of their purposes is to support further discussion about future research and policy.

One finding is by no means new, but its far-reaching implications warrant restatement here. This investigation has revealed that despite the fact that every person in the world wanted a particular end, there was no guarantee that it would necessarily be achieved. More specifically, even though a stable atmosphere was desired by all, actors were, over many years, unable to escape sub-optimal outcomes on issues of global atmospheric change. Indeed, a number of momentous hurdles had to be overcome before actors were finally able and/or willing to modify their established policies, which were furthering the destruction of the earth's protective ozone layer. Meanwhile, the fact that the difficulties on the climate change issue have not yet been resolved serves to strengthen this finding. In short, this examination reinforces the belief that the members of international society will not necessarily co-ordinate their actions in order to prevent the destruction of collective goods. Indeed, Machiavelli's warnings, cited in the Introduction of this book, should continue to be heeded.

Let me now turn to the way in which scholars investigate the processes associated with international co-operation and discord. In Chapter 1, I proposed a set of hypotheses for international co-operation. They were distilled from the established literature, with further insights provided by a number of independent observations. The elements of this framework were then tested against the experience of two issues of global atmospheric change. In the strictest sense, each hypothesis has been refuted – that is, in every instance, an event that disproves the hypothesis was found. This does not necessarily, however, impoverish them completely. Their spirit, if not their letter, intimates a measure of association – that is, a degree of correlation. In this way, the four hypotheses should be viewed as heuristic devices to structure the investigation, rather than hard and fast statements which must necessarily be discarded once a single refutation is discovered.

Nevertheless, measures of association were indeed found. Although it was recognised that each simple hypothesis failed to tell the whole story (problems were illuminated in the final chapter of each part), each one nevertheless directed attention to important elements of the processes associated with international co-operation. More specifically, the degrees of correlation on the ozone layer issue was at least moderate to high for each of the first three hypotheses. The degrees of correlations on the climate change issue were somewhat lower, though still significant. With respect to the fourth hypothesis, meanwhile, the importance of political entrepreneurs and non-governmental organisations as catalysts was confirmed. The influence of issue tangibility, meanwhile, may best be incorporated into other elements, while the importance of a conducive international environment could not be determined. These results are summarised in the table opposite.

In order to assess the relevance of these findings for international relations more generally, two assumptions must first be made. First, it is assumed that the application of the evidence – that is, each of the chapter's individual stories – has not been manipulated to conform to the theoretical expectation. And, second, it is assumed that the selection of the two particular case-studies did not unduly prejudice the investigation. If these two can be accepted, then the findings from this examination give the proposed set of hypotheses sufficient weight to justify further study.

Proceeding upon the belief that these two assumptions are tenable,

Hypothesis	Degree of correlation	
	Ozone layer depletion	Climate change
A consensus regarding the problem's causal relations is necessary for international co-operation.	moderate to high	moderate
A situation in which all key actors, operating as self-interested utility maximisers, calculate the benefits of co-ordinating their policies to be greater than the costs, is necessary for international co-operation.	high	moderate
Adequate resolution of North–South issues – that is, developing countries' concerns about 'equity' – is necessary for international co-operation.	high	unclear
The prospects for international co-operation will increase when any of four catalysts are present:		
political entrepreneurs	moderate to high	moderate
non-governmental organisations	moderate	moderate
issue tangibility	high	low
conducive international environment	moderate to high	unclear

I turn to consider the range of issues against which this framework might be applied. Although this book has been primarily concerned with two specific issues – namely, ozone layer depletion and climate change – it has often been pointed out that they are subsets of larger classes of problems. With increasing generality, these larger classes are: global environmental issues, international environmental issues and international collective action issues. To which of these might this framework be applied? Given that a number of independent observations also contributed to the framework, my confidence is greatest for the first of these three classes. Nevertheless, the set of hypotheses may be able to help to advance understanding on any or all of them. Regardless, their application to other issues would help to advance our theoretical understanding of international co-operation (by either falsifying or further strengthening the set of hypotheses).[1]

Before proceeding with further applications of the framework, however, it is useful to reflect upon its elements. How might the framework be improved? Given its use to study the two issues of global atmospheric change in this book, I advance two major suggestions – one related to the ways in which the elements of the framework interrelate, and the other related to the object of the analysis. Let me consider each of these in turn.

One of the major motivations for this study was the belief that a multi-dimensional approach to the study of international co-operation was necessary. This investigation has confirmed the value of such a technique. A commitment to any one of the established approaches – be it power-based, interest-based or knowledge-based explanations, or some variation thereof – would have constrained the analysis of the politics of global atmospheric change. In much of the international relations literature, however, any kind of heterogeneous approach is not generally endorsed, let alone used in original research. Despite the fact that some theorists occasionally make favourable references to such analyses, they nevertheless contend that the scholar must exhibit a steadfast commitment to only one approach – usually, one 'level' – during the study of any particular issue. The results of this investigation, however, give further support to the challenges to this conventional wisdom.

Single-level, or, indeed, single variable, investigations are attractive, for they proffer explanations that are precise, parsimonious and easily testable. Indeed, even the first three hypotheses proposed in this study together presented a seductive package. Each comprised a step in a levels-of-analysis staircase. Moreover, each also represented a discrete fragment across time. Finally, each was made up of a distinctive bite-size discipline. Together, then, the first three hypotheses produced an image consisting of various tripartite divisions: the scientist working away on her or his own, striving to discover the natural laws governing the atmosphere; then the economist would take over, determining the aggregate interest for the country by costing out policy alternatives; and, finally, the politician, negotiating in international fora, would strive to ensure that some sort of equity was achieved.

Scholars investigating global atmospheric politics, however, should resist the temptation to put such elements into their own different packages, because unfortunately (at least for those seeking elegant hypotheses), the world is considerably messier than this. This type of parcelling breaks down – across levels, across time and across disciplines. Let me consider each of these in turn.

First, global atmospheric issues contained linkages that cut across the traditional levels of analysis. While the individual–state and state–international links were the most obvious, connections between the individual and the international were also evident. Consequently, attention to only one level of analysis would have been destined to be only partially useful, at best.

Second, one of the most striking differences between the two issues of global atmospheric change was with respect to time. The ozone layer debate did develop in a predominantly serial manner, while the climate change debate progressed in a parallel fashion. In other words, the first three hypotheses were addressed, to a significant extent, in a sequential way on the ozone layer issue: scientists identified a problem; *then* domestic costs were brought down to a tolerable level; *then* questions of global equity were considered. In this way, there was some measure of time parsimony. The climate change issue, however, unfolded quite differently.[2] The issue became highly political – both domestically and internationally – soon after the potential consequences of the natural science problem were recognised. Instead of a serial consideration of the first three hypotheses, all three attracted significant political attention simultaneously. Consequently, packages of issues divided by time in the study of global atmospheric politics have only limited utility as well.

Finally, boundaries have been broken down between the disciplines as well. Because every human activity is affected by global atmospheric change, a wide range of social science, applied science and natural science knowledge had to be utilised in order to understand fully the politics of these two issues. Indeed, in this work, ideas about the distribution of costs, capabilities, consciousness, clauses and chlorine were all critical, confirming the need for at least a measure of knowledge in economics, politics, sociology, law and chemistry. Consequently, traditional academic divisions no longer hold – they are all blurred.

Because the packages were found to be so permeable – across levels, across time and across disciplines – the framework for analysis used in this study would have benefited from a more explicit acknowledgement of this. Although recognised to some degree in this investigation, greater attention should have been paid to the ways in which the four hypotheses – that is, science, interests, equity and catalysts – affected one another.[3] Conceivably, the catalysts – those factors that were included because, at least partially, of a perceived neglect in the literature – might have effectively been absorbed by the three other hypotheses. (Indeed, it was found that 'issue tangibility' was sufficiently related to interests to be included there. Additionally, different aspects of NGOs' activities could possibly have been incorporated into each of the other three hypotheses.) Greater recognition of the interrelationships would improve the value of the framework.

The second suggestion I advance regarding the framework relates to the object of the analysis. Although I explicitly stated that 'international' (rather than 'intergovernmental') co-operation was the dependent variable for which I was searching, much of the analysis focused on the state. Whereas this concentration remains defensible for the moment (for reasons I present below), it may well not always be the case. Therefore, rather than suggest a major modification to the framework, I simply wave a flag of warning to scholars engaging in such studies in the future. Let me elaborate by considering the role of the state in the politics of global atmospheric change.

This investigation into the politics of ozone layer depletion and climate change has revealed that the state remains a key entity. It was the predominant object of persuasion: those who wished for co-operative action on issues of global atmospheric change attempted to influence and to sway government officials' beliefs and preferences. These observations thus vindicate a focus upon the state, such as was primarily employed in this study.

Recognise, however, that states were predominantly reactive. In order to explain outcomes, some attention had to be focused elsewhere so that the forces that precipitate state action and thus international co-operation could be identified. In this study, a variety of other locations were investigated – they included scientists, industry representatives, individual political entrepreneurs, environmental pressure groups and the media. Consequently, any study of global atmospheric politics that focuses upon the state as the primary *independent* variable should be challenged, because it appears that a wide variety of inputs to state behaviour must be accounted for.

This is a somewhat paradoxical report on the importance of the state: it was the key dependent variable, yet perhaps an unimportant independent one. Consequently, the evidence from the study of the politics of global atmospheric change suggests that states acted as 'gate-keepers' between, on the one hand, the desires for an international co-operative arrangement and, on the other hand, the tangible formation of one. States did not initiate demands for co-operation, but nevertheless acted as filters, with the result being that only some aspirations were fulfilled.

This conclusion about the state is, however, by no means categorical. Rather, it may be the case that the 'success' on the ozone layer issue has lulled us into thinking that history will automatically repeat itself on the climate change issue. Indeed, Ted Hanisch reveals that '[p]erhaps one reason why expectations were so high [in the climate change case] is the success of negotiating the Montreal Protocol. . . . Environmental NGOs and negotiators moved from ozone to climate change, many of them expecting the second shot to be much like the first one.'[4] The two issues are conceptually similar, but they have important differences, which have been revealed in this investigation. Thus, to date, focus upon the state is warranted, but that may not hold for ever in the future. (I return to this point below.) The difference between 'international co-operation' and 'intergovernmental co-operation' should therefore remain near the forefront of the analyst's mind.

In the final parts of these Conclusions, I would like to return to the experiences on the politics of global atmospheric change, but no longer with reference to the framework for analysis and its constituent hypotheses. Rather, freed from this point of reference, I would like to make a number of more general observations – observations that have pertinence for the study and practice of international relations more generally.

One recurrent theme throughout the book was that the issues of global atmospheric change are complex. Indeed, they appear to possess characteristics that are unprecedented: they are global in scope and systemic in nature. Let me consider each of these aspects in turn.

First, there is the characteristic of 'global scope'. These issues have a geographical reach that is – with the possible exception of nuclear war – unparalleled. Because every person, and thus every state, has the means to exacerbate these atmospheric problems, an effective response to them requires the constructive participation of *every* actor in the world. Arguably, no individual can cut themselves off from the actions of others. The two issues therefore extend beyond 'the international' to 'the global'. They cannot be contained to either the local level, the national level or the international level narrowly defined – that is, two or more, but nevertheless a limited number of states. Instead, all peoples and consequently all states play a role. This in turn means that the marginalisation of particular regions of the world can no longer take place.[5] Foreign policy must now consider the global dimension in addition to the international.

Second, there is the quality of 'systemic nature'. Because of the extensive lifetimes of many gases in the atmosphere, these issues have considerable lag-times associated with them – that is, the full impact of today's activities will not be experienced for many years. The most significant repercussion of this is that current human activities are limiting society to only a restricted set of possible futures, no matter what actions might be taken in later years. The consequence for the practice of international relations is that decision-makers may be forced to consider issues, and perhaps to control activities, before the full consequences of society's actions have been demonstrated and perhaps even before full proof of causation is undeniably demonstrated – that is, they may be forced to have their activities guided by the 'precautionary principle'.[6] The requirement to act in this way may conflict with some traditional ideas about foreign policymaking. In the short term, customary conceptualisations of crisis management and brinkmanship have to be re-evaluated, because the inertial forces that drive the systemic issues are likely to become inexorable. By curbing the ability of humans to intervene, decisions will be much more difficult to reverse. In the longer term, meanwhile, questions of intergenerational equity will have to be considered much more deeply than heretofore. This, however, is also problematic: traditional 'discount rates' may not be able to deal with things that are 'unique' and 'irreversible', yet a high proportion of environmental capital has both these properties. In short, systemic issues pose unprecedented, and academically interesting, challenges to conventional policy practices.

Indeed, this opens up a much broader discussion about humans' relationship with their surroundings. Recently, the prevailing (or at least, 'Western') understanding of this relationship has been that 'humans have supreme authority over the earth and all of its living things, both plant and animal'.[7] This view may be under challenge, however, for the empirical findings from this study suggest that human society has disrupted equilibria in nature: while the system searches for its new equilibria, humans no longer exercise supreme control over it.[8] Thus, political agendas and choices may, to some extent, be falling under the control of natural systems. If this is indeed taking place, then there may be profound implications for thinking about human beings' relationships with their sur-roundings.[9]

With these problems possessing such unique characteristics (and other issues potentially echoing them), a key question for inter-national relations scholars relates to the most appropriate response. More specifically, is the present structure of international society well-suited to deal with this new generation of international issues? There is an argument to suggest that it is not. The nation-state system, many argue, is responsible for the problems that we are facing today. We should not, therefore, expect it to be able to propose and implement solutions. Indeed, it appears clear to some that the state may not be fit to deliver the goods, for it is both too large and too small for the task at hand. It is too large in the sense that successful 'sustainable development' requires bottom-up solutions. It is too small because the generation of global problems requires truly global co-ordinated responses. A world of selfish and competi-tive states can only, therefore, exacerbate the existing situation.

Ronnie Lipschutz and Ken Conca, for example, reinforce this sentiment. While examining the implications of global environ-mental change for international relations, they:

> suggest the emergence of a fundamentally new social dynamic, with which governments, their critics, and their observers may be poorly equipped to deal. We will argue that this new dynamic, which we label *global ecological interdependence*, consists of two seemingly countervailing trends: tighter systemic binding among actors in the prevailing international system, and the simultaneous decay and fragmentation of the traditional authority structure of world politics.[10]

Additionally, Marc Levy and colleagues contend that they already see a withering away of state sovereignty:

> In a world of genuinely independent states, legal freedom of action may be a precondition for effectiveness in goal attainment; but under conditions of high interdependence, maintaining such operational sovereignty may prevent effective action by anyone. Thus, inter-national environmental interdependence and negotiations about it reinforce formal sovereignty while limiting operational sovereignty.[11]

Finally, Brian Wynne provides additional evidence, citing pressures from 'below':

> Conventional models and styles of 'rational' institutional authority are already seen to be under extreme strain in modern society, as people alienated from existing public institutions and their scientific modes of legitimation seek new forms of association with which they can more closely identify. Environmental organisations are seen as the epitome or leading edge of these new social movements.[12]

For such scholars, the nation-state system is ill-equipped to respond to the challenges. Instead, social movements (and 'civil society', more generally) will bring about the required changes. Evidence to support this claim is already apparent: transformation in social behaviour is often 'ahead' of governments' policies. Consequently, any preoccupation with 'intergovernmental co-operation' is doomed to neglect key developments. Consider, for example, the coverage given to the 'famous five' outputs from the Earth Summit (that is, the Conventions on Climate Change and Biological Diversity, the Forests Statement, the Rio Declaration and Agenda 21). An alternative interpretation holds that such attention was misplaced: these intergovernmental agreements may one day be overtaken in significance by the 41 'alternative treaties' agreed by NGOs at the Global Forum. Because environmental issues are too important to be left to the state, the state must be left behind.

Others, however, disagree. Given the size of the challenges ahead, the state is the only entity with sufficient resources and legitimacy to tackle them head on. Moreover, a state-led response might not, after all, be such a bad thing. The record of the state-system is not, as some would have you believe, desperate – it has already registered a number of successes.[13] Anyway, those who lay charges against the capacity of the state-system to deal with global environmental problems have misdirected their fire. They do not truly want to do away with the state. Rather, what they really want is a new and improved (perhaps more democratic and decentralised) state.

Regardless, it seems that the state is going to attempt to retain its importance. The 'mainstream of sustainable development'[14] is, after all, about 'managing', with the state serving as primary manager.[15] The Earth Summit helped to reinforce this: states revealed that they were not willing to give up any measure of authority without a fight. In spite of a range of wonderful-sounding intentions,[16] numerous caveats throughout the agreements reinforced the sovereign rights of states, thus rejecting any third-party arbitrators, any supra-national body with authority over reporting, monitoring and inspection.

Regardless of their view about the longer-term ability of the state system to deal with such problems, most would probably agree that the state retains a significant measure of importance in international relations study and practice today. Consequently, I now propose a number of implications for international relations in the shorter term.

Any remaining illusions that a unitary, rational state universally exists should have been comprehensively dispelled by the experiences of global atmospheric change, for a variety of reasons. The investigation of scientific consensus in Part II revealed the importance of perceptions and interpretations. Intangible factors of this sort are often overlooked when international relations scholars employ cost–benefit analysis (CBA) in order to explain state behaviour. Indeed, this study has shown that scientific relativism at the level of the individual, organisation and state can contribute to scientific non-consensus and thereby affect political processes in ways unanticipated by some rational choice theorists.

Additionally, the study of equity in Part IV demonstrated that history is an important consideration in the formulation of policy. Actors in international society do not simply take snapshots of the present distribution of costs and benefits on any issue in order to determine a negotiating position. Instead, they look back over time to discern how events have structured the present arrangements. Once again, a traditional CBA, such as is used by some scholars, does not usually consider such historical, and often non-measurable, factors. Their method of analysis would consequently be unable to make sense of some of the politics of global environmental change.

Finally, findings from Part III of this investigation revealed that politics at the domestic level can be significant in the formulation of states' policies on global environmental issues. A number of different groups make their views known to decision-makers. And, although decision-makers still use some notion of 'national interest' in order to formulate national policy, the concept is much more complex than suggested by traditional scholars who assume the existence of a unitary, rational state. With claims being made by a vast range of groups within a society, interests will not aggregate nicely. Consequently, a variety of other factors – illuminated by studies of the society and its politics – will influence perceived interests.

Let me also consider the most important resources with which actors attempt to influence others in international society. To phrase this in more common international relations terminology, consider the tools of power. An understanding of power as military might is not particularly useful in relation to the issues of global environmental change. Instead, money is one of the most significant levers with which one actor is able to influence another. This is evident at all levels – individual (e.g. green consumerism), inter-state (e.g. trade balance considerations) and global (e.g. resource transfers). In fact, it may well be that states have lost their power, to the market and the players in the market. Thus, the need to identify and to recognise the importance of economic power in the processes of international co-operation – a need that has been accepted in the study of some other issue-areas – has been reinforced by this investigation.

The study, however, also revealed that power went beyond merely economic considerations. The findings reinforce the view held by some scholars that 'knowledge is power'. Knowledge took a variety of forms. Not unexpectedly, those who were able to discover previously unknown natural relationships or physical changes (and thus environmental problems) were able to determine, to a significant extent, whether or not certain issues spilled over from the scientific agenda to the political agenda. In addition, those who were able to disseminate this new-found knowledge effectively were able to determine, also to a significant extent, the position to be occupied by that issue on the political agenda. Additionally, however, those who were able to claim expertise in the 'costing' of the various policy alternatives were also able to determine, to a significant extent, the hierarchy of policies on political agendas. Therefore, it appears that those who can both gain and transmit knowledge exercise profound power in the international system. In this way, scientists and economists in particular, and leaders of environmental pressure groups and members of the media in general, may be able to exercise a new-found amount of power in international politics.

Perhaps, however, the most consequential finding emerges from the dissolving of boundaries noted above in these Conclusions. It was argued that the issues of global atmospheric change – and potentially a whole range of other issues – challenge traditional academic divisions. Knowledge from a range of disciplines was required. At the very least, this suggests that research requires a multidisciplinary approach.

Terms like 'multidisciplinary' and 'interdisciplinary' have often been advocated with evident enthusiasm in academic discourse. In spite of this, however, there is little agreement about what they mean, let alone about what their full-scale and professional adoption might imply. This assertion is supported by the fact that borders between disciplines appear to be fervently defended in many institutions of higher learning. Even within international relations – a subject that would seem to be a natural home to interdisciplinary efforts – much time and energy are spent upon works that set out the parameters of the discipline. Such efforts should not be criticised in their own right, and, indeed, those that seek to define the field of study may simply be responding to broader institutional pressures, not unlike those that are discussed in Chapter 4. Nevertheless, it appears that research efforts that both draw upon and integrate traditional disciplines may be needed. It remains to be seen if such efforts will be encouraged, or even tolerated, for at present, there exist significant obstacles to a wholly committed interdisciplinary approach.

This book has not examined every aspect of the issues of global atmospheric change, let alone every aspect of the debates surrounding either the determinants of international co-operation or the evolution of international environmental politics more generally. Indeed, a vast number of questions remain unanswered; even more questions remain unasked.[17] Nevertheless, this book has striven to elaborate a viable framework for the analysis of international co-operation and to apply it to the two issues under consideration. By focusing upon the theoretical dilemmas and the historical evidence, it has attempted to contribute to the general discussion as the members of international society seek to build co-operative structures to address not only the challenges of climate change, but global environmental issues more generally.

Notes

1   Further application would also be able to discern the extent to which each of the first three hypotheses is truly necessary but not sufficient conditions for international co-operation (as is implied in this framework).

2   This is despite the fact that international society's initial response to the challenge of global warming embodied this linear approach: Working

Group I of the IPCC considered the science; Working Group II, the impacts; and, Working Group III, the responses.

3 This reinforces one of the most important findings from a recent study, which placed emphases upon substitution and interaction effects. (Oran R. Young and Gail Osherenko (eds), *Polar Politics: Creating International Environmental Regimes* (London, Cornell University Press, 1993).

4 Ted Hanisch, 'The Rio Climate Convention: real solutions or political rhetoric?', *Security Dialogue*, 23:4 (December 1992), p. 64.

5 This is not meant to suggest that all actors in the world will have significant leverage on these issues, but they will nevertheless have to be accounted for.

6 Principle 15 of the Rio Declaration states that:

> In order to protect the environment, the precautionary approach shall be widely applied by States according to their capabilities. Where there are threats of serious or irreversible damage, lack of full scientific certainty shall not be used as a reason for postponing cost-effective measures to prevent environmental degradation.

As Chapter 4 elaborated, 'certainty' should consequently no longer be demanded by policy-makers. Instead, policies should be explored by use of scenarios with varying (yet explicit) assumptions.

7 Arthur H. Westing, 'Constraints on military disruption of the biosphere: an overview', in Arthur H. Westing (ed.), *Cultural Norms, War and the Environment* (Oxford, Oxford University Press, 1988), p. 6.

8 See, for example, J.E. Lovelock, *Gaia: a New Look at Life on Earth* (Oxford, Oxford University Press, 1979).

9 In this way, there may be important implications for our traditional Cartesian interpretation of the relationship between subject and object. Indeed, an interesting parallel with the study of 'Earth Science' is suggested by the comments of one of the world's foremost atmospheric scientists. Michael McElroy, of Harvard University, maintains that, unlike other 'traditional' scientists, earth scientists do not have the luxury of working in the laboratory, where they 'would have hypotheses, . . . would do experiments, . . . would manipulate the experiment and . . . would learn about the processes by the conventional iteration of theory and experiment' (quoted in Cheryl Simon Silver with Ruth S. DeFries, *One Earth One Future: Our Changing Global Environment* (Washington, DC, National Academy Press, 1990), pp. 20–1). Thus, just as applied and natural scientists are considering the need for a 'paradigm shift', social scientists might also be forced to reconsider their traditional worldviews.

10 Ken Conca and Ronnie D. Lipschutz, 'A tale of two forests', in Ronnie D. Lipschutz and Ken Conca (eds), *The State and Social Power in Global Environmental Politics* (New York, Columbia University Press, 1993), p. 9.

11   Marc A. Levy, Robert O. Keohane and Peter M. Haas, 'Improving the effectiveness of international environmental institutions', in Peter M. Haas, Robert O. Keohane and Marc A. Levy (eds), *Institutions for the Earth: Sources of Effective International Environmental Protection* (London, The MIT Press, 1993), p. 416.

12   Brian Wynne, 'Implementation of greenhouse gas reductions in the European Community: institutional and cultural factors', *Global Environmental Change*, 3:1 (March 1993), p. 127.

13   See, for example, the contributions in Haas, Keohane and Levy, *Institutions for the Earth*.

14   See, for example, W.M. Adams and D.H.L. Thomas, 'Mainstream sustainable development: the challenge of putting theory into practice', *Journal of International Development*, 5:6 (1993), pp. 591–604.

15   See, for example, World Commission on Environment and Development, *Our Common Future* (Oxford, Oxford University Press, 1987).

16   Principle 21 of the Rio Declaration, for example, states: 'The creativity, ideals and courage of the youth of the world should be mobilized to forge a global partnership in order to achieve sustainable development and ensure a better future for all.'

17   With a range of international environmental agreements having been agreed, the question of compliance – that is, issues of implementation, enforcement and dispute settlement – deserves greater attention.

Index

Note: Page numbers followed by 'f' refer to figures; page numbers followed by 'n' refer to notes.